W9-BDU-078

The Natural Superiority of
MULES

A Celebration of One of the Most Intelligent, Sure-Footed, and Misunderstood Animals in the World

Second Edition

JOHN HAUER

Edited by Sena Hauer

Foreword by Sue Cole

Skyhorse Publishing

Copyright © 2006, 2014 by John Hauer

All Rights Reserved. No part of this book may be reproduced in any manner without the express written consent of the publisher, except in the case of brief excerpts in critical reviews or articles. All inquiries should be addressed to Skyhorse Publishing, 307 West 36th Street, 11th Floor, New York, NY 10018.

Skyhorse Publishing books may be purchased in bulk at special discounts for sales promotion, corporate gifts, fund-raising, or educational purposes. Special editions can also be created to specifications. For details, contact the Special Sales Department, Skyhorse Publishing, 307 West 36th Street, 11th Floor, New York, NY 10018 or info@skyhorse-publishing.com.

Skyhorse® and Skyhorse Publishing® are registered trademarks of Skyhorse Publishing, Inc.®, a Delaware corporation.

Visit our website at www.skyhorsepublishing.com.

10 9 8 7 6 5 4 3 2 1

Library of Congress Cataloging-in-Publication Data is available on file.
ISBN: 978-1-62636-166-9

Printed in China

The Natural Superiority of

MULES

DEDICATION

In the early 1900s, hundreds of thousands of mules were purchased all over the southern United States, assembled in the Guyton and Harrington stockyards in Missouri and shipped to foreign countries on chartered steamships. Great Britain alone purchased 180,000 mules from this exporter.

Adventurous young men were "engaged as caretakers of the mules at very modest wages."* These stewards were assigned about fifty mules each to feed, water and care for on the twenty-four-day trip "across the pond" to Spain and other countries. "Some were city boys, some were college students and some didn't know which end ate the hay." When they arrived in Spain, the young men were given fifteen days to tour Europe on their own and then got free passage back to the United States on a returning mule boat.

This book is dedicated to one of those young men who did know which end ate the hay, a farm boy and college student from Speed, Missouri: Charles Eugene Hauer, my dad.

*Quotes are from *The Missouri Mule: His Origin and Times, Volume I*, by Melvin Bradley.

PURPOSE

The purpose of this book is to enhance the image of the mule and to provide a source of information for people who are interested in learning about mules. It is also intended to honor mules for the contributions they have made to civilization, and to make mule owners better informed and even more proud of their long-eared companions.

The book is a compilation of articles, essays and stories by a full spectrum of mule lovers, from leading experts in the mule industry to beginning mule aficionados. Readers may notice differences of opinion among authors. In some cases, differing opinions will be true for a given mule in different circumstances. After all, no two mules are alike, and no mule acts the same all the time. There is also some repetition in the book, since authors often agree on the traits that make mules special.

Contents

MULE MATTERS

MULE STORIES

Foreword

I began riding a mule almost forty years ago and purchased *Mules and More* magazine in 1990. Both riding a mule and having the privilege of helping educate others about their wonderful attributes has been a wonderful experience for me. I remember the first thing I did when I purchased my first mule was get an encyclopedia to learn about what I actually bought. Back then, there wasn't a lot of information published about mules.

Today, my family is very involved in the mule industry. My granddaughter, Cori, has taken over the reins of *Mules and More*, bringing the magazine to a new level in design, quality, and information. She, along with her daughter, Camri, find time to trail ride and show their mules at a few events throughout the year. Loren's son, Cole, has joined his dad training mules for clients all across the country. They both enjoy trail riding and hunting wild hogs while riding mules. Loren's wife takes photos and writes articles for the magazine during the summer months.

I still have my palomino mule, Star, who we purchased twenty-eight years ago. She is thirty-seven years old as I write this and is in good health. I can't imagine my life without a mule or two around.
–Sue Cole

Through mules, I was able to meet John Hauer at a mule show in Pueblo, Colorado in 1997. I have had the opportunity to watch John's knowledge and love of mules grow throughout the years.

I was thrilled in 2001 when John contacted me to let me know he was planning on writing a mule book. At that time, he asked for help from my family, knowing they were involved with mules in several aspects. My son, Loren Basham of Pair A Dice Mules, was training mules full time, and he was traveling across the country with his wife, Lenice, and children, Cori and Cole. Loren was into gymkhana competition and roping with his mule, Jessie; Cori was just moving on from gymkhana into Western and English events; and Cole was beginning to take an interest in gaming events. John asked Loren and Lenice to write a chapter for the book on eventing and provide photos for his book.

John was instrumental in helping Loren get started with his training business by inviting him to bring a load of good mules to his ranch in South Dakota. John placed an ad in a local newspaper and provided the clients, while Loren provided the mules. At one point Loren and his family traveled to the Hauer home in Moab, Utah, to ride with John.

It seemed like years before John finally called to let me know his dream of a mule book was finally becoming a reality in 2005. When his book arrived, I was amazed at the quality. Not only does this book contain a wealth of knowledge, but it is also one you would want to leave out on your coffee table or office desk for others to thumb through and enjoy.

John's second edition is still the same high quality and contains new information and photos of what's taking place in the wonderful world of mules today.

The versatility of the mule provides people in many walks of life an opportunity to own and use them for their personal needs and activities. When handled and trained properly, the mule is almost dog-like in its devotion and affection to humans. Mules are very intelligent and cautious, sometimes called stubborn, when they are only handling the situation in what they consider to be a safe manner.

– Sue Cole
Senior Editor, *Mules and More*

Introduction

I have ridden horses all my life—from Arabians to Standardbreds retired from the track, to Quarter Horses that were better trained mounts than I was a rider—and I love them all. But when I moved to a new town and looked for a place to board my Arabian, I phoned John Hauer, and he asked me if I'd ever ridden a mule. "No," I replied, hoping he couldn't hear my snooty tone over the phone.

"We're riding into Angel Arch next Thursday. Would you like to ride a mule?" Okay, if that is what it would take. Angel Arch is an immense formation of red rock poised far back in Canyonlands National Park, a place inaccessible to vehicles and too far for me to hike. Twenty-six miles round trip, in one day, through a deep sand creek bed and thigh-high water. Fine, I'd ride a mule.

That day I learned a few lessons about mules. It was a very good day indeed, and Angel Arch was truly spectacular. The mule's gait didn't leave me aching the next day. She didn't spook at anything. She was sweet and responsive, and I found I didn't mind those big ears a bit. They swung happily back and forth with the rhythm of her gait. She cantered easily when I asked. I'd thought mules just plodded along.

I was also curious about the mules' condition the day after such a hard ride, but when I checked their legs, they were sound and cool, not filled with fluid from pulling through the sand. I silently wished my endurance horse were this sound, but I had not yet become a Mule Rider.

My tutelage continued as I rode more with Hauer. I ventured from Sassy to Raven, and then to other mules of Hauer's. Those mules carried me with unwavering sure-footedness into the highest reaches of the twelve thousand--foot La Sal Mountains, through Nevada's burning desert, and up Colorado canyons. They did not get sick. They did not go lame. They never missed a step, nor did they slip on rock. Their ground-covering walk left horses far behind, but they would stay patiently behind if asked. Ultimately, I even bought my own mule to take her place in the group.

After three years of riding mules, I realized that I had become a Mule Rider. On that occasion, two friends, both riding horses, and I were on a precipitous

Sharon Northrup is a lifelong horsewoman. Her career as a college administrator has taken her riding in Montana, Colorado, Texas, and Utah. She currently lives on a ranch in western Colorado, using her mules for ranch work and trail riding in the nearby mountains.

trail high in the mountains. I was enjoying the scenery, and my heart was not pounding in the least as my mule navigated the trail. Actually, I wasn't paying any attention to her—the trail was her job. My job was to sit squarely and lightly balanced so she could do her job. Ahead, I saw my two friends dismount and begin to lead their horses, and I momentarily wondered why. Then I remembered what they were doing—exactly what I would do, if I were still riding horses. The trail was too rugged, and they were getting off. Without thought, I gave my mule more rein so that she would have greater freedom to handle the jump-downs ahead. It didn't occur to me to get off. I knew she could handle the trail better than I could.

When I first became interested in mules, I devoured every book and article I could find, and wished I had the definitive work on mules. The books and articles were helpful, and Hauer was more helpful, sharing everything he had with me. The mules were the ones who taught me the most, but I still wished for the definitive volume.

What Hauer did for me was give me his broad knowledge of mules, gleaned not only from personal experience, but also from reading every volume about mules that he could get his hands on. He is indefatigable in finding information, talking to old timers, searching out those with experience with mules. The result is this book, a compendium of mule knowledge, the book I wished I'd had when I first became acquainted with mules, the book I am glad to have now. The information ranges from the serious exploration of mule hybrid vigor to wry comments about people too asinine to appreciate the value of mules. Whether you are newly curious about mules or have enjoyed mules for years, Hauer's book is one that must grace your bookshelf. It is the ultimate mule book. And if I could give you a benediction, it would be this: I hope you have the opportunity to become a Mule Rider. This book will help you.

– Sharon Northrup

A Note From Sena Hauer

For as long as I can remember, I've been crazy about horses. When I was five and had just started kindergarten, I became best friends with a girl whose family lived out on the desert about 30 miles from where I was raised in Moab, Utah. I spent as many weekends with her family as I did with my own, largely because I could get my fill of riding. They had a herd of quarter horses and appaloosas and one funny donkey named Sister Sarah. I learned to ride on those critters on that desert—and begged and begged my parents to get me a horse of my own.

Little Sena.

One of my favorite childhood books was *Brighty of the Grand Canyon* by Marguerite Henry. When I turned ten in June of 1973, my parents gave me an old palomino gelding and I chose to name him Brighty. The Brighty of Grand Canyon fame was of course a donkey, but it didn't matter to me. He was an equine, and I loved anything that resembled a horse.

Of all the characters in Walt Disney's cast, my fondest has always been Eeyore the Donkey, simply because he is the most horse-like of all. Although Eeyore was actually the brainchild of A.A. Milne, who created Winnie-the-Pooh and all of his friends, he rose to fame with the help of Disney.

I watched old Westerns on TV with my dad when I was a little girl only because I could watch the horses and dream which one would be mine if I had my pick. I didn't understand the plots, but it didn't matter. I just enjoyed watching those horses run around. Pa Cartwright of the old television serial *Bonanza* and Matt Dillon of *Gunsmoke* fame both rode buckskin horses, so that has always been my favorite color of horse. But I also loved the orange cartoon character Pokey, and I even named a horse after him. I'm a horse freak.

Mules have not been an exception to my love of equines. As a college-aged teen, I had a volunteer summer job on the La Sal Mountains near Moab wherein I could ride the century-old trails, marking old aspen trees with new Forest Service blazes and building up rock cairns to help travelers find their way. In exchange for my work, the local district ranger hauled my two horses up to the mountain where there was an old guard station and spring-fed corral. The horses and I stayed there off and on all summer, and I scouted trails and had a grand old time.

One day while riding the rough alpine routes, I came upon a man on a mule. I didn't know anyone in Moab  who had mules—donkeys yes, but I'd never seen nor learned about mules close up. That man turned out to be the local government trapper, and he proceeded to tell me why he rode a mule as opposed to a horse for his solitary and rugged line of work. I was intrigued and sold on the mule's virtues in riding the country I loved so much.

Years passed, but I didn't cross paths with another mule man for more than twenty years. During that time, I raised and rode a couple of quarter-appaloosas that were descendants of my friend's desert herd. I'd moved away from Moab with those horses, then come back, and I was itching to ride those old mountain trails. I soon met a new friend who shared my passion for riding, and he introduced me to mules.

The first time I met John Hauer, he asked if I liked to fish, hunt, or ride equines. Replying yes to the latter, he invited me to go riding, as he so frequently invited others, and I took him up on the offer. That began a roundabout way of having John, and mules, in my life.

Fast-forward fifteen years to 2013. John and I have been married a decade and now share a herd of horses and mules which we use in our little dude string based on the Colorado River. I've learned a lot about mules, first by spending many hours in the saddle with them, and also by helping John finish the first edition of *The Natural Superiority of Mules*.

That first book endeavor was spawned by John's passion and appreciation for mules, and his belief that the intelligent hybrids have been much too maligned for too long. John, at the encouragement of his late and dear wife Nancy, started gathering information twenty years ago for that first edition. Book projects are huge, and although Nancy had wanted to see the book in print before her passing in 2002, it wasn't to be.

After Nancy's death, I took a closer step into John's world, and the mule book, as we call it, became one of our many joint ventures. While John had single-handedly assembled most of the book's content in the years leading up to its publication in 2005, my experience in the newspaper business gave the project a nudge toward final edits and layout. And off to the printer it went, with Lyons Press printing and reprinting the book several times before retiring their rights to it in 2012.

When it comes to mules and stories, though, there are always more tales to be told. My personal gratification about having mules in my life is as much for the animals as those who love and own them. I have followed John to Bishop Mule Days in California, Jake Clark Mule Days in Wyoming, and smaller mule events in Colorado and Arizona. People from all over the United States and farther reaches of the globe have come to our ranch to meet us and the mules. And I can testify that mule people are a special breed! My most near and dear friends today are those whom I have met due to our association with mules. Several of these dear friends appear in this second edition of the mule book. They are mule experts and advocates, and most of all, they are mule lovers and salt-of-the-earth people.

The mules in our dude string anchor the safety and satisfaction of our ride program. Many trail ride outfits have age limits on who can ride, but we have yet to turn away even the smallest smiling face that wants to climb up on the Grand Dames of our stables—Honeybee and Jeanne—who at thirty-plus years are still framing a view of the desert through their long ears for visitors from around the world.

The mules in our dude string also have the most charisma in our herd.

This is Sena today, almost grown up. The photograph at left is of John and Sena Hauer riding in the Flat Tops Wilderness of Colorado.

Johnny Reb the jumping mule is particularly fond of eating Tootsie Pops, including the stick and the wrapper! That antic never ceases to get a chuckle out of our visitors and me.

These colorful characters have certainly made my life more interesting and more blessed. I consider some of our dude string horses members of our family. All of our mules are members of our family. My relationship with mules and horses brings to mind a quote from the aforementioned A.A. Milne, who in Winnie-the-Pooh's voice wrote, "Some people talk to animals. Not many listen though. That's the problem."

The Natural Superiority of Mules

MULE SENSE

Photo provided by Charlie Leonard.

RAVENSWOOD FARM MULE BARN

When I was growing up, Ravenswood Farm in Missouri was owned and operated by my dad's sister, Mary Ellen, and her husband Charles Leonard. The farm had been in the Leonard family for several decades.

I rode a horse for the first time at Ravenswood. My cousins who lived on the farm taught me that you don't need a saddle to ride a horse. Although there were no mules on the farm at that time, the mule barn was still there in all its splendor.

In the late 1800s and early 1900s, the Leonard family was very active and well known in the mule business. In 1870, Charles E. Leonard was elected president of a newly formed mule owners association, which was organized to enhance the reputation and value of mules.

In the early 1900s, an architect in Kansas City was hired to design the mule barn. It was built, burned down a few years later, and then rebuilt. In that era, there was no shortage of beautiful mule barns. It was often said that if a farmer's barn was nicer than his house, it was a sure sign that he was successful. It was sometimes true that the mules were better fed and cared for than the family, because they were the ones that fed the family.

Unfortunately, the barn in the photograph burned down about twelve years ago. The fire was caused by modern equipment in the form of an electric branding iron that was accidentally left on.

The Natural Superiority of the Mule

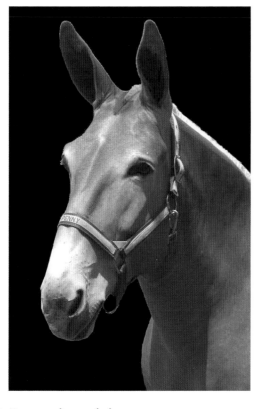

Ms. Penny, as photographed by Tony Leonard of Lexington, Kentucky. Leonard is recognized as being one of the greatest Thoroughbred horse photographers in the world. Among his achievements are capturing the last living portrait of the great racehorse, Secretariat. Ms. Penny is owned by J. Mack Bohn.

Let's start at the beginning. A mule is the progeny of a male donkey (a jack) and a female horse (a mare). In contrast, the union of a male horse (a stallion) and a female donkey (a jenny) produces, if anything, a hinny. Because conception is difficult for the female donkey bred to a male horse, there are very few hinnies. Hinnies are slightly more horse-like in appearance than mules, but it is difficult to tell them apart. Like most hybrids, both mules and hinnies are sterile. Since it takes about a month longer to make a donkey than a horse, one might expect a certain degree of superiority on the part of the mule.

…It all starts at birth: Baby mules are just a bit more precocious than other equine creatures. Of course the most obvious physical advantage of the mule is those magnificent ears! It is true that when shown a mule, a donkey and a horse,

BY JOHN HAUER

John Hauer is the owner and operator of two ranches, a 1,400-acre ranch in the Black Hills of South Dakota, and a ranch located on the banks of the Colorado River north of Moab, Utah. In the past, his ranching operations have used Quarter Horses, Appaloosas, Morgans, and Peruvian Pasos, but since his "conversion," the focus is exclusively on mules. John and his wife, Sena, buy, sell, raise and ride mules on their "Back Country Mules" ranch north of Moab. John has co-authored college textbooks on travel and tourism, and has had articles about mules published in *The Saturday Evening Post* and in *Mules and More*, a monthly publication for the mule aficionado.

an artist, poet, or engineer will recognize that the mule's ears are in better proportion to the head than either the donkey's or the horse's. Many horses display a very hostile attitude toward mules. Their hostility may be attributed to "ear-envy."

Both the mule's hearing and ability to express emotions are enhanced by those graceful and flexible appendages. Some old-time mountain men believed that the mules' ears also account for their great sense of balance on narrow mountain trails, and that the long ears serve the same function as the balance pole carried by high-wire acrobats.

A rider who watches his mule's ears will have otherwise unnoticed wildlife, people and other things of interest pointed out to him. It is said that mules can "see" as much with their ears as with their eyes. And, when a mule's ears are flopping in rhythm with her gait, it is a sign that the mule feels that all is right in the world. (I have a slight preference for female mules [mollies] and use feminine pronouns when referring to mules.)

Going to the underside of the mule, you will find small, slightly constricted but very hard and durable hooves. One veterinarian compared the composition of mule hooves to ivory, noting that they rarely crack or split. It is often not necessary to put shoes on a mule, and those "bare feet" have great traction.

Speaking of veterinarians, unless you have a crush on yours, this is good news: Mules are much less likely than horses to injure themselves, colic, or contract laminitis, navicular syndrome or ringbone. They have a hefty sense of self-preservation, and rarely go over backward with a rider, run through fences or injure one another by kicking. If a mule gets a leg caught in a barbed-wire fence, she will either figure out how to free herself without injury or will wait stoically and patiently for help. The mule rarely overeats to the point of detriment or drinks too much when overheated. A horse veterinarian once told me that if everyone rode mules she would soon be out of business.

People who do not know much about mules usually ask, "Aren't they stubborn?" The answer is, "Depends on your definition of stubborn." If you mean, "Do they have minds of their own and do they think for themselves?" then the answer is yes. If you mean, "Are they unreasonably obstinate?" then the answer for most mules is no.

How then did mules get such a universal reputation for being stubborn? In the days when mules were used primarily as working animals, the people who used them were often ignorant and inexperienced, thinking that if brute force and mistreatment did not get results, more force and mistreatment were called for. In other words the "two-by-four mentality" prevailed. Those "mule skinners" didn't realize that "you have to treat a mule like you should treat a horse."

Loren Basham, a professional mule trainer in Bland, Missouri, says, "When I train a mule, I try to make the mule think that everything I ask her to do is her idea. A horse can usually be intimidated and forced to do things that he perceives to be either senseless or potentially harmful to herself. However, a mule may 'balk' or become 'stubborn' when asked to exceed her capacity to perform or to do something unnecessarily dangerous. For example, mules have rarely been used as war animals that are expected to

John Hauer continues the imprinting process with a two-day-old paint molly mule.

charge headlong into enemy fire, because the mule will very likely decide that such activity could endanger her well-being." (Remember that strong sense of self-preservation?)

Here are some other examples of so-called stubbornness: Most mules cannot be "ridden to death" as horses can. When a mule is ridden to the point that she feels her health is in danger, she will stop, perhaps lie down and refuse to go on until sufficiently rested. It takes a tremendously long ride to get a well-conditioned mule that tired.

If a pack mule is loaded with more weight than she can safely carry, she may lie down or just refuse to move. When the load is reduced to within her self-preservation limits, she will carry it willingly.

When asked to cross a stream or ditch, the mule may notice a safer or easier crossing and try to convince the

Fording the Colorado River where John Wayne crossed in the movie Rio Grande.

rider that there is a better place to cross. Most mule riders eventually learn to heed the advice of the mountain men: "Trust your mule."

People who have had little or no contact with mules often have interesting misconceptions about them. Some will look at an average-sized mule and say, "I didn't know mules were that big." Others have said, "I didn't know mules were that small" in reference to the same mule. Still others have said, "I thought mules were ugly" or "I didn't know mules could trot–I thought they could just walk really slowly."

I took two mules to a trail ride in Wyoming where most of the other riders were from Jackson Hole and owned very

fancy horses. None of them had ever seen a saddle mule before. They were surprised that the mules were not as "ugly as sin." To their dismay, there was not a horse on the ride that could keep up with the mules.

The next week, a friend who had ridden one of my mules was told by a horseman from the Wyoming ride that he was surprised to see the mules there and said, "It must take a lot of self-esteem to ride a mule." This is probably true, because of all the "cute" and deprecating comments a mule rider hears about his or her mount from the uninformed. Most mule riders do seem to have a fair amount of self-esteem, a good sense of humor, and more *joie de vivre* than the average person.

The attitude of old-time cowboys toward mules is illustrated by the following story, told by Max Harsha of Cliff, New Mexico: "An old boy told me he always liked to ride mules but they were kind of like your girlfriends: It was nice to have 'em around, but it was embarrassing to get caught on one." Max says that attitude has changed, and today it is fashionable to be seen on a nice mule.

One old-time cowboy is reported to have told people he rode a mule because he was too poor to ride a horse and too proud to ride a cow.

What superior traits does the mule inherit from her sire, the donkey?

Intelligence. Padre Antonio Vieira, a Brazilian priest, wrote a volume described as the most complete book ever written about the donkey. Vieira said the donkey "has this extraordinary ability to absorb instructions within a very short period of time."

The fact that mules get bored easily may be another sign of intelligence. Jerry Villines, a well-known mule trainer in Coffeyville, Kansas, said, "Nearly all trainers use the method of repetition for training mules. There is a fine line that you have to be careful not to cross, when repetitive training ceases to be learning and starts to become boredom. One should have a variety of activities in order for the mule to maintain a good attitude toward the training process."

Sure-footedness. Mules are safer and more sure-footed in steep and rugged terrain than horses. This trait and their hard hooves are derived from the donkey.

Toughness. Mules can go longer and farther without food and water than either horses or oxen. In the 1800s, the Oregon Trail was littered with the bodies of dead horses and oxen, but only rarely did a mule die on the trail. Extreme heat doesn't affect mules as much as horses. Because mules do not sweat much, they do not require as much water as horses. Their ability to survive and work under adverse conditions was one reason American Indians thought so highly of the mule. In a trade, a Navajo would get two horses for a mule.

Endurance. Arabian horses excel in relatively short races (thirty to one hundred miles), but in a really long contest the mule may have an advantage. The Great American Horse Race was held in 1976 to commemorate the nation's bicentennial and the role played by equines in the settlement and development of the United States. The event started in New York and ended in California. Several Arabians competed in the race, but the winner was a mule.

General George Custer (riding a horse) and Buffalo Bill Cody (on a mule) had a long, friendly and informal race across some very rough country. They finished the duel together, but when Cody went to see Custer the next day, he learned that the General's horse had died during the night. It had literally been ridden to death. Cody's mule was fine.

"Endearance." There is no such word, but there should be. It is descriptive of the way in which many people react to mules: they often want to hug and even kiss them. It is partly that "doleful, soulful countenance" that they inherit from the donkey and partly the fact that many mules are very affectionate and seem to real-

ADVICE CORNER

Mules get due apology from Ann

DEAR ANN LANDERS: In a recent column, you described a man who was determined to have his own way as "stubborn as a mule." Actually, Ann, mules are not stubborn. They are highly intelligent animals. When ordered to do something they perceive to be potentially harmful to themselves, they appear to be stubborn. Mules have a strong sense of self-preservation and cannot be forced to work themselves to death, unlike horses.

The mule is the most under-appreciated, maligned domestic animal in the country. Their service in the U.S. Army alone has never been granted. More than 500,000 mules served the allied armies in World War I and II. Thousands of mules were killed in action. The American Legion considers those mules to be veterans.

You owe an apology to our long-eared servants.
— *John Hauer, President, Mule Riders of America, Moab, Utah*

DEAR JOHN HAUER: I apologize to all the mules whose feelings I hurt by focusing on their alleged stubbornness. Little did I know that the American Legion considers them veterans. Thanks for enlightening me.

In January 2002, the author wrote a letter to Ann Landers in defense of mules. The letter and Landers' apology prompted a cute follow-up story from Illinois.

Dear Ann Landers: I enjoyed the letter you printed about mules and their service to our country. It reminded me of an incident in my childhood.

My father never praised me as a child. He often said I was "as stubborn as a mule" and a rotten kid. After enduring his verbal abuse for several years, I looked up "mule" in the dictionary and showed my father the definition. It said a mule had a horse for a mother and a jackass for a father.

He never compared me to a mule again. — *Feeling Better in Illinois*

Dear Illinois: You certainly had the last word. How sweet it is!

Honeybee

FROM THE MULE'S POINT OF VIEW

Some time ago I read an article that explained that equines do not see things the same way humans do. This is not only true in the physical sense of seeing, but psychologically as well. The mule's eyes are much farther apart than ours, so she has a wider angle of vision. Because of the distance between the eyes, objects directly in front and close to the mule are in her peripheral vision and are not seen clearly. There are undoubtedly other physiological differences in the structure of eyes that cause objects to appear different to various species. For example, color vision is very likely not the same in mules as in people, and mules have much better night vision than we do.

Psychologically, the mule sees the world from the perspective of an animal whose ancestors have been chased or bushwhacked, attacked and eaten by flesh-eating animals for thousands of years. On the other hand, humans have done much more attacking than being attacked. Flight was never a practical defense for humans, since almost all of their animal enemies were much swifter than our ancestors. In other words, mules see their environment as being filled with things that might harm or eat them (the attitude of a prey animal), and humans see the world almost exclusively as full of things to be dominated and eaten (the predator attitude).

An example of an object that the mule and her rider will often see from different points of view is a blacktop highway. When approaching the road and preparing to cross, the rider sees a black, solid, smooth, flat surface that will be easy and safe to cross as long as there is no traffic. The mule may see a long, narrow, unending, black, bottomless pit that is impossible to cross without the ability to fly. The rider who does not appreciate another point of view will often try to prove to the mule that his judgment cannot be trusted; the rider will urge the mule to cross before she has figured it out through careful study.

Two other senses that create differences in viewpoints are smell and hearing. Those big, beautiful ears aren't just for decoration. I know for a fact that my mules can hear much better than I can. Quite often my favorite molly, Honeybee, will obviously hear a truck or car approaching from the far side of a hill long before I do. I haven't been able to find scientific information about the mule's sense of smell, but it is almost certainly much more highly developed than ours.

Now, apply the senses of hearing and smell to the problem of getting your mule to cross that long, narrow, unending, black, bottomless pit that you know as a highway. The mule may refuse to cross because she can hear a truck coming that you will be unable to hear or see for a minute or more. She may also perceive that the terrible stench coming from the asphalt (even humans can smell asphalt) is caused by the rotting carcasses of all the mules that were foolish enough to have attempted to cross this mule-eating pit in the past.

A similar difference that I have often noticed between what I see and what my mule sees is our reaction to shadows. I ride in an area where there are rocks of all different sizes. It is not unusual for Honeybee to suddenly show concern about a rock she has walked by dozens of times in the past with no concern at all. Before I learned to appreciate the mule's point of view, I thought she was being silly or stupid by shying away from a rock that didn't worry her at all the day before. After studying the situation, I realized that because the time of day was different, the rock was casting a shadow that had not been there the day before. Like the highway, the shadow may have appeared to be a black hole that could house a wolf, a lion or some other creature that could be hazardous to the health of a molly.

In addition to their keen senses of hearing and sight, mules have an uncanny knack for avoiding injury. An example is an incident involving a rider, a wooden bridge crossing a small stream, a mule and a horse. The rider frequently crossed the bridge when riding his mule and his horse. On one occasion, his mule absolutely refused to walk across the bridge, and the rider allowed her to pick a different place to cross the stream. A few days later the rider's horse willingly started across the bridge only to have a front leg injured when a rotten board gave way. By being considerate of his mule's point of view, the rider avoided a confrontation and probably earned the respect of his mule.

Perhaps there is a message here for humans regarding interpersonal relationships. If we were all more tolerant and understanding of the other person's point of view, we might not have to worry about terrorism, war or simple assault.

It might also be a good idea for anyone choosing a mate to give each prospect a mule and watch how he or she handles the relationship with the mule before taking a walk down the aisle.

ly like people. They especially like people who brush, scratch and feed them. Explaining why he preferred mules, one old timer said, "They can do anything a horse can do; they can do some things better; and they'll love you like a dog." Some mule lovers tell equestrians who are acquiring their first mule that they should treat the mule more like they treat their dog than the way they treat a horse, which means spending a lot of time with the mule when you are not riding or schooling it. "Brush 'em, pet 'em, talk to 'em and let 'em know you love 'em."

There have been several reports of mollies giving birth to baby mules, and nearly all have actually been "adoptions." Apparently some mollies have such a strong desire to be mothers that they will steal a newborn mule baby from its real mom. In many well-documented cases the mule foster-mother has produced normal, wholesome milk for her adopted foal. The American Donkey and Mule Society has a photo of a molly suckling a calf–that molly had a super strong desire to be a mother!

Disposition. The mule isn't as philosophical and laid back as the donkey, nor is it as "full of prance and fart" as the horse. Mules have a businesslike attitude and seem to possess something like a sense of humor. They notice everything, but an object or event rarely bothers them more than once, if at all. Most mollies do not have a heat cycle, so they do not have periodic bouts of the crazies like mares. Many people prefer mollies to johns. Mollies that are strangers can be corralled together and will usually not injure one another. They do a lot of bluffing, but seldom do any real damage to their pasture mates. Virtually all johns are gelded at an early age.

Natural Cautiousness. When a donkey sees, smells or hears something that it doesn't recognize it usually stands its ground while cautiously evaluating the situation and determining whether the unknown presents any danger. If there is danger, the donkey may freeze, flee or attack. Donkeys are very brave and can be quite ferocious when they decide that attack is their best method of self-defense.

From the donkey, mules gain the wisdom required to evaluate strange situations without a great deal of fear and agitation. If they decide there is danger and that flight is their best defense, it is not blind flight that may cause injury. They very rarely run through fences or off cliffs, but rather choose their retreat with concern for their safety.

Gait. Mules have, on average, smoother gaits than horses. Many people are surprised to learn that mules go faster than a slow walk or shuffle. Actually, the mule gets her easy, smooth gaits from the donkey. And donkeys can be bred to any of the gaited horse breeds (Missouri Fox Trotters, Tennessee Walkers, Peruvian Pasos, Paso Finos, etc.) with a good chance that the mule will have a gait similar to that of her dam. Yes, mules can trot, canter and gallop. The mule's gait makes her a superior pack animal, because the eggs and other items in the pack get a very smooth ride.

What superior traits does the mule get from her dam, the horse?

Speed. Mules are faster than their sires, and the fastest mules can outrun most horses. Of course if you want to run on a quarter-mile track or in the Kentucky Derby, there are horses that excel. Very few riders need (or want) to go faster than a mule will carry them. Mules can outrun cows, and many ranchers and cowboys in the West prefer to ride mules for their ranch work, including roping calves and even pasture-roping cows that need to be doctored in the field.

Conformation. The mule's dam gives her a more refined body and head than the donkey's has. It is said that Quarter Horses are built like weightlifters, and mules like long-distance swimmers. Padre Vieira said of the donkey, "its physical build is anatomically perfect."

Agility. This trait is enhanced by the mother horse, and balance and careful sure-footedness by daddy donkey. This combination results in an incredibly safe ride. Many people underestimate the ability of their mules to negotiate rough terrain without hesitation or panic.

HYBRID VIGOR Mule traits of superiority due to hybrid vigor (the tendency for hybrid animals and plants to be stronger, healthier and hardier than either parent, and to inherit many of the good traits of both parents) include the following:

Longevity. On average, mules live (and work) seven to nine years longer than horses.

Teeth. Mules generally have healthier teeth than horses. Since mules live longer, it makes sense that nature equips them with harder and better teeth. A veterinarian told me that when you look at a mule's teeth to determine its age, she will appear to be a year younger than a horse the same age.

This little molly can jump as high as her back. Here she is competing in the coon jumping event at Bishop Mule Days.

LEFT: *Mules at their best...on the trail in the scenic West.*

Jumping ability. No one I have talked to knows the source of the mule's exceptional jumping ability, so I chalk it up to hybrid vigor. Whatever the source, mules can jump! In the southern states, coon hunters ride mules because of the animal's ability and willingness to jump fences. When the mounted hunter comes to a fence, he doesn't need to look for a gate. He dismounts, climbs over the fence, cues the mule to jump the fence, and they are on their way to the next fence that has to be crossed. The world's equine jumping record of over eight feet was set by a United States Army mule.

Mules do not need a running start in order to jump. They jump "flat-footed" and gracefully, like a deer. Many mules can jump a six-foot-high fence, and some of them love to jump out of their corral or pasture and go visiting. I watched one of my john mules jump over a five-foot corral fence and six pasture fences in order to fraternize with a neighbor's donkeys. Mules can also jump with riders on them, and when permitted to compete with horses in steeplechase and other jumping competitions, they hold their own.

THE MULE AS KING MAKER When David was the King of Israel, he promised Bathsheba, one of his wives, that her son, Solomon, would be king when he, David, became too old to rule. The Bible reports that when King David was "old and well advanced in years, he could not keep warm even when they put covers over him." Luckily the King had some loyal servants who recruited a lovely young virgin, Abishag, to "lie beside him so the king may be kept warm."

While King David was distracted by his efforts to keep warm, one of his ambitious sons, Adonijah, said, "I will be King." "So he got chariots and horses ready," planned a big party to declare himself King of Israel and invited almost everyone but David and Solomon. When Bathsheba learned of Adonijah's plans, she went to King David and reminded him of his pledge that her son, Solomon, would be the next King.

King David's response to Bathsheba was, "I will surely carry out today what I swore to you...Solomon your son shall be king after me, and he will sit on my throne in my place." Then David called in the prophet, the priest and other officials and commanded, "Set Solomon my son on my own mule and take him down to Gihon." After this was done the report reached ambitious Adonijah that there was bad news for him. "King David has made Solomon king... they have put him on the king's mule, and...have anointed him king." When the news was received Adonijah's guests "rose up in alarm and dispersed."

Although the Bible doesn't report what happened to the mule, it is safe to assume that he lived happily ever after.

Understanding the Mule

Recognized from early times, the physical characteristics of the mule made it superior to either parent for domestic purposes. Therefore, intentional mule breeding was started a long time ago.

The mule is, in a sense, one of mankind's earliest attempts at genetic engineering. It is a hybrid cross between the horse and the ass (donkey). Physically and mentally, the mule is a blend of its two parents, with sometimes the characteristics predominating of its maternal parent, the mare, or sometimes its paternal parent, the ass. But there is something more. We call it "hybrid vigor." It is this hybrid vigor that has made the mule so useful to mankind, because in meeting human needs, the mule often exceeds either parent in its qualities.

The horse evolved in North America as a grazing animal on the vast, grassy plains and disappeared about 15,000 years ago after the last Ice Age. The reason

BY ROBERT M. MILLER, DVM

Dr. Miller is founder of Conejo Valley Veterinary Clinic, Thousand Oaks, California. He has served on the editorial staff of Veterinary Medicine, Modern Veterinary Practice, Veterinary Forum and Western Horseman. He has published twelve books, including *Most of My Patients are Animals, Ranchin', Ropin' and Doctorin'*, and *Understanding the Ancient Secrets of the Horse's Mind*. A noted veterinary lecturer, he has traveled all over the world to share his expertise in shaping animal behavior, veterinary philosophy, horsemanship and ethology. His distinguished service to veterinary science has earned him the Bustad Companion Animal Veterinarian of the Year, American Veterinary Medical Association President's Award and the North American Saddle Mule Association Lifetime Achievement Award, among others. Dr. Miller rides mules and his well-known molly, Jordass Jean, was inducted into the Mule Hall of Fame during ceremonies at Mule Days in Bishop, California, in May, 2004.

for its disappearance is controversial, but I believe it was due primarily to predation by the many species of large canine and feline predators that inhabited North America at that time. Human predation was an additional factor that probably helped lead to the extinction of the horse in North America. However, long before its extinction, horses had migrated over the Bering land bridge into Asia and from there into Europe and down through the Middle East into Africa. Only the New World, North and South America, was devoid of horses. It was not until the sixteenth century that the horse was introduced by the Spanish conquistadors into the New World.

Over the millions of years during which this all took place, the horse evolved into a variety of forms that included the zebra, the ass and the onager. The ass, then, is actually a more highly evolved form of animal than is its predecessor, the horse. In fact, the horse was on its way to extinction in Europe and Asia and was probably only saved from that fate by domestication.

Even though the horse and the ass are different species with different chromosome counts, they are capable of breeding and producing a hybrid offspring that is almost always sterile. These offspring we call the mule (mare plus jack) or a hinny (stallion plus jennet, or jenny). This hybridization occurs in nature, but because the offspring are sterile, it is usually a dead end. Even so, mankind recognized early on the physical characteristics of the mule that made it superior to either parent for domestic purposes. Therefore, intentional mule breeding was started a long time ago.

Evolving as a plains-dwelling creature, the horse, surrounded by hungry predators, developed flight as its primary survival behavior. This is in contrast to most other grazing animals, which are equipped with horns to defend themselves. Members of the cattle family–for example, the *bovidae*, such as bison, Cape buffalo, musk ox, or yak–are extremely aggressive and use their horns very effectively to defend themselves. Domestic cattle have for thousands of years been bred for docility and are therefore less

aggressive, with the exception of the Spanish fighting bull. That's the real cow!

Cattle, like other ruminants, have a compartmentalized stomach, fill it when grazing, and then rest while they ruminate, chewing the cud and reprocessing the food. If, during this process, a predator threatens them, they are quite capable of arising and defending themselves with their horns. The horse, on the other hand, with an overly full stomach, is handicapped in flight. Therefore, the horse has a different digestive system and a different lifestyle. It eats all the time. Its stomach never completely fills or empties. Wild horses will graze ten to eighteen hours a day, depending on the available vegetation. Because the stomachs are never full and because they do not have to ruminate, they are capable of instantaneous flight whenever threatened. In order to understand the horse, it is essential to realize that it is a flight creature and, in fact, the only common domestic animal that in the wild state uses flight as its primary survival behavior.

The ass, on the other hand, evolved in arid, rugged terrain and is much less flight oriented than is the horse. When frightened in the wild state, a horse will resort to instantaneous blind flight and may sustain injuries. The wild ass views this as possibly calamitous, and therefore, when alarmed, it will assess the situation and make a decision to do one of three things: to flee as would a horse, or to stay put because it is safe in its particular location (this is where the reputation for stubbornness comes from), or third, to attack. This choice may be made in a fraction of a second, but it is particularly un-horse-like behavior, and it is this decision capability that gives the ass and its hybrid offspring, the mule, its wisdom and judgment. This explains why a runaway horse will often run through a barbed-wire fence or off a cliff, whereas mules will rarely do so. Even though a mule runs off with its rider, it rarely runs blindly and it is usually thinking all the way. It is the reason that a mule, when trapped in wire, will usually freeze and assess the situation or wait for help, whereas horses will usually struggle and injure themselves severely. It is the reason that an overloaded mule will balk and refuse to go on, whereas a horse will usually go on until it drops. It is the flightiness of the horse that causes it to injure itself so frequently and to injure the people who work around it. Ironically, this flightiness is also the reason that the horse is so useful to us. In domestication we harness that flight instinct and we direct it down the racetrack, into the harness collar, after the cow, over the fence, around the barrels and so on. Being less flighty, if the mule does not enjoy what it is doing, or if it feels overburdened, it will make a decision and refuse to go on.

As a veterinarian I have treated hundreds of thousands of horses, but a much smaller number of mules, so my experience medically with mules is fairly limited. Even if mules were as abundant as horses, I would have far less experience because they simply do not get themselves into trouble as frequently as do horses. The horse, being so much more flighty than the mule, suffers a far greater incidence of injuries. The sure-footed abilities of the mule, derived from its asinine father, are another reason that they are injured less often than the horse. One of the most common ailments of the horse is colic. Indeed, most horses die of intestinal obstruction because horses are programmed to eat all they can whenever they can. The mule, like its paternal parent, is a more selective and discriminating eater and will rarely overload its digestive tract. Therefore it is much less susceptible to common veterinary problems such as colic and laminitis.

The hybrid vigor of the mule makes it resistant to many of the infections and afflictions that we see so commonly in horses. The fact that mules are judgmental and are capable of making decisions helps keep them from overexerting themselves, and this is probably one reason they are less susceptible to the many orthopedic problems that we see in horses.

The large ears of a mule radiate heat, allowing the mule to withstand heat.

Pound for pound, mules are generally stronger than horses.

Donkeys have 62 chromosomes, horses have 64 chromosomes, the mule or hinny has 63.

Mules tend to live five to ten years longer than a horse.

Mules can jump as well as horses, and their speed and agility is equal to a horse.

Mules inherit their sure-footedness from the donkey.

14

Thus, the horse may run its heart out on the track or in the rodeo arena, often suffering leg injuries as a result, whereas the mule, which is capable of running just as fast as the horse, will often spare itself the extreme exertion that causes break-downs. Mules, therefore, even racing mules, are much less susceptible to leg problems.

Because their ancestry evolved not on turf, but on rocky harsh terrain, mules usually have a bet-ter texture to the structure of their hooves. Because the ass evolved in hot, desert climates, it is capable of withstanding environmental heat much more effectively than can the horse. The large ears of the ass are, like those of many desert animals, designed to radiate heat in order to keep the body temperature normal.

There are only a few medical conditions to which the ass and the mule are *more* susceptible than the horse. These include habronemiasis, also known as summer sores, jack sores, or bursatti. Habronemiasis is a skin disease of *equidae* caused by the larvae of stomach worms (habronema) carried by flies to wounds in the skin. They cause severe inflammation and nasty sores. Horses, mules and asses are all suscepti-ble, but the ass and mule more so than the horse, hence the name "jack sores." There are now modern medications that help to heal these sores; they may be largely prevent-ed by treating wounds promptly and by the use of fly repellents on the animal during warm weather.

The ass and the mule are also more susceptible to lungworm infestation than are horses. However, the

The first mule I ever treated was when I first moved to Thousand Oaks, California. An elderly couple had a small farm and called me to geld a two-year-old mule. I arrived and gelded it just as I would a horse. When I was done, I told them I wanted them to wait twenty-four hours and then start exercising it about twenty minutes twice a day to keep the swelling down. They whispered together and seemed to have a problem with that. I said, "Well, I don't expect it's broke to ride; I don't expect you to ride it." I said, "You can put it on a lunge line or pony it from another horse, just so it moves around and gets some exercise." They replied, "Well that's not the problem. You see, it doesn't belong to us and the owner doesn't know we had it castrated." I looked at them, horri-fied. They went on, "See,

it belongs to the place next door and it keeps coming over the fence to breed our mares, so we decided to have it gelded. The owners are so dumb they probably won't know the difference." I said, "You know what? You didn't tell me this, and I don't know anything about it. I don't want to hear another word about it!" So, I am not so sure the owners were that dumb; they may have figured out a way to get the neigh-bors to pay for the castration.

Another story is that many years later there was a man who had six miniature mules just up the

street, walking distance, from our hospital. He used these six little johns in a team. He came over one day and said, "These little guys are getting so rambunctious I think I ought to geld them. What would you charge me to cas-trate all six?" Well, we were charging at that time one hundred dollars to castrate a grown horse and I thought, gosh, they are so small and there are six of them and he can walk them right over to the clinic, I don't even have to drive to his place. I said, we'll do

them for twenty-five dollars apiece. Oh, what a mistake I made! They were a cross between a Shetland pony and a Sicilian donkey and they were a handful.

I think I could have done six Percheron horses in the time it took me to do those six little mules.

modern vermifuges, or anti-worming medications, have greatly minimized this problem.

Another condition, somewhat more common in mules than in horses, is neonatal isoerythrolysis. This is a serious condition of newborn foals that can cause a fatal destruc-tion of the red blood cells. The condition has also been called foal anemia, foal jaundice and erroneously, RH factor. With the exception of these few conditions, mules have far fewer medical problems than do horses.

Mules in general are more difficult patients for a veter-inarian than horses. On the one hand, they are capable of withstanding high levels of pain. Balking mules have been whipped severely and yet they will still refuse to move. On the other hand, they do not like to be hurt and can be very refractory to anything that either causes pain or that they think may cause pain, including an ordinary injection. For the veterinarian as well as for the trainer, the old saying that "mules must be treated the way horses should be treated" holds true.

Scooter, at three weeks of age, was bred out of a Quarter Horse mare. Patient training that occurred since this picture was taken has made her into a wonderful mule.

Horses have remarkable memories, rarely forgetting anything, but they are forgiving creatures. This is fortunate, or most horse trainers would be incapable of training horses because the methods they use are coercive and less than optimum. Mules similarly do not forget anything, but they also do not forgive. If mistreated, mules will wait until the opportunity arises for them to get even. This is the reason that all mule lovers are horse lovers, but not all horse lovers are mule lovers. Many successful horse trainers dislike mules and will not handle them. I believe one of the reasons the mule is rapidly regaining popularity as a recreational animal is because the training methods that are now sweeping the world—called variously "natural

horsemanship," "new age horsemanship," and "progressive horsemanship"—are so much more appropriate for training mules. Even more than horses, mules respond to solicitous, gentle, persuasive training methods rather than the use of force and coercion.

Horsemanship changed tremendously in the last decades of the twentieth century, and there is every indication that it will continue to change as traditional methods, largely involving the use of force, are being abandoned while more scientific and humane methods are becoming popular. The reasons for these changes are many. First, a horse owner in our society is now usually an educated person. This was not true in past centuries, when most people working with horses were uneducated and often illiterate, a situation that continues in some parts of the world. Second, the communication explosion that has affected all technologies has also affected horsemanship. Videotapes, the Internet, periodicals, books and clinicians traveling all over the world are rapidly teaching better methods of horsemanship. Very significantly, for the first time in human history women now dominate the horse industries in countries such as the United States, Canada, Western Europe, Australia and New Zealand. And women, as a general rule, are more accepting of persuasive methods of manipulating equine behavior than the traditional coercive methods. This revolution in horsemanship, as I call it, has been of great benefit to the horse, but it is of even greater benefit to the mule. Were it not for this change in horsemanship that is so rapidly spreading all over the world, the increasing popularity of the mule would never have occurred. Once again, horses never forget, but they do forgive. Mules never forget and they *do not* forgive. Remember, the wild horse startled by a predator will always flee, whereas the wild ass startled by a predator will often attack the predator.

I have found the training methods taught and advocated by Pat Parelli, of Pagosa Springs, Colorado, to be especially effective in the training of mules. Mules are highly sociable animals and bond strongly to horses in particular, but

THE BABY-SITTER
© HARVEY RATTEY 1998

also to other mules and to humans. Even though mules that have never been taught to accept dogs will often show aggression to them, mules will often bond with dogs if given the opportunity to, especially if exposed to them while quite young.

I do not know why, but I have observed that a majority of the best performance mules in all disciplines (jumping, racing, roping, reining, cutting and so forth) have been mollies. There have also been many outstanding johns. The mule that converted me from horses to mules was a seventeen-year-old john mule named Jerry, but still I find that the mollies outnumber the johns greatly when it comes to successful performance. I do not know why that is.

As saddle animals, mules are capable of doing anything that a horse is capable of doing, although generally, horses will excel. There are some exceptions. Mules are, as a rule, definitely superior for backcountry trail riding, being very sure-footed. They also tolerate hot weather better than horses will. Pound for pound, they are stronger than horses. As draft animals, they excel. As show animals, horses will generally outperform mules, but mules seem to have a greater versatility than horses, being able to do a greater number of things

ODE TO THE MULE RIDER

When you are tense, let me
    teach you to relax.
When you are short-tempered, let me
    teach you to be patient.
When you are shortsighted, let me teach
    you to see.
When you are quick to react, let me teach
    you to be thoughtful.
When you are angry, let me teach you to
    be respectful.
When you are self-absorbed, let me teach
    you to think of greater things.
When you are arrogant, let me teach you
    humility.
When you are lonely, let me be your
    companion.
When you are tired, let me carry the load.
When you need to learn, let me teach
    you.
After all, I am your mule.

And now the REAL story....

When you are tense,
let me teach you that there are dragons
    in the forest, and we need to leave
    NOW!
When you are short-tempered,
let me teach you how to slog around
    the pasture for an hour before you can
    catch me.
When you are shortsighted,
let me teach you to figure out where,
    exactly, in the 40 acres I am hiding.

When
    you are quick to react
    let me teach you that herbivores kick
    MUCH faster than omnivores.
When you are angry,
let me teach you how well I can stand
    on my hind feet because I don't FEEL
    like cantering on my right lead today,
    that's why!
When you are worried,
let me entertain you with my mystery
    lameness, GI complaint, and skin dis-
    ease.
When you feel superior,
let me teach you that, mostly, you are the
    maid service.
When you are self-absorbed,
let me teach you to PAY ATTENTION.
    I TOLD you about those dragons
    in the forest.
When you are arrogant,
let me teach you what twelve-hundred
    pounds of a YAHOO-let's-go mule can
    do when suitably inspired.
When you are lonely, let me be your
    companion. Let's do lunch.
Also, breakfast and dinner.
When you are feeling financially secure,
let me teach you the meaning of "veteri-
    nary services."
When you need to learn, hang around,
    bud. I'll learn ya.

—AUTHOR UNKNOWN

than horses are capable of. Most horses are more specialized. In a show arena mules probably will excel in trail classes, being less flighty than horses, if properly trained. Mules can jump as well as horses and sometimes higher, although not always as beautifully as horses. Their speed and agility are equal to those of horses, but it takes an exceptional trainer to get the mule to perform to its fullest extent.

About forty years ago I developed a method of training newborn foals. I call this method "imprint training" because the foal sees whatever is moving around it and is automatically bonded to that. This method of training newborn foals has been slowly accepted all over the world by all equine disciplines, although it is by no means yet prevalent. It has even been accepted by the racing Thoroughbred industry which was at first very resistant to the concept. However, mule breeders have been the most enthusiastic of all breeders to accept this training method. This verifies, once again, the old adage that horses should be trained the way mules *must* be trained.

I have long been a proponent of not riding horses under the age of three years. Stressing immature horses does nobody any good save for the veterinarian, who is being constantly presented with orthopedic problems, many of them very serious, which are due to too much work for too young a horse. Because mules are so physically durable, I once thought that mules would be an exception to this principle and could be safely started as two-year-olds. I have changed my mind. Not only should mules be allowed to mature as fully as horses before they are worked hard, but, in fact, they are slower maturing. And perhaps one should wait

Our world champion performance mule, Jordass Jean, is now retired and in her twenties. She was nominated for the Hall of Fame for the 2002 Bishop Mule Days and inducted in 2004. When she was in her prime, we were at the Los Angeles County Draft Horse and Mule Show. My wife was in the warm-up ring preparing for an English class. Two young women about twenty years of age came along and they were standing by me. They did not know I was the owner. One of them said, "That is the most bizarre thing I've ever seen!" The other one said, "What?" Her friend said, "That's a mule! Get a load of the English get-up." And the other one said, "Yeah, but that's a good-looking mule!" The first one responded, "I bet it's half horse."

And as a matter of fact, I think a minority of horse owners know what a mule is. Most of them are confused between a mule, a burro and a donkey. Of course the donkey is the domestic ass. The burro is the Spanish word for donkey, and the mule is a hybrid. They will often see one of our mules and say, "I didn't know they were that big."

Of course, they are thinking about burros.

Debbie Miller, wife of Dr. Robert Miller, riding Jordass Jean at the 1984 Olympics. Jordass represented the American Mule in the cavalcade of horses at that event. She was the only mule invited to do exhibition jumping.

a little bit longer. There is so much valuable training that can be done on the ground before a horse or a mule is ridden that there is no reason to regard it as a waste of time to wait until it is a little more mature. Extending the useful life of the animal will more than compensate for the delay. Many horses break down before they reach their prime because they have been ridden too early. Moreover, mules tend to outlive horses by five to ten years, and if not injured early in life, there is a good chance they will remain sound until they are quite old. I have found that mules go through certain changes in their personality as they mature. Six years of age is a turning point, as it is in horses, but then I find that mules settle further at about ten years of age. Somewhere between ten and thirty years of age may be the very best years of performance for a mule. So why hurry and push them too hard when they are young and still growing?

Mules have a different body structure than horses, and there are some training aspects I have learned that should be given consideration. I find that a lot of mules do not like the simple snaffle bit and respond better to a more flexible bit such as a Dr. Bristol snaffle. Mules can be nicely started in a halter or hackamore and not put into the bit until they are performing well. Mules tend to be slightly more stiff-necked than horses and less accepting of excessive contact and harsh hands. They compel us to be better horsemen, using our legs and other aids rather than relying upon the bit.

Many mules, probably the majority, are built in such a way that an ordinary saddle, even with a mule tree, will tend to slip forward on them, necessitating either a crupper or a britchin'. Western saddles, especially those with Quarter Horse trees, often do not properly fit mules—even those mules that are born of Quarter Horse mares. It is important that the saddle fit the mule's back.

It is a myth that mules do not have to be shod, although it is true that their feet tend to be more resilient and tougher than horses' feet. If used on abrasive surfaces, mules will have to be shod. It is also a myth that

Dr. Robert Miller ropes off of Sally, the 25-year-old mule in this photograph. Sally was out of a Tennessee Walker and lived to be 34.

mules will not founder and become lame. Although they are less greedy than horses and less susceptible to grain-founder, they can and do founder, especially if they are overweight and overfed. Mules require the same preventive medical care that horses do: the same vaccinations and the same worming program as dictated by local conditions.

Since johns have no breeding potential, there is no reason to delay castrating the male mule foal. Many people do not realize that foals can be successfully castrated shortly after birth. I have done quite a few castrations. There are those who believe this actually produces a larger mule, and I tend to agree with them. It is the increase in testosterone at puberty that slows and stops bone growth. This is the reason that steers grow larger than bulls. I believe this is true of the horse as well. All of the colts younger than one week old that I have castrated grew to a larger size than anticipated. Other than that, there is no disadvantage to castrating very young foals. In the case of mules, I definitely recommend it. I have gelded them as early as two days of age with no ill effect. Nobody can look at a five-year-old gelding and tell if it was castrated when it was one day, one week, one month, or one year of age.

In the case of well-bred horses, if there is any possibility of producing an outstanding stallion, I recommend that castration be delayed. In the case of mules, however, there is no similar reason. By gelding them early, we can prevent a lot of undesirable behavior problems later on. The exception is where a small gelding mule is desired. In that case, I would recommend delaying castration until after puberty. Several authorities have reported a higher incidence of inguinal hernia following very early castration. This has not been my experience, and I believe that careful surgical technique can minimize this possibility.

Although I am a mule enthusiast, I do not recommend mules for most horse owners. I am not sure that I would have been able to get along well with mules when I was younger, having been a normal young male. On the other hand, in my mid-twenties I discovered what is now called "natural horsemanship" and was starting colts using these gentle, kind and non-forceful methods. So perhaps I would have been better with mules than I think.

Mules will test your horsemanship. You must be patient, kind, gentle, consistent and very persuasive in order to train mules and get along well with them. They separate the "men from the boys" when it comes to horse trainers. This is one of the reasons that I am a mule fan. Other reasons are their resistance to lameness. They are so much less trouble than horses and less temperamental than horses. A well-trained mule can be laid up for many weeks or even months and then when you go back to ride that mule, it will usually act just as if you had ridden it the day before. Again, this relates to the fact that mules are less flighty. This does not mean that green or poorly trained mules will not run away. They *will* run away and are, in fact, more difficult to stop than a horse, but they rarely run blindly, they watch where they go, and they are thinking all the time. They are less likely to buck than horses, but I can tell you from personal experience that there are exceptions to that rule, too.

I have heard people say that mules are just like horses, only more so. I think that is a good description of their personality. I kind of consider the mule a super-horse. I have been involved with mules as a breeder and owner for about a quarter of a century and people often ask me, "Why do you like mules?" I say to them, "If you knew a man who would rarely start a fight, but was always capable of finishing one, who had very good judgment, high intelligence, a tremendous work ethic, but would never allow himself to be taken advantage of or overworked, what would your opinion of that person be?" Most people say that sounds like a person with character. Well, that perfectly describes mules and that is why I like and respect them. The longer I am around them, the more I respect them.

Let me say something about the people who ride and like mules. I like them. They tend to be the salt of the earth. There are a lot of horse people who ride because of ego or social standing. They ride to project an image of success, aristocracy, or superiority. People who are involved with mules are not interested in it for ego or for money; they just like the mules. That is why my wife and I rarely attend horse shows anymore, but we really do enjoy the mule shows. We like the people and we like the animals. Mule owners tend to be unpretentious, kind, sociable and tolerant. If everybody were that way, this would be a far better world.

WHY I'M NOT HORSING AROUND ANYMORE

BY RON SCHARA

Ron Schara is a well-known outdoor writer and television personality. His nationally broadcast program, Backroads with Ron and Raven, airs on ESPN2 and has consistently been one of the highest-rated shows on the outdoor block. Schara's programs are seen on national cable outlets The Outdoor Channel and on Kingdom Vision Network.

There's a new way to get around in the boondocks. Just remember you heard it here first. Well, okay, it's not exactly a new mode of backcountry transportation, but it seems to be moving faster than a racehorse. We're talking mules. Yes mules, those colorful steeds with long ears and a reputation for stubbornness.

Have I got mule stories to share with you. Horses are out; mules are in. But first allow me to apologize to Midnight and Cowboy, a couple of mountain horses. In autumns past, I have trusted my life to Midnight and Cowboy and a smattering of other horses whose names escape me. They have carried me across godforsaken ground in the darkest of nights; they have led me home on trails I couldn't remember.

I like horses; now I like mules more. And I'm not alone. This is a trend. Maybe even a hee-haw movement. My friend John Hauer used to be a horseman who would accept any reason to saddle up. He loves riding. In short, John has pitched his share of hay bales and horse manure. Over the seasons, we have ridden together on hunting trips from the antelope prairies of Wyoming to the deer draws of the Black Hills, and always on horses. But no more.

Some time ago, my hunting companion became an unabashed owner, rider and promoter of nothing but mules. "When you compare the advantages and disadvantages of riding mules versus riding horses, you saddle up on mules," Hauer insisted.

It was like a reincarnation. John meant it. He sold his horses and bought mules.

At first, I thought Johnny had lost a marble or two. Then one fall shortly thereafter, John and I planned on gathering in the Colorado Rockies at Dick Dodds' Elkhorn Outfitters to ride into the high country near Craig, Colorado, in search of bull elk.

John said he would bring a couple of mules. What would Dick Dodds think of such a sight? "Mules?" Dodds said, happily. "That's what I ride, too."

Holy hee-haw. Had I uncovered a four-legged scoop?

Dodds, who has sixty thousand acres of hunting ground limited to foot or horseback (muleback?), had also become a mule man. "I just realized that mules hold up better. You can ride a mule day after day and it holds up," Dodds explained. He said the mules also are a better fit for his elk-hunting customers, most of whom don't know rein from rain or stirrup from syrup.

"You can ride a mule for hours and never feel sore," Dodds added.

Having sat on a mule now for three days, I can testify to the absence of an aching crotch. If you know what I mean, this is a remarkable achievement. The credit for this goes to Sassy, a molly with an attitude and a pair of long, pointed ears. For three days, Sassy trudged up and down the high plateaus of elk country carrying me, a backpack, and a seven-millimeter Remington. Together, we plunged through deep snow and encountered the wonders of mountain wildlife ranging from flushing sharptails to bounding mule deer.

Sassy and I walked where many a Jeep would fear to tread. None of this surprises mule men. As John explained, mules are stronghearted and sure-footed. Although a mule is what happens when you cross a mare with a jack, Hauer says the result is the best of both animals. Little things, such as a tangled lead rope that might make a horse stampede, simply don't faze a mule, Hauer insisted. "Mules will figure things out," he said.

Dodds, a former Minnesotan, said his decision to abandon motorized vehicles in favor of mules has made vast improvements in the quality of his hunting experience and for the hunters he guides. No pistons, just hooves. "It's just a better hunt. It may not be for everybody but a hunt on muleback is the way we like to go," said Dodds.

Count me in.

Sassy didn't break my neck or bruise my rump. By riding and walking, I bagged a nice bull elk and felt it was a trophy I had earned. And that's the point. I'll never forget the hunting horses of my past but I'm a mule man now. It's just good horse sense.

Ron Schara and John Hauer on a successful hunting trip in the foothills of the Rocky Mountains in Colorado.

Mules Are the First Cloned Equines

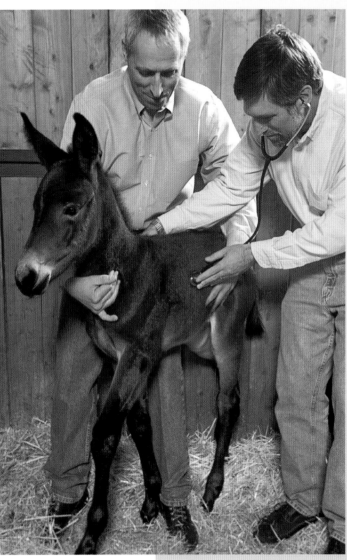

Idaho Gem receives a careful examination from University of Idaho research scientists Dr. Gordon Woods (left) and Dr. Dirk Vanderwall.

In their first year, the identical triplet mule clones of Project Idaho proved more than worth their weight in entertainment and publicity for the University of Idaho in Moscow. Idaho Gem, the firstborn, made news worldwide after the official announcement of his birth on May 29, 2003. He was at once endearing, comical, good looking and a scientific marvel as the first equine clone.

The team of scientists, Dr. Gordon Woods and Dr. Dirk Vanderwall, both professors and veterinarians from the University of Idaho, and Dr. Ken White, an animal reproduction scientist from Utah State University in Logan, Utah, finished first in the international race to clone a member of the horse family. They won by a matter of weeks in a long-term endurance race that began with the 1997 announcement of the cloning of Dolly the sheep by Scottish scientists. Dolly was the first mammal cloned from an adult cell—in her case, a mammary cell.

Italian scientist Ceasare Galli finished a close second in the equine race and was the first to clone a horse. Prometea, named for the titan who stole fire from the gods to give comfort to man, was born to a Haflinger mare on May 28, twenty-four days after Idaho Gem's birth. Her birth occurred the day before the

BY BILL LOFTUS

Bill Loftus is a science writer at the University of Idaho.

world learned of Idaho Gem. A publication on the website for *Science* magazine, the pinnacle of American scientific publishing, served as a prestigious birth announcement.

Forging a new trail through the highly traditional world of equine reproduction proved full of excitement. The Project Idaho team, which included the scientists and a bevy of university administrators, advising veterinarians and a large support crew, believed there was a race afoot. Common acquaintances with Galli's group relayed veiled progress reports back and forth across the Atlantic.

Once May 4 dawned and Idaho Gem began to show his vigorous, healthy promise, the fear grew that the mule could win the race but be trumped in the quest for the attention he was due by a later-arriving horse. The scientists decided that the scientific rigor of peer review for their article and publication in one of the world's top journals was their main goal. The cameras could wait.

Both the scientific and the publicity arms of the American Association for the Advancement of Science (AAAS), the publisher of *Science* magazine, knew they had a winning science story and a winning personality when the first photos of Idaho Gem arrived at the AAAS office in Washington, D.C. The review of the equine cloning publication sped through channels with nearly the same speed as a report about the sequencing of the genome of the SARS virus.

Three weeks after Gem's birth, the scientific article was scheduled for publication, and word began to filter out to reporters worldwide through the AAAS network. Reporters from London and Australia called to talk with Woods, the team leader. The *Wall Street Journal* put a reporter on the story. The story was also covered by the *Los Angeles Times* and *New York Times*. A report by a science writer for the Associated Press found its way around the world on the news wires. Suddenly, mules were cool. In fact, CNN declared the birth of Idaho Gem its "Cool Science" story of the week.

Twink Allen, one of the world's foremost equine reproduction scientists, served up the best compliment from among the leaders of rival teams. Allen, frustrated by bureaucratic controls that hobbled his own efforts at cloning, combined British humor, grace and charm in his comments to London's *Guardian* newspaper: "I have to say the key drive until now has been scientific arrogance; we wanted to be first. I am feeling very cheesed," he said. "But they deserve great credit. I am just jealous as hell of them."

Others were less gracious. The *Wall Street Journal* tapped into a vein of mule prejudice from a horse expert chagrined by defeat. "It's a big step," said Katrin Hinrichs, a professor at Texas A&M University in College Station, but "it's a little disappointing that it's a mule." Hinrichs' own attempt at cloning ended bitterly later in the year with the loss of a nearly full-term pregnancy of a clone of a horse ridden by her daughter. The article declared, "Cloning horses could one day be a big business; some top jumpers and dressage animals are worth millions."

The excitement was in part generated by the remarkable run of a magnificent gelding, Funny Cide, who romped through the Kentucky Derby and Preakness before losing in the Belmont Stakes, another victim of the Triple Crown curse. Funny Cide attracted widespread attention both as the first gelding to win the Derby since 1929, when Clyde Van Dusen did the deed, and for his pack of high school buddy owners, who proved that regular guys could still buy a contender.

The only way to bring Funny Cide's superior ability back into Thoroughbred bloodlines would be through cloning, to recreate a genetic copy of a gelding that would be born again as a colt. Not that the Jockey Club would allow it, of course. The official arbiter of Thoroughbred racing made it clear as soon as the topic sprang up that it was natural service or nothing. Idahoans had their own horse to ride in any debate about the potential for cloning Thoroughbreds. Buddy Gil, an Idaho-trained gelding, made a strong showing in Funny Cide's Kentucky Derby, finishing sixth.

Defenders of Kentucky bluegrass blueblood studs no doubt cheered comments from Dr. Ernest Bailey, an expert on horse genetics at the University of Kentucky, in the *New York Times.* He noted that the clone of a champion racehorse would not necessarily be a winner itself and reiterated points that the Project Idaho team also made: nature (or genetics) and nurture (or environment) both rule an organism's development.

Don Jacklin poses with Idaho Star and his surrogate dam, Idaho Dawn.

Even identical genes turn on and off during different times of an animal's development. Bailey responded to the Funny Cide discussion with professorial authority in his comments to the *New York Times.* "If you had a race with ten Secretariats, they wouldn't cross the finish line at the same time." He claimed cloning would steal the magic from the success of the breeders who produced Funny Cide.

The *New York Times* reported Bailey saying, "If they had done that with a clone of Secretariat do you think people would care? Even worse, what if they raced a clone of Secretariat and lost? People would think they were idiots."

Mule people cared little about such concerns. Don Jacklin, a Post Falls, Idaho, businessman and president of the American Mule Racing Association, was an unabashed fan of Idaho Gem. Jacklin, who owns a stable of racing mules, should have been. He donated much of the private funding that allowed the project to proceed. Jacklin enjoys sharing his passion for mules and mule racing. Idaho Gem and his identical triplet brothers were from the same cross of the Quarter Horse mare Mesmerizer and the Spanish jack Coaley McGhee that produced several of his other racers, including his best, Taz, and a promising new brother, Chinook Pass.

The DNA for Idaho Gem and the other clones, Utah Pioneer and Idaho Star, actually came from fetal skin cells. There were concerns shortly after the birth of Dolly the sheep that she might have been "born old" because her DNA was from a six-year-old ewe. In 1998, when Jacklin challenged Woods to produce the world's first equine clone, the scientists decided to go to the youngest possible source of somatic or differentiated, adult cells, the fetus. The mules were cloned from skin cells taken from a forty-five-day-old fetus that resulted from mating Jacklin's favorite mule parents.

Mule racing and Jacklin's Taz inspired passion in a lot of race fans in 2002 when the rivalry between Taz and Black Ruby, a molly mule who outran him as often as not, won the TVG television racing channel's Viewer's Choice Award for the top rivalry in horse racing. Mule racing is gaining popularity throughout the country, particularly in the West where it began, Jacklin said. California racetracks such as Los Alamitos, Pomona and Del Mar have scheduled mule races with strong fan support, including a daily record turnout at one track.

The TVG vote was exciting, Jacklin said, because it showed broader interest. "They picked up eastern fans that didn't even know that mule racing existed ... Seeing the Taz–Black Ruby rivalry attract so much attention was surprising because they were up against the best races, the best horses and the best jockeys in the world."

The strong will that makes mules famous also makes them intense competitors, Jacklin said. "People were amazed these two mules would compete so hard."

Mules are fast, though not as fast as Thoroughbreds. They can beat some horses such as Paints, Arabians and Appaloosas but typically run in the middle of the pack when racing against Quarter Horses. Mules typically race their best over short distances of 300 to 440 yards.

Jacklin has long supported research by Woods, a University of Idaho professor of animal and veterinary science and a veterinarian, who directs the Northwest Equine Reproduction Laboratory on the Moscow campus. Jacklin donated funds to directly support Vanderwall, a UI assistant professor of animal and veterinary science. Woods said Vanderwall's expertise was essential to the project.

In 1994, Jacklin and Woods represented the UI program when it was chosen to be grand marshal of the Bishop Mule Days Parade in central California. The focus of the program then was using pioneering embryo transfer techniques to produce four siblings within months of one another.

Jacklin makes it clear that he is proud to have been a sponsor of the research that led to the first cloned equine, and proud that it produced a mule. He is more proud to support the people. "Even though the animals are important, what this is really about is the opportunity to work with quality people like Gordon Woods, Dirk Vanderwall and other members of the team," Jacklin said.

When asked the now-familiar question about why the team chose a mule as the focus for its cloning project, Woods has developed a stock answer. "Do you want the smart-ass answer or the real one? The smart answer is because mules are sterile and can't reproduce, so we decided to give them a hand. The real answer is that our work was supported by Don Jacklin, and he asked us to make sure mules finished the race first," said Woods.

Horsemen around the world and far removed from Kentucky are interested in cloning. Eric Palmer traveled from Sonchamp near Paris, to Moscow, Idaho, weeks before Idaho Gem was born to visit Woods. Palmer sees an important future for cloning in Europe's refined world of competitive horsemanship. The reason is simple: most of the top champions in dressage, jumping, eventing, equitation and similar events are geldings, which are genetic dead-ends. In Europe, athletic performance in competition is what counts. Equine champions can come from any breed.

Unlike the racing world, where a champion stallion's progeny are tested by age three or four on the track and can then be retired for breeding, Europe's champion horses take a decade or more to develop, undermining the ability to quickly test the performance of a stallion's offspring. That produces the irony that brings Europeans like Palmer to America in search of a successful method for cloning horses.

Palmer's interest in cloning horses arose long before the run for the roses in 2004. Long an academic researcher, Palmer shifted gears to commerce and formed a company, Cryozootech S.A., based in Sonchamp, France, to rescue the genetics of gelded champion horses.

"So now we come into cloning; why is cloning an interesting business? It's another way to solve the problem of some totally infertile animals. Among these infertile horses are all the geldings, all the horses that have been castrated. And some of them, after they have been castrated, you find they are very, very big champions. And their potential is being a stallion."

Cloning offers a tool to turn back the clock to recreate the stallion that became a gelding that became a champion. The performance of the cloned stallion in athletic events will be less important than his ability in the breeding shed to pass on his unique carbon copy DNA to improve traditional breeding lines.

Palmer's own stature in equine science is unique. In 1990, he produced the world's first test-tube foal produced by in-vitro fertilization—uniting egg and sperm outside the mare's body to ensure fertilization. It is a last-ditch solution for infertile mares. His team produced another test-tube foal, and no one has reported success with the technique since. Embryo transfer, wherein horse embryos begin life naturally within valuable mares and are then moved to less-valuable surrogate dams, has become routine. With embryo transfer, a valuable mare can produce many more offspring than she could otherwise.

And while artificial insemination and embryo transfer have made advances in horse breeding, Palmer is excited about the impact of cloning. "If you can take one of these big champions that has been castrated but is at the top of the genetics, there is potential for improving genetics and a business potential," he said.

"I am working with people in quantitative genetics. They made some calculations according to the type of populations and in some of the disciplines like dressage, endurance, and eventing, ninety percent of the big champions are castrated horses. In this situation you can improve genetic progress, and accelerate genetic progress by fifty percent if you are able to make stallions of these big champions," Palmer added.

Although business prospects were apparent to Woods, Vanderwall, and Jacklin in particular, Woods made it clear that equine cloning opened new doors to his own scientific understanding of horses and human health. The intersection of the two, he believes, may prove the key to understanding how some types of cancer, diabetes and other age-onset diseases begin. Woods had taken an interest in basic horse physiology after becoming intrigued by the observation that stallions do not develop prostate cancer. The horse's basic metabolism is "slow" compared to humans and many other mammals, Woods said. He speculated that differences in cellular activity might play a role in both cancer development and reproduction. He formed an outside company, CancEr2, to investigate that observation. The studies showed a fundamental difference between men and stallions in the calcium concentrations within the cells and surrounding fluid. Woods said the team would explore other lines of scientific inquiry opened by the cloning success.

The births in 2003 of Utah Pioneer on June 9 and Idaho Star on July 27 soon followed that of Idaho Gem the previous year. The mule foals quickly began to attract the public's attention. Woods and the University of Idaho devoted resources to take the mules on the road to help the public understand science and the potential benefits of research, focusing attention on the possible medical benefits that could follow the research. The first appearances were modest: Idaho and Washington state 4-H members visited the campus weeks after the May 29 news conference. A regional gathering of Rotarians also welcomed a visit from Idaho Gem.

In August 2003, the road trips began in earnest with a swing south to Boise and the Western Idaho Fair for Gem, then on to the California State Fair at Sacramento for a stand outside the CalExpo racetrack, where Idaho Gem's brothers Taz and Chinook Pass took their turns out of the starting gate. More than five thousand people on peak nights filed past Idaho Gem on their way to the races. Very few objected to the idea of equine cloning. Even so, with public reaction uncertain, the racing staff provided full-time animal handlers and armed security guards to watch over Idaho Gem during his visit. Caustic commentators were few and admirers many.

That pattern held during Idaho Star's visit to the Eastern Idaho Fair at Blackfoot, while Idaho Gem soaked up the California sun. It was the same at the Lewiston (Idaho) Roundup, Woods' hometown and at Sandpoint, Idaho, home of the International Draft Horse and Mule Show. Utah Pioneer took his turn on the road in early October, visiting Utah State University's homecoming in honor of White, a crucial member of the cloning team. The three clones were kept separate from public viewing until the University of Idaho's Ag Days in mid-October. In November, another long journey from Moscow to Pocatello for the Idaho Horse Expo and its strong contingent of mule fanciers served as the 2003 finale for clone events.

Throughout the public travels, thousands of people had gathered to learn about mules, cloning, and the potential benefits of the research for human health. Few, perhaps no more than a few dozen, had voiced disapproval of cloning. One of them condemned even mules created the conventional way as abominations of divine law.

In January 2004, the foals received an invitation showing that scientific curiosity in their birth and development, and the implications of cloning, remained keen. As officials for the AAAS planned the world's largest scientific organization's February annual meeting in Seattle, they included Woods among the panelists invited to speak during a session on cloning. The organizers also invited Woods to bring along the three clones and to display

them in the Washington State Trade and Convention Center exhibit hall during Family Science Day. Attended by nine UI student employees, the clones were a hit, generating a new wave of worldwide news and acquainting more than three thousand visitors with the world of mules. Not that all visitors quite understood all the details. Jessica Marquardt, who was studying for her doctorate in animal physiology at UI with Vanderwall, was perplexed for a time by one comment. "Someone came up and complimented us for our excellent English. It turned out he thought we were from Moscow, Russia."

The *Chronicle of Higher Education*, the gazette of academe, leapfrogged off the students' Seattle experience and sent a reporter along with the student crew to the Idaho Horse Expo in Caldwell in April. The reporter shared droll insights about horse talk and horse people, the "dauntingly early" hours of clone field trips, and the public life of the foals. The reporter also wrote respectfully about the time and effort devoted to public outreach and training students to communicate science to the public.

The next major step for the mule clones will be when at least one will be trained for racing. The mule's DNA represents the best traditional attempt to breed for athletic performance. One test of their genetic fitness for that task will be to take them to the track, Woods said. It is likely that will be done through an arrangement with Don Jacklin. The University of Idaho will continue to view and keep the clones as research animals for the indefinite future in order to study the effects of cloning and basic questions about nature and nurture. Most visitors view them simply as interesting animals. "They look like mules," said one youngster, giving voice to popular sentiment. And so they are. And very special mules at that.

Triplet mule clones, from left, Idaho Star, Utah Pioneer and Idaho Gem with University of Idaho student employee handlers. Jessica Marquardt, far right, is a PhD student who served as Idaho Gem's main trainer and handler.

A Compilation of Interesting Facts (and a Few Opinions) About Mules

BY JOHN HAUER

George Washington, the father of our country, was also the father of the mule business in this country. America's mule industry started with a large jack that was a gift to Washington from the King of Spain. Washington named the jack Royal Gift.

He found that when the jack first arrived in this country he was a "shy breeder" of mares and "was perhaps too full of royalty to have anything to do with a plebeian race." Later, Royal Gift redeemed himself and Washington "sent the stud on a triumphant one thousand-mile breeding tour through the southern states."

Shortly thereafter, the Marquis of Lafayette gave Washington a smaller Maltese jack that Washington named Knight of Malta. Knight proved to be well suited for the breeding of saddle mules.

Washington believed that horses "ate too much, worked too little, and died too young" to be productive farm work animals.

General George Crook, considered to be the best Indian fighter on the western frontier, rode mules, and attributed his success in the Indian wars to the outstanding pack mules used by the army to pursue the Apaches.

During the Civil War, the rebels captured forty mules and an army general. When Abraham Lincoln heard the news, he is reported to have said, "I'm sorry to lose those mules."

In 1850 there were six hundred thousand mules in the United States. By 1920, the number had increased to six million, and by 1954 it had decreased to about 1.5 million. Today there are fewer than eight hundred thousand, but more mules are used for pleasure riding than ever before.

In World War I, the allied armies used approximately three hundred thousand mules, and

two hundred thousand mules saw service in World War II. Thousands of the mules used by the allied forces in Burma were de-voiced so their braying wouldn't give away their position. It is said that the United States has never lost a war in which it utilized mules.

In Switzerland, all mules, like all young men, are enlisted in the army, and like the men, the mules have serial numbers. The mules' serial numbers are branded on their hooves.

Alexander the Great rode a mule into battle; twelve mules pulled his war chariot. Sixty-four mules adorned in gold harnesses pulled his funeral bier.

Napoleon rode a mule when he crossed the Alps.

When Sam Houston retreated across Texas with Santa Anna hot on his heels, he rode a mule most of the way. Just before entering a village, he would change to a prancing stallion

for the ride through town. Then when out of sight of the town folks, he would get back on his trusty mule.

Mules were so valuable to American soldiers in the Spanish-American War that, when ambushing a pack train, the Spanish soldiers (who also rode mules) would shoot the mules first and then try to kill the soldiers.

In the 1970s and 1980s, the United States exported mules to the freedom fighters in Afghanistan, who used them to outmaneuver the Soviet troops in the mountainous areas where Jeeps, tanks and even helicopters were ineffective.

In old-time western movies, the sheriff usually rode a fancy white or buckskin horse. In real

life, the hero sometimes rode a mule. Such was the case of the straight-shooting deputy sheriff of Jerome, Arizona. In 1891, Jim Roberts was a mule-riding deputy in that Arizona mining camp where, prior to Roberts's arrival, the law was little respected and the miners mostly enforced their own laws.

A short time after Roberts arrived in Jerome, he arrested a desperado named Dud Crocker and chained him to a wagon wheel because there was no jail. With the help of a man named Sid Chew, Crocker cut his chains and the two men proceeded to murder the local blacksmith and Deputy Sheriff, Jim Hawkins. The murderers stole two horses and headed for a camp on the Verde River. A short time later, Roberts, riding a big white mule and leading a pack mule, started on their trail.

A report of the event states, "It was mid-afternoon when Roberts rode back into Jerome on his big white mule, the bodies of Crocker and Chew draped over the back of the pack mule he was leading."

A few months later a man known only as Chappo killed a local bartender, threatened

to kill Roberts if he came after him, and left Jerome headed for Prescott. Chappo "returned to Jerome a short time later draped over the back of Roberts' pack mule, dead from a single shot."

Heck, Gene Autry probably rode a mule on his day off.

Almost everyone is familiar with the Pony Express, but few are aware that mules preceded it. The Overland Mail, nick-named the Jackass Mail Service, blazed the trail for the Pony Express to follow.

The first mail service between Sacramento and Salt Lake City followed a route par-alleling modern Interstate 80. The Jackass Mail was misnamed, because the monthly mail ser-vice actually utilized carriages pulled by mules. The Jackass Mail carried the post from 1851 to 1860 and used just one major supply station for the journey of nine hundred miles. The compa-ny lost one of its owners, fifteen employees, and about three hundred mules and horses to hostile Indians.

Horace Greeley rode a Jackass Mail coach to California, as recounted in his book, *An Overland Journey*. Greeley tells about one part of his trip

on which he and his fellow pas-sengers started out in a wagon drawn by four mules, and when they reached a deep, narrow canyon, "we left our wagons, saddled the mules and forded the creek—and it was all our mules could do to stem its impetuous current."

Greeley also related the following story: "Mr. Villard, of Cincinnati, who, riding at some distance from all others, was thrown by his mule's sad-dle slipping forward and turn-ing under him, so that he fell heavily on his left arm, which was badly bruised, and thence was dragged a rod [16.5 feet] with his heel fast in the stir-rup. His mule then stopped." Lucky for Mr. Villard that he wasn't riding an Arabian.

When the United States government canceled the Jackass Mail Service contract in 1860, the contract was awarded to the Pony Express, which took over all of its way stations and stock.

Some mules don't tend to be as "barn sour" as other equines. I frequently take two to six of my mules on short loop rides starting where they live in the corrals and sheds by the barn. At first I was surprised that they usually don't seem to be in big a hurry to get back home, and, even more surprising, they sometimes slow their pace a little when we turn back toward the corrals.

Mules often become very attached to one or more mem-bers of their herd. They may develop an even greater attach-

ment for mares, as illustrated in the famous painting by Fredric Remington called The Bell Mare, which depicts a grey mare with a bell around her neck being fol-lowed down a trail by a string of pack mules. Mules can be turned loose to graze almost anywhere as long as their favorite horse is kept confined by the wrangler. The mules can be trusted to stay close to the horse and not head for home or just wander off, a trait used to good advantage by outfitters in the mountains of the West.

Selecting your first mule is very important. Unless you are a trainer, your first mule (and maybe all of them) should be six years old or older. Mules mature both mentally and physically later than horses, and most are not as safe and dependable as

By George! It's **MAD** Mule Appreciation Day OCT. 26

ON OCT. 26, 1785, THE JACK "ROYAL GIFT" ARRIVED IN BOSTON HARBOR, A GIFT FROM SPANISH KING CHARLES III TO GEN. WASHINGTON. THIS JACK BECAME THE START OF THE GREAT AMERICAN MULE.

you probably want until they "have some age on 'em."

People selling young mules may tell you, "She's only four, but she has the attitude (or disposition) of a ten-year-old," or, "Attitude's more important than age." Maybe, but look for attitude, disposition and age, and the experience and maturity that go with age. Since mules are long-lived, a twenty-year-old mule is a great choice for a child or a person with limited riding experience. More than half of the

trainers I know would also recommend buying a molly first.

There is a saying that sums up what many people have learned the hard way: "A mule shouldn't be born until he's six years old."

The tack used on your horse is unlikely to fit your new mule. The mule should certainly have a saddle built on a tree with mule bars. A saddle that fits most horses may cause a great deal of pain to a mule. Circle Y makes a mule saddle, and several very good custom saddle makers advertise mule saddles in nationally circulated mule magazines.

Because of the lack of pronounced withers on most mules, you will also need to use a britchin' or a crupper (both of which attach to the saddle and go around the mule's rump or under the tail) to keep the saddle from sliding forward.

The reason for the mule's sterility is that the mare has sixty-four chromosomes and the jack has sixty-two. The mating of the horse and donkey leaves

the mule with sixty-three of the gene-carrying chromosomes, and reproduction requires an even number.

The first depiction of a mule is found on an Egyptian stone carving dating back three thousand years. This carving shows the Egyptian goddess of fertility riding a mule, suggesting that the artist had a sense of humor.

Mule twins are more common than horse twins and have a better rate of survival.

In the Del Mar All Breed Classic equine show that features six events, the all-around prize was won for five consecutive years by mules.

Throughout history, the Pope has ridden only mules.

Mules' ribs aren't "sprung" like those of a horse, so their bodies are narrower. This configuration makes for a more comfortable ride, and a ride on a mule doesn't usually make the neophyte rider saddle-sore the next day.

The first wheeled vehicle to cross the Rocky Mountains was pulled by mules. It was a cannon-on-wheels owned by a party of fur trappers.

The mule has been the mascot for the United States Military Academy at West Point,

New York, and its Army athletic teams since 1889. Just before the Army vs. Navy football game that year, Army fans agreed that they needed a mascot to confront the Navy team's goat. An Army team fan donated a mule to serve as the mascot. At that game, the mule gained permanent Army mascot status by kicking the charging Navy goat into the stands. It is said that the mule represents what the Army and West Point stand for: strength, persistence, tradition, heart and resolve.

It was a long, uphill battle to finally have the mule named the state animal of Missouri. Republicans in the state legislature felt that mules were all Democrats, and it was well known that the mule was Harry Truman's favorite animal.

In 1995, a group of mule devotees explained to the state legislature why the mule deserved the honor of being named the state animal of Missouri. They told the legislators that in the 1930s, 1940s and 1950s, mules generated a great deal of income for many Missourians. They cultivated the fields, carried food to market, stood beside soldiers in war, hauled heavy artillery, carried in supplies and took the wounded to medical attention.

Representatives of the American Legion testified that the mule is considered a Veteran of Foreign Wars. Their testimony was persuasive, and the mule earned the title of the state animal by the Missouri Legislature.

Charles Darwin loved mules. From 1831 to 1836, before he became famous for his theory of evolution, Darwin toured the world with a British surveying expedition. Part of the tour in South America was accomplished with the help of mules that Darwin and two companions rode and packed.

In his journal, Darwin related that ten mules and a madrina accompanied him. "The madrina (or godmother) is a most important personage: she is an old steady mare, with a little bell 'round her neck; and wherever she goes, the mules, like good children, follow her … It is nearly impossible to lose an old mule; for if detained for several hours by force, she will, by the power of smell, like a dog, track out her companions."

Darwin was quite impressed with mules: "Each animal carries on a level road a cargo weighing 416 pounds … yet with what delicate, slim limbs, without any proportional bulk of muscle, the animals support so great a burden! The mule always appears to me a most surprising animal. That a hybrid should possess more reason, memory, obstinacy, social affection, powers of muscular endurance, and length of life, than either of its parents, seems to indicate that art has here outdone nature."

Many people think those beautiful and functional extra-wide streets in many of our western towns and cities are the result of good planning by local engineers. Not so. The main street in those towns had to be wide in order to facilitate a U-turn by a sixteen-mule train.

Mules are not exclusively "manmade." They do occur in the wild, where feral horses and donkeys occupy the same range. In 1994, the Bureau of Land Management roundup of wild horses and burros netted more than thirty mules. It is claimed that jacks often attack wild stallions in order to breed a mare or even a harem of mares.

In its 1983 issue, the Smithsonian Institution's magazine, Smithsonian, featured a beautiful photograph of two mules on the cover. Inside, a nine-page article with eleven photographs discussed "The return of the mule." The article stated: "Consigned to the 'killer man' for slaughter when tractors growled across the landscape in the late 1940s, the mule has come back from cast-off beast of burden to popular beast of pleasure." The article also stated: "Common sense is the mule's greatest asset."

THE GRANDDADDY OF THEM ALL— BISHOP MULE DAYS!

Bishop, California, is a scenic, sometimes sleepy, little town in the foothills of the Eastern High Sierra Mountains. Since 1969, on Memorial Day Weekend Bishop wakes up with a resounding bang, or should we say with a prolonged braaaay! That is the time Bishop hosts Mule Days—a six-day event in which approximately 700 mules compete in more than 160 events to entertain and astonish in excess of thirty thousand fans. The purpose of the event is to demonstrate the versatility and value of mules and to make the eyeballs bug out on thousands of spectators.

Mule Days includes almost every event seen at horse shows, a few rodeo-type events, and the wildest, funniest, noisiest event to be seen in any arena in the world … The Packers Scramble. In this wild and wooly spectacular, ten teams of four packers per team compete against one another with more than one hundred mules and horses running loose in the arena, being encouraged to go crazy by the clowns and their loud and smoke-belching shotguns. The participants are professional men and women packers who work for outfitters that provide pack trips into the back country of the High Sierras. It is this event with all its good-natured competitive spirit, its wrecks and its displays of professionalism that qualifies Bishop Mule Days for the title, THE GRANDADDY OF THEM ALL.

Logical Long Ears:
Resistance-Free Training Techniques

A lot of people send their equines to trainers, which does not often work well with mules and donkeys. Equines tend to bond to the person who trains them, so the owner really needs to take part in the training process. Owners who do not participate in the training process often get along with their animals for a while after training, but may experience a deterioration in obedience over time. It is best when they train the animal themselves. Clinics, due to a limited amount of time, cannot possibly provide one with all the information necessary to completely train an animal. Thus, many owners may experience frustration when they go home and try things they have observed in the clinic. In extreme cases, they may even get hurt trying.

Animals, like humans, need to work a predictable routine, one that progresses in a natural order, much like grade school. This provides a good foundation from which to work, and eliminates confusion, which can lead to resistance. The formal term for what I do is called behavior modification.

You define acceptable behaviors for your animal at each level of training beginning with the simplest of expectations and working forward from there. Each level of training presents certain tasks for the animal to accomplish. For each accomplishment, there is a reward to reinforce the correct behavior. When an animal responds negatively, there is a disapproving consequence called negative reinforcement. These kinds of negative reinforcements are short and to the point. The focus is on the positive behavior. Each behavior in us elicits a certain response from the animal. Thus, we also learn to be more meticulous about our own way of asking the

BY MEREDITH HODGES

Meredith Hodges has written numerous articles and books about mule and donkey training. She has also developed a video training series for equines. Hodges's Lucky Three Ranch in Loveland, Colorado, is well known for its production of top-quality, athletic saddle mules and donkeys.

Meredith Hodges riding Lucky Three Sundowner, a two-time third level dressage world champion, and world champion reining mule.

the animal, since we are not always able to feed the reward the minute the desired behavior takes place.

Many people have expressed a fear of adverse behavior or have objected to this kind of training because they say it is a form of bribery. There is a big difference between bribing animals to do something and rewarding them for something they have already done. If an animal does become aggressive for the reward, he is negatively rewarded, defining a limit to his aggressive behavior. He will respect this limitation if the negative reinforcement is applied correctly, firmly and without malice.

These techniques have been proven effective over years of use in dealing with any living being: dogs, cats, lions, elephants, horses, donkeys, mules and even humans. If applied correctly, these techniques work across the board and provide a productive and happy life for those living beings. We are teaching them the best ways to be able to cope with all that they may have to face in their lives.

animals to perform. We become more aware of our animals and ourselves, and learn to act in an appropriate and timely fashion.

The reward is important. It needs to be something the animal loves and will work for, yet it needs to be something that is nutritionally sound. In the case of equines, it would be rolled or crimped oats. If you use something that an animal likes—for instance, alfalfa cubes—but is a little high in protein, the result will be an animal who will perform a few things, then tire of the reward, or worse, will eat so much that it will become hyperactive and will not pay attention. It is much the same as offering a boy candy for numerous rewards, then asking him to listen after he has eaten so much that he is hyperactive. The other danger is that an animal will tire of things that are too rich and will cease to work. It is physically impossible for such an animal to remain still long enough to listen. So you choose a reward that is tasty, yet harmless. We teach verbal commands to elicit certain responses in the animal and attach the word "good" to the reward when it is doing precisely as we ask. In this way, we are able to pinpoint the exact behavior for which we are rewarding

REINFORCING BEHAVIOR The behaviors we adopt in life are perpetuated by reinforcements. There are positive reinforcements and negative reinforcements. Positive reinforcements are those things that give us some kind of pleasure that will cause a specific behavior to occur again. This is true in all healthy living things. An equine that is rewarded for performing a certain task will be willing to perform that task again and again in anticipation of the payoff. Negative reinforcements are such things as a blow, yelling or any of those things that cause one to want to avoid repeating the behavior that elicited that response.

Negative reinforcements cause discomfort to the individual and discourage the chance of that behavior occurring again, but will not always stop it. If too much attention is given to negative reinforcement, it can actually cause repeated bad behaviors or desensitize the animal from achieving desired behaviors. For example, if you kick your mule to go forward and he does not respond, it is clear that a stronger reinforcement is needed if you are to proceed forward. This is what a crop is for, to back up your leg cues. One well-placed tap behind your leg should send the animal forward. If you were to simply keep kicking him, he would ignore your kicking. In addition, more than one appropriately used tap with the crop could cause some desensitization from the crop and could result in severe avoidance behavior.

Reinforcements need to be given the instant the behavior is taking place for the animal to understand completely. For this reason, we use our voice as a positive reinforcement, saying "good" when the animal is doing well, then stopping him and giving him the reward for good behavior. The food reward reinforces the value of the word "good." The animal makes the association, and you are thus able to get certain behavior without the food reward for sustained periods of time. Clicker training applies these same concepts, except that the clicker is used in place of the word "good." Because it is difficult for many people to respond at the right time or with the right inflection in their voices, the clicker is a useful tool for training.

When you first begin training, the mule will need to be reinforced every time he performs a desired response with both the verbal reinforcement and the food reinforcement. As he learns more, you can reinforce the already learned behavior less frequently and focus on rewarding the new desired response. The animal becomes satisfied with the verbal reinforcement for the established behaviors and will comply for longer periods between food rewards.

In the learning stages of any new behavior, you will have to use a predictable, or fixed, schedule of reinforcement. That is, you would reward the animal every time for a given behavior. After a behavior is learned, he only requires a variable schedule of reinforcement. That is, you can reward the animal less frequently and less predictably. As the animal learns more—for example he is making the transition from lunging to riding—the animal will be asked to perform for a certain time before the reinforcement is given. Where he was being reinforced after each set of rotations in a round pen, he is now ridden through his entire thirty- to forty-minute session before receiving the reward.

There is a phenomenon called delayed gratification. If the time limit is overly long before the reinforcement is given, it can actually prevent the animal from getting started. This is why it is prudent to give the animal a quick reward at the beginning for something simple before going on to the lesson. You know yourself that if you are faced with a task as overwhelming as cleaning the garage, it is sometimes difficult just to get started. Animals experience the same kind of reaction.

Reinforcement is an event that occurs upon completion of a certain behavior, thus increasing the likelihood that the behavior will occur again. Negative reinforcement is not the same as punishment because it discourages a behavior from recurring. Punishment will stop the behavior from occurring, but it may create other undesirable behaviors.

Reinforcing too early is ineffective. The animal should only be rewarded immediately after the desired behavior has taken place. An animal that is rewarded too soon can start to exhibit more aggressive and undesirable behaviors. The term most commonly used for premature rewards is bribery. The animal will learn to take the reward and may refuse to perform the desired task.

SHAPING BEHAVIOR When we talk about shaping behavior in an animal, we are talking about taking a tendency of the animal to perform in the right direction and shifting it, one step at a time, toward our ultimate goal. This is called successive approximation. For instance, if you are teaching a turn on the haunches on the lead line, you need to ask for a step forward first, before the turn, then walk toward the mule's shoulder and ask for the turn. If you just kept walking toward the shoulder and elicited the turn, he would most likely complete the turn, but would not do it correctly by planting his pivot foot. In order to teach him to plant the foot, this process needs to be broken down into smaller steps. You would ask for the step forward, then reward him for that immediately. When he is doing this correctly, you can move on and

TEN LAWS FOR SHAPING BEHAVIORS

1 Establish and raise your criteria in small enough increments that your animal has a reasonable chance at success, so you are able to reinforce the positive response. If the criteria are too high, the animal may fail and give up trying.

2 Train one aspect of behavior at a time. Do not try to do more than one thing at a time. When training for a dressage test, for example, do not practice the whole test with all the parts every day. Take a few sections of the test and work on those. Practice straight lines as you go up and down the centerline. Practice twenty-meter circles. Practice the right amount of bend as you go through corners. These are all components of the ultimate goal and will fit together nicely once you have achieved success in the

smaller components. However, if you are riding the test as a whole, the quality of the smaller components will decrease.

3 Before you increase the criteria of any behavior, put that behavior on a variable schedule of reinforcement. You would use a fixed schedule of reinforcement on any new behaviors, but once the animal "gets it," you need to reward less often and randomly. Then you would add the new behavior and reinforce that behavior with the fixed schedule while you randomly reward behaviors he has already learned.

4 When introducing new behavior, relax the expectations on the old ones. What was once learned is not for-

gotten, but under the pressure of learning new behavior, the old ones sometimes fall apart temporarily.

5 Stay ahead of the animal. Should your mule have a sudden breakthrough and perform the next step easily, you need to keep him challenged to maintain his interest.

6 Do not change trainers midstream. The animal/trainer relationship is a process in itself, and changing trainers results in the necessity of establishing a whole new bonded relationship.

7 If one shaping process is not working, try another. Individuals learn in different ways. Find the way that works best for your animal at any given stage.

8 Do not interrupt the training process

gratuitously; that constitutes a punishment. If you are training your animal, do not stop to talk to a passerby. This is more than good manners. When you enter into a training contract with anyone, you are obliged to reinforce the good behavior, and you cannot do this when you are not paying attention. You may inadvertently punish a good behavior that you desire at the time of interruption, which reads as punishment to the trainee.

9 If a learned behavior begins to deteriorate, just review and reinforce it the way you did initially. The re-learning time should be considerably less. Sometimes side effects from punishment can cause this to occur, but if you stay calm and willing as you review the behavior, you should have few problems.

10 Quit while you are ahead. At the beginning of the next session you will most often see the improvement over what you were asking for in the previous session. Overworking on a desired behavior will make the animal tired and less willing to perform. Better to quit with a good assimilation of what you were asking.

Lucky Three Mae Bea C.T. and Lucky Three CIJI, Lucky Three Mule Ranch's driving team.

ask for one step forward followed by one step to the side, and then reward him. Then you would ask for one step forward, with two steps to the side and reward him. Soon, the animal will take as many steps as you desire. He is also learning to step over only as many steps as you ask. If you were to allow him to turn indiscriminately, you would not have control of how many steps he takes. The success or failure of our attempts to shape behavior does not depend upon our expertise, but rather on our patience and persistence during the process.

Different individuals learn in different ways, so it is important to know that when one approach is not working, there is another way available to you. The most obvious example that I have encountered is in the case of teaching a donkey to canter. Many people tried to tell me that donkeys do not canter, but I knew this was not true because they canter when they are free. I ultimately set the goal at cantering a circle, but first I had to get my jack to can-

Little Jack Horner, the only formal jumping donkey in the world, clears a jump.

ter. Kicking did not work, the crop did not work, and no one could run fast enough to stay ahead of him with grain, so I had to come up with something else. I finally put some cycling broodmares in a pen at one end of the hay-field and I took him to the other end. When I asked him to canter toward those mares, he most certainly did! I reinforced his behavior with the words "good, good, good" while we were cantering and gave him the food reinforcement when we had stopped at the pen. The next time we did the same thing, only I turned him in a large half circle toward the pen and rewarded again the same way. Then, the next time I asked for a little more of a circle and got it. Several times later, I was able to canter an entire circle before we ran the line to the pen with the mares in it. Once I had him cantering, I did not need the mares around anymore. I took him into the arena and began trying to canter the perimeter. At first, he cantered a few strides and then dropped to a trot. Each time he cantered, I praised him verbally, and when he broke to trot, I would finish the circle, stop him and praise him with the food reward. It seemed as though we were getting nowhere the first few tries, until I started counting strides and realized he was adding one more stride at canter with each attempt. Before long, he was cantering the circle with ease. Training him like this has enabled my donkey, Little Jack Horner, to perform successfully in trail, reining and even in jumping to a level of four feet. For a thirteen-hand equine that is really quite remarkable, especially for a donkey!

As you begin to understand the principles of shaping and modifying behavior, it is important to realize that it is a lot like dancing; even though you need to think about these things, there is no forward progress without actual practice. The more practice you get, the better trainer you will become. You have the opportunity to reinforce behavior in all the individuals in your life: the cat, the dog, your wife or husband, your children. It becomes a game of noticing and praising the positive things in life. In practicing, you will increase your awareness and thus, your skill.

Tennessee Walking Horse Mare

Thoroughbred Mare

Quarter Horse Mare

BY LOYD W. HAWLEY

Loyd Hawley is a well-known breeder and trainer of mules. He lives in Prairie Grove, Arkansas.

Perfect Mule Mama

When selecting a mare for mule production, first decide what type of mule you want and how you plan on using it. Next, become familiar with the breed of horse you have selected. You need to know what is available in that breed, the ideal type for that breed and the characteristics to look for. For instance, if you like an animal that is very correct in the hind legs, the breed you have selected may not offer many individuals that meet your ideal. The Tennessee Walking Horse, for example, is typically sickle hocked. If you want a mare that is straighter legged and wider between the hocks, you might have to search a bit longer.

I have a grey mare Tennessee Walking Horse mare that has given me a good number of foals. When I was buying Walking mares, I looked for mares that were more Quarter Horse type. By that I mean they are smaller in the head and ear, fuller in the hips, have straighter legs, and are wider between the hocks. It was not easy to do, but I managed to acquire seven or eight mares like the one in the photograph. I had a number of breeders tell me that the mares had to be crooked legged and sloped off in the rump in order to "gait," or produce a running walk. This is simply not true. Also, notice that the gray mare has a higher head set, which is desirable in gaited animals.

I have raised a lot of mule foals from Thoroughbred mares. They have many appealing characteristics. They are longer bodied, have long, clean necks, high, sloping withers and clean, flat bones. They usually have long strides and a flat-kneed trot and canter. If you are look-

MULE VERSATILITY

BY JOHN HAUER

As pointed out by Dr. Robert Miller in his chapter, Understanding the Mule, horses will generally outperform mules in horse show and rodeo events. Exceptions may be in the various pleasure classes where the mule's laid-back and relaxed demeanor are an obvious advantage.

However, one trait that makes mules so much fun is their versatility. Whereas most horses are entered in one or two horse show or rodeo events, mules are often entered in all events for their age and size. A given mule may be entered in pole bending, barrel racing, Western pleasure, trail class, keyhole race, and coon jumping. Then, with a different saddle and tack, she may be ridden in an English pleasure and/or trail class. The same mule may then be dressed up like a moose and ridden in a costume class by a 6-year-old girl or boy. The surprising thing to those who are not knowledgeable about the versatility of mules is that mules will often perform exceptionally well in all of those events.

Mules seem to be able to shift gears and attitude from a frothing-at-the-mouth, wild-eyed, hell-bent-for-leather barrel racing machine to a relaxed, sleepy-eyed pleasure craft being enjoyed in a trail class by a teen-age rider.

Not many riders are as versatile as the mule, but if you want to be in every event at the show, either take a mule or a trailer full of horses.

CLOCKWISE FROM LEFT: *Vince Hawley and Ciera run the poles; Loyd Hawley bends poles on Clematine My Darlin; Loyd takes Clematine through the keyhole event; Lou Moore participates in the English riding event.*

38

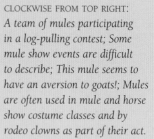

CLOCKWISE FROM TOP RIGHT:
A team of mules participating in a log-pulling contest; Some mule show events are difficult to describe; This mule seems to have an aversion to goats!; Mules are often used in mule and horse show costume classes and by rodeo clowns as part of their act.

ing for an animal to use for English-type events or endurance riding, a Thoroughbred mare is an excellent choice. However, mules from Thoroughbred mares can often be too "hot" for the average trail-riding situation, and most of them do not have enough width and strength to produce a good halter animal. The sorrel Thoroughbred mare pictured on page 34 has produced national "under saddle" as well as grand champion halter mules.

Quarter-type mule

The buckskin/dun mare is a foundation-bred Quarter Horse mare. She stands fifteen hands and weighs about fourteen hundred pounds. She is wide, straight and strong and still maintains a lot of style and balance. This is the type of mare that would be most suitable for the majority of people. Usually, Quarter Horse mares have a calmer disposition and produce a more versatile mule.

After selecting which breed you want, the second most important consideration is disposition. For the most part, the mare is going to pass on her disposition to the foal. You can correct or change this to some degree with imprinting and proper handling, but why chance it? Start with a mare that has a willing attitude and a good disposition.

Third in importance is conformation. Regardless of which breed you select, conformation traits are the same. You have to live within the limits of the breed, but always select from the top end. You want a mare that stands straight on all four legs, is wide between the hocks, and has full hips with as much muscle down the leg as possible. High withers with long, sloping shoulders, a long, clean neck and a smaller head and ears top off the package of the perfect mule mama.

Most of the people who call me looking for mules start off by saying, "I'm not looking for a show mule," but when they come to my farm, they pick out the best-looking mules. Some want a good-looking mule so they will not be embarrassed or because of pride of ownership. Whatever the reason, conformation is important and is worth extra time and dollars. Conformation also plays a role in how well your animal performs.

The fourth consideration is color. You have to decide what color you like or want to breed for, and buy accordingly. Some colors, such as palomino, are hard to breed for and may not be worth the extra time and expense. You have to live with the color for many years, so it does deserve careful consideration.

Fifth on the list brings us back to the beginning: What do you want to do with your mule? Within each breed there are certain bloodlines that have been bred to be better at a certain event or activity. For example, some Quarter Horses are better than others at cutting, reining, and so on. If you want your mule to specialize in a certain field, you should select a mare that has proven herself in that area or is bred to be good. If done properly, the breeding and raising of a colt is very expensive and should start with top-quality parents.

While this essay is about mule mamas, I have to add a word or two about mule papas. Mares are very important, but no more so than the jacks. Because most people are more familiar with horses, the mare gets more consideration. In my opinion, you need a medium-sized jack about fourteen hands high. Just as with a mare, you are looking for correct conformation and a good disposition. Select one that has the stature you want, because the jack pretty much determines the bone size. With a jack of this size and conformation, you can control the size of your mule with the mare. A medium-sized jack will usually sire a mule about ninety percent the size of the mare.

My perfect mule formula is a running-bred Quarter Horse mare bred to a large, standard gaited jack. That combination should result in a mule with Quarter Horse looks that will also gait nicely.

We always knew our mamas were important; now you know how important they are to your mule, too!

Know No Boundaries —Ride a Mule

If trail riding is your special passion, then join the club. When you go out on the trail do you have an itch to see what's around the next curve, across that rockslide, in that small cave yonder? If you do, that is what some people call "pushing the envelope." I call it riding with no boundaries. That's why I ride a mule.

Mules race, rope, team pen, barrel race and coon jump. They show in halter, Western pleasure, English pleasure, reining and dressage. If it can be done on a horse, someone can do it on a mule. Mules are the equine version of a sport-utility vehicle. Most of all, mules excel on the trail. With their sure-footed and easy way of moving, mules set the standard for comfort over the long haul. It makes no difference whether your choice is an endurance race, competitive trail event or everyday pleasure riding, you will enjoy it more with a mule.

Today, mule prices soar into the five-figure range. Ten years ago, such price tags were unheard of. The number of people buying mules for the first time has doubled, even tripled, in the last three years. Why? Maybe it's because mules today are bred from higher-quality mares using some of the top bloodlines from different popular breeds. Maybe it's because mules are unique and attract attention. Maybe it is because of their versatility. But why is not the point. The point is mules make extraordinary mounts no matter what you choose to do with them. But for those of us who simply love trail riding, choosing to ride a mule means the mule is doing what comes naturally. Before you choose your first mule, there are some things you should consider.

SOME POINTS TO PONDER First of all, mules are hybrids, and therefore sterile. When you purchase a mule, whether male or female, it's like buying a gelding. What you see is what you get. The mule has many pluses, as she inherits the best qualities from the horse and from the donkey. Some mules look

BY BETTY ROBINSON
Betty Robinson is a professor and freelance writer who thinks life should be about doing what you love. For her this is riding her mule, searching out new trails, and writing about those trails to share with friends. A native Oklahoman, Robinson came to Arkansas in 1970 where she fell in love with the rugged mountain trails and never left. She has written for Horse Illustrated, Equus, and Western Horseman as well as other national publications. She is a staff writer for Mules & More magazine.

much more horse-like, while others exhibit features that are more predominant in the donkey. The big difference between a mule and horse is intelligence. No matter what they look like, all mules are "thinkers." The mule with the most donkey characteristics will be a "long thinker" and will require a great deal of time and patience to train. You might ask yourself whether you have enough patience to work with a mule.

In working with trail mules, you will find that the learning curve is slightly different for mules than horses. When you begin training a mule, he will first appear confused, unsure how to react. A little patience and assurance gets you past this step. Next, the mule will understand what you want, but he won't believe you mean it. Here he may try avoidance and resistance while he considers the situation. Finally, once the mule is sure you know what you have asked for, if you have earned his respect, he will comply. The length of time necessary to accomplish each step will vary with each mule.

Not every mule begins with the temperament to be a safe, dependable trail mule. Fun trail riding is created through teamwork—a relationship between one mule and one rider. No special pedigree is better suited for trail riding than another. The "right" mule is actually, like your taste in music, a personal preference. Even though no specific trail breed exists, some common characteristics might make one animal a better choice than another.

HEIGHT A trail mule can be any size or shape. When looking at size, usually only the height is considered. Many riders, particularly teens through those in their thirties, tend to think tall. You often hear, "I just don't think a little mule can carry me all day long." Some folks,

many women included, don't think you are well mounted unless your mule is fifteen hands or taller. These are the riders who also stop frequently to pick up hats dislodged by low limbs.

A good rule of thumb when deciding what size trail mule to purchase is to consider the age of the rider. Then, decide on the size of the mule. Young riders develop independence more quickly when they can mount their own mule without adult help. Research also indicates that older riders have completed the "impress everyone" stage and are back to reality. They accept the fact that shorter mules are easier to mount and know it requires less energy when you don't need to constantly duck limbs on the trail. Seniors often prefer a mule that stands somewhere between fourteen and fifteen hands (usually closer to the short end).

John mules tend to be more rambunctious and playful in the pasture than do mollies.

GENDER With a mule, there are two choices: a john, which is a gelded male, or a molly, which is a female. Because mules cannot reproduce, males are always castrated. Mules have tenacious personalities and super intelligence; therefore, an uncastrated male mule can quickly become a rambunctious rogue. Mollies still come in heat just like mares, so some people prefer to ride a john or to have the molly spayed. Again, this is a personal preference. But with the modern spaying procedures, the operation is a viable option, especially since mollies can't conceive anyway. A molly that has been spayed usually demands a higher price in the marketplace. In my experience, johns tend to be a little pushy on the ground. When

Mules don't drink every time they are offered water. They tend to know when they need it.

the spirit moves them, they will shove you out of their way and go on about their business. Mollies, more often than not, exhibit better ground manners. Johns also cause more problems in the pasture. Being bored drives them nuts. They will invent their own games, such as, "Watch me open the gate and let every one out," or "Let's chase the calves," or…well, you get the idea.

AGE The best recipe for determining what age mule to buy is "the younger the rider, the older the mule." In the sport of trail riding, older mules remain useful much longer than they do in speed events or stressful arena work such as team roping. Trail riding extends the useful lifespan of many mules by keeping them active. Young mules and young riders seldom make a good match on the trail. One or the other in the partnership needs to have enough experience not to be unduly upset by a crisis. Even though a mule's actual productive work span is much longer than that of a horse, mules for trail riding are seldom as solid as you would like until they reach eight or even ten years old. Eight years of age and older are prime years for a mule. It is not uncommon for mules to still be in use at thirty-five.

CONFORMATION Everyone likes a mule that is pleasing to the eye. This is usually at least partially affected by color and conformation. However, when looking for the perfect trail mule, remember, color is only the wrapping paper; what counts is what's inside. A mule with at least marginally good conformation is a plus on the trail. The mule needs a good set of withers to help hold the saddle in the proper place. Round, mutton-withered mules are an aggravation to mount. No one enjoys a saddle that slips every time you put weight in the stirrup. A poor set of withers also lets the saddle slide forward. Such movement necessitates the use of a crupper or britchin' or you will have to stop frequently to adjust the saddle. Round withers in mules are common; they won't keep a mule from being good to use on the trail, as long as you tack her up correctly.

Because good conformation qualities vary with each equestrian sport, discussing all these qualities is beyond the scope and purpose of this chapter. If you are new to the sport of trail riding and maybe to mules in general, ask a person you consider an expert to help you find a mule, or ask him or her to look at one you have found. Veterinarians or trainers often provide this service for a

44

Mules that are frequently used on the trail will require shoes. Their hooves are tough, but not indestructible.

fee. Purchasing a mule is like going to the doctor; it never hurts to get a second opinion.

Talking about conformation naturally leads to "way-of-going." This means focusing on how the mule travels, not just the gait. Watch how the mule actually moves his feet and how he looks when he does it. Way-of-going is affected by conformation. You don't want a mule that wings or paddles because of poor leg structure. This lateral movement is considered inefficient. Mules with poor structural conformation in the legs often interfere, which means they clip the cannon bone or fetlock of one leg with the hoof of the other. Such mules may also forge or overreach, striking a forefoot with the hoof from the back. Any of the problems mentioned can be coped with by adding boots or wraps or by proper shoeing, but, given a choice, you are better off to avoid purchasing a mule with these undesirable traits.

Two common misconceptions plague the mule when it comes to the discussion of hooves. While most folks have heard that sound feet are a primary asset of a mule, many falsely then assume that mules don't need shoes. While it is true that most mules have strong, black hooves that can take a great deal of wear, the relevant issue remains: wear the hooves within reason. Mules that are frequently used on the trail, especially in rocky terrain, will require shoes. Do not let the lack of shoes ruin a good trip. For example, while I was visiting the Gila Wilderness in New Mexico, I met two gentlemen from Texas who had come to do some trail riding over a long weekend. They made one ride and had to find a farrier. Where they lived, shoes were not necessary, but in the Gila they are. The men spent most of their vacation trying to find shoes for their mules.

A second misconception about shoeing mules is that a mule needs to be shod only in the front. I realize that mules, like horses, carry sixty percent of their weight up front. But I also know that wherever the front of my mule goes, the back end tends to follow. So the back end takes as many steps on as many rocks as the front. If you ride a mule hard, he will require shoes all around. Because this is such a controversial issue, I have tried it both ways. To answer this question for your personal situation, you must consider where you ride, how far you ride and how often you ride. Mules' hooves can and will stand much more abuse than horse hooves, but they are not indestructible.

On some rides, if the flies or ticks are bad, I have seen horses stomp hard enough to crack big chips out of strong hooves. I have never seen that happen to a mule. Losing a shoe in remote backcountry can lead to serious problems. With regular farrier care, mules seldom lose shoes. Always check whether the mule you want to buy has had shoes on before. Some mules don't wear shoes because the farriers won't put them on. A good modern trail mule will stand as well for the farrier as most horses.

GAIT Gait is another characteristic to consider when selecting a trail mule. Many times, trail riders want a mule with more than the typical walk, trot and canter. They pay extra for a mule that does a single-foot, fox trot, rack or some combination thereof. However, for the basic trail rider, a mule's walk is the most important gait. You do not want a mule that jigs or plods. The jig, although rare in mules, is a short, fast, up and down, dicey trot that jars your teeth and wears you out. Because a jig exhausts both the animal and the rider, you will seldom find this trait in the mule. A plodder is your basic deadhead. She must be prodded every step of the way. The plodder never moves fast enough to tire herself out, but she can wear out even

Trail mules learn to stand in camp as quietly as they do for lunch breaks on the trail.

an experienced rider. A good trail mule should not require a kick for every step.

PERSONALITY Certain personality characteristics create unwanted changes in a mule's gait. For example, some mules plod away from the trailer or barn, but turn into jiggers or pullers on the return trip. A mule that exhibits these characteristics is a good candidate to become "barn sour." The barn sour mule is one that has learned if he throws a big enough fit, he will not have to leave the barn. This kind of mule is never recommended for a novice rider. While the problem can be corrected, it usually takes a great deal of experience combined with patience.

Some mules form very strong friendships with paddock partners or stable mates. This is known as "buddying." The result is a mule that paws, frets and calls all the time. Leaving a buddy at the barn and hauling one mule away to the trail is bad enough. Both mules will continue to call and fret in the other's absence. Separating buddies on the same trail can be even more disastrous. Riders have been thrown and hurt while trying to ride one buddy away from another on the trail. Most mules buddy only with an animal they have come to know well, either a mule from their own farm or stable, or one they trailer with on a regular basis. Some mules can leave a buddy at the barn and pick up a new one the minute they unload at the ride. A mule that does this is usually insecure, can't think for himself, and wants to just follow blindly along doing whatever the mule in front of him does. Avoid this kind of mule if at all possible.

A good trail mule should be happy wherever he is placed in the group. The rider chooses the speed and location. The mule complies. The mule should travel wherever he is asked, in the front, back or anywhere in between. An "alpha" mule, one that strives to be herd leader, does not make a good mule for pleasure trail riding because he constantly fights to lead. This mule is like a Dr. Jekyll and Mr. Hyde. He changes from a docile companion when you ride alone to a frantic, sweaty beast when put in the

This mule does double duty. When he isn't pulling a wagon he serves as a riding mule. Right now he's begging cookies.

middle of a pack. Such personality traits do not add pleasure to a ride.

The very best trail mules learn early to conserve energy. They prefer to adopt the speed and gait that is most comfortable for them, but they are flexible enough to adjust their speed to the terrain and the group. A mule that gallops to the top of every hill to get the work finished sooner does nothing but wear himself out. A steady pace over the long day is the best plan. In addition, good trail mules take rest breaks seriously. They stand tied without excess fidgeting or pawing. If offered the opportunity, they graze quietly even when hobbled.

ATTITUDE The primary characteristic I look for in a trail mule is a willing attitude. This mule is usually friendly and easygoing, and learns to trust quickly. A good trail mule has to have an attitude that keeps him putting forth his best effort until the task is done. The trail mule's work may last six, eight or ten hours with brief breaks. These mules do not have the luxury of carrying their load a few

hundred yards over level ground. Their job requires them to safely transport some usually sizable rider over rough, remote, even mountainous terrain. We call this mule dependable. He always gets you home.

The very best trail mule has a distinguishing physical and mental temperament that enables him to be hauled long hours, unload relaxed, and be ready to eat, drink or hit the trail. In contrast, some horses are much too fussy for this grueling schedule. They go off their feed and often colic from the stress. Mules maintain their composure and exhibit what old-timers call "bottom." They travel all day, sleep hunkered at the fringes of the campfire all night, and are ready to go again at first light.

To be enjoyable, a mule should stride confidently down the trail, passing "mule-eating" stumps, rocks, old cars, barking dogs and other natural trail obstacles without panic or undue excitement. Blind obedience is not the answer but being bold enough to trust the rider's judgment without a great deal of hesitation is a big plus. As a herd animal, the mule's survival instinct is "fight or flight." It takes true courage for a mule to put trust in his rider and face new and unknown situations on the trail.

EXPERIENCE When you are in the market for a trail mule, a good question to ask the current owner is, "How much trail experience has this mule had?" Nothing prepares a mule for the actual experience of the trail like having been there and done that. A calm, cool, collected show mule may or may not demonstrate the same characteristics

This mule lost an eye by accident. With teamwork and trust, these two ride trails as much as ever.

on the trail. Barking dogs, wildlife and multiple trail users with backpacks, bikes, or four wheelers add spice to the everyday trail experience. Most of the time you will find the need to have an inverse relationship between how much experience the rider has and how much the mule has. The more experienced the rider, the less experience is required of the mule. If the rider has little or no experience, he or she should find a mule that knows what to do.

BOTTOM LINE The equation for purchasing the best trail mule might look something like this: Attitude plus Way-of-Going times Experience equals A Good Trail Mule. Never be rushed into a decision. Do not let the excitement of the moment push you into making a pur-

chase you may regret tomorrow. Some sellers try to clinch the deal by telling you another buyer is coming to look at the mule the next day. Be willing to walk away. There is always another mule down the road.

Let me emphasize that you personally need to test-ride the animal on the trail, and you need to know what the owner's return policy is. What happens after you ride the mule for two weeks and discover the two of you just cannot get along? Can you get your money back or does the owner only allow an exchange for another mule? Is this acceptable to you?

It is impossible to discuss in detail all the characteristics and special skills to consider when selecting a good trail mule, but a checklist will help you remember some of the most important items. Be sure to add questions of your own, but before you write that check and load your new trail companion into your trailer, look for satisfactory answers to the following questions:

- Does the mule load well?
- Does he haul well in a standard trailer?
- Does he stand tied?
- Is he easy to shoe?
- Does he stand quietly while you mount?
- Is he or she an alpha mule in a group?
- Does he have a current Coggins and health certificate?
- Will the mule hobble or picket?
- Does the mule cross water easily?
- Is he ear shy?

If you still like the mule after your riding experience, you may have found the right one. Take him home and good luck. And never miss a chance to ride a new trail.

The Beast

By Brenda Worley

After achieving a certain age, I decided to switch from thoroughbreds to mules. I was looking for a used car for my daughter when my eyes veered to the Livestock Column.

FOR SALE – 16 HAND MOLLY MULE, $2500.

When I pulled in the driveway, she was doing laps around the pen and she was gorgeous, but with longer ears than I was accustomed to. The owner caught her and we took her to the round pen. She scooted away from the saddle several times; he acted surprised and said, "She's never done that before."

"That's no big deal; I can fix that," I thought to myself.

After a short ride, I took her back to the corral; she got a half a head in front of me and took off running. Her nose went up, her trot got really big, and she laughed and hee-hawed at me. This was my introduction to one of her favorite tricks and there would be no catching her until I could get my pride and temper under control. The Beast had a lot to teach me, and I'm still learning.

One of the first and most important lessons: Adjust your clock; you are now on "mule time." There is no making up for lost time. If you are running late, well, don't even consider making up for it by a quick catch, load, saddle, or anything that even vaguely pertains to your mule. All of your riding buddies need to be clued in to "mule time," also. If you're early, there's more time for the important things like listening to your mule contentedly munching grass, grooming, or even cleaning up after a nice roll in the mud.

When The Beast finished with this lesson, I quickly realized how right she was. Relax, smell the hay, and set your watch ahead an hour or two, depending on your level of training.

Brenda with her Beast. Photo courtesy Brenda Worley.

The Natural Superiority of Mules

MULE HISTORY

Mules and the Grand Canyon

"For far longer than Grand Canyon has been a national park, mules have carried people and supplies into and out of the canyon. Early miners also used mules to haul ore to the rim. Since 1887, mules have carried terrified tourists down and up the trails, and beginning in 1902, the Kolb brothers made their living photographing mule-mounted 'dudes.' Today, in this age of space travel and the Internet, mules perform the same roles they have for more than a century at Grand Canyon. For saddle-sore tourists who have braved a journey into the canyon astride a mule, the memories of their exhilaration from the ride and awe from the view will stay with them for a lifetime."

The Park Service has reduced the number of mule rides allowed in the canyon, and it is rumored that they may eliminate them completely. If you care, you can contact the Grand Canyon Association at www.grandcanyon.org.

BY BETTY ROBINSON

Every day a few hardy souls grab life by the saddlehorn, trust their lives to a mule and ride off down the Grand Canyon. Trusting the mule is easy. Handling the height is hard. However, this tradition has been going on year-round for decades.

HISTORY In about 1540, as part of Coronado's legendary expedition, the first Europeans arrived at the Grand Canyon's south rim. For the next three hundred years the canyon became an approach-avoidance issue for the missionaries, trappers, explorers, government surveyors and soldiers who passed through that part of the country. The early exploratory men of fortune who ventured into the canyon added little to what was known. Such men spoke little and wrote less. Until 1869, practically nothing was known of the Colorado River or the Grand Canyon, through which the river runs. The canyon and its river remained a source of mystery and fear. No evidence existed to prove anyone who entered by river ever came out alive. However, the excitement of facing the challenge of the canyon, and witnessing the unparalleled beauty for the first time, created a magnetic force that tugs as strongly today as it did when Major John Wesley Powell made his first successful boat trip.

The promise of mineral resources, mainly copper and asbestos, became the catalyst for the first settlements on the Grand Canyon's rim. Entrepreneurs in search of fortunes established camps wherever feasible, packing supplies in and resources out on the backs of burros. However, early settlers discovered that tourism was far more profitable than mining. Even though the only method of travel at the time was by stagecoach, locals recognized that the call of adventure and the heart-moving beauty of the canyon enticed people to visit no matter what grueling physical discomforts had to be endured to enjoy it.

We found ourselves face to face with a barrier more formidable than the Rocky Mountains — an abyss 280 miles long containing an unbridged, unfordable, dangerous river.
—F. E. Matthes

THE FIRST MULE TRAIN ACROSS THE CANYON While various individuals began to travel the Colorado River through the Grand Canyon as early as 1869, the first pack train of mules did not cross the canyon until 1902. F. E. Matthes, team leader for the U.S. Geological Survey, was assigned the task of making topographical maps of the canyon area. His party started work on the south rim with the intention of crossing to the north. But at that time, no trail existed from rim to rim, nor was there any type of bridge to expedite passage over the Colorado River. This early survey crew found itself facing what the local Paiute Indians called the Kaibab, or "mountains lying down"–an abyss 280 miles long, containing an unbridged, dangerous river that could not be forded.

After much deliberation, Matthes decided to take his group down the Bass Trail. This was merely a burro trail and still unfinished at the lower end. The Shinumo Trail, which would be used to ascend to the north rim, was little more than a faint, rarely used track. The trip began with a pack string of ten mules. Little information exists about the actual descent. At the bottom, arrangements had been made to use a homemade boat, owned by a local prospector named Bass, to transfer goods from one shore to the other. Mules were expected to swim behind. It was an easy matter to transfer the gear to the other side; however, convincing hot, overworked mules to jump into a surging river was another matter.

At long last, Matthes resorted to subterfuge. In his 1927 manuscript, "Breaking Trail through Bright Angel Canyon," he wrote, "The mules were led one at a time down a rock platform, ostensibly so that they might quench their thirst. Then suddenly, they were pushed into the swirling flood." Matthes stated that it was some kind of a battle getting the mules across the water, even once they were secured behind the boat. Some animals tried to swim back to shore, tugging the boat with them. Others tried to get in the boat and ride across. With much effort on everyone's part, all the mules arrived safely on the north side. The ascent to the rim of the Kaibab Plateau took another day and a half of exhausting work.

During the ten weeks of mapping on the north rim, no one considered sending back across the canyon for supplies. No two men could do it, and with only four on the team the idea was not feasible. Instead, a pack string was sent to Kanab, Utah, seventy-five miles away. The trip took a packer seven days to get there, shop and return.

In early autumn, the team realized it was time to leave if they planned to beat the snows, which come early on the Kaibab. The survey had progressed as far east as the head of Bright Angel Canyon, and the men were directly opposite the south rim station, thirteen miles by air.

Matthes stared into Bright Angel Canyon and planned their retreat. Because the canyon is carved along a great fault and the lines of cliffs are consequently broken, it was possible to build the old Bright Angel Trail, now familiar to millions of tourists.

At the time when Matthes planned his route, two haggard men and a weary burro emerged from the head of Bright Angel Canyon. These men, Sidney Ferrall and Jim Murray, had explored the canyon and fought their way up the fault zone. This heartened the members of the survey team, but they also knew that taking a pack string where a single small burro could travel was an entirely different matter. Two of the team immediately set about cutting out brush and rolling logs and boulders to make a reasonably clear path for the pack train. The trail was so steep that in many places the animals slid down on their haunches. It was often so narrow between the rocks that the larger packs could not pass through and had to be unloaded. Matthes recorded that there were more accidents than could be chronicled, but none of them were of a serious nature.

The mule carrying the most precious burden—the instruments and the newly made maps—was led with particular care, but she lived up to her reputation and made the trip without a stumble.

After a couple of nights spent mapping the bottom of the canyon, the team crossed the river without mishap. The mules seemed to have lost their fear of the river and were eager to be on the trail toward home. Soon after crossing, the group scrambled up the steep burro trail and without serious misfortune reached its goal on the south rim.

The following year, when the survey was extended, Bright Angel Trail became the regular route of travel across the Grand Canyon, both north and south, though the terrain remained as rough as ever.

Some years later, in order to increase tourist traffic, the town of Kanab improved the trail and spanned the river with a steel cable along which a traveling cage large enough to hold a pack animal could be pulled across. When the National Park Service took over in 1919, Bright Angel Trail became the main avenue for travel. The cable was replaced with a suspension bridge.

TOURISTS COME BY THE MILLIONS In the 1900s, the Fred Harvey Company set a goal to provide the Grand Canyon's visitors with fine services. A Harvey Hotel opened at the south rim in 1905. In 1908, President Theodore Roosevelt, a noted outdoorsman and canyon visitor, changed the canyon's status from national forest and game reserve to national monument. In 1919, the United States Congress upgraded the monument's status to that of a national park. By 1920, the Harvey Company was the principal concessionaire at the south rim. In addition to good food and good service, the Harvey Company's entertainment grew to include the Grand Canyon mule rides. The first mule trips began descending the canyon even before the ranch at the canyon's bottom–known as Phantom Ranch–was completed in 1922. When Phantom Ranch began accepting

Former President Theodore Roosevelt, followed by John Hance, prepares to descend the Bright Angel Trail, March 17, 1911.

54

lodgers, it gained a reputation as the deepest ranch in the country and became a mecca for the rich and famous. The ranch's guest register includes a long list of notables.

Today, Grand Canyon National Park entertains five million visitors each year. This means that on any given day there will be a crowd. Reservations for camping, lodging or mule rides are essential. Expect traffic congestion and parking problems. A trip to the bottom of the canyon and back, whether you walk or take a mule, will take two days. Hikers who walk from rim to rim usually take three days. Rafters often take as long as two or three weeks. With proper permission and permits, you may use your own mules to traverse the canyon. With these arrangements, you may stay longer than two days.

Ron Clayton, former livery manager, and two of his charges.

John Hance, left, and a three-dude mule party prepare to descend the Bright Angel Trail. Note the boarding platform in the foreground. Circa 1902

THE GRAND CANYON AND ITS MULES Mule rides are now part of Grand Canyon culture. One can hardly think of the canyon without thinking of the mules that walk in and out, up and down, every day. Ron Clayton, longtime manager of the mule barn and mule remuda, was fond of saying, "These mules don't want to go to the bottom of that canyon. They have already been there. They go only because you want to." And go they do; some of the mule string make this walk every day.

Many folks think, erroneously, that mule rides began when the canyon became a national park. In fact, "Captain" John Hance is the man whom history records as having taken the first paying passengers into the canyon on mules. He used the primitive Hance Trail, which lies some fifteen miles west of the trail used today. Being an early entrepreneur, Hance advertised in the local newspaper for customers: "I have a fine spring of water near my house on the rim and can furnish accommodations for tourists and their animals." Such early trips into the canyon were "unnerving for all but the most fearless of travellers."

A Grand Canyon party. Bill Bass, famous guide, is on the left. Circa 1890

An early journalist for the *Saturday Evening Post* indicated that the fearless were not the only ones who made the mule journey down the canyon wall; others, like him, were carried along with the group because they were too afraid to turn back.

Hance was only one of the early pioneers to take advantage of the canyon's attraction to visitors. Wallace Bass turned to tourism, and spent the better part of fifty years accommodating visitors at his various camps, both in the canyon and on the rim. Ralph Cameron, later a United States senator from Arizona, capitalized on his mining claims along the Bright Angel Trail and designated the trail a toll road. He charged one dollar for a walker, or a mule and rider. This practice quickly led to a battle over control to access of the inner canyon.

The essence of all this history is to make the point: "When the going gets tough, those 'in the know' go it with a mule." To quote Clayton, "Mules are well suited for travelling the trails of Grand Canyon. Mules are stronger than a horse, more sure-footed, intelligent and trainable. Their supposed stubborn nature is due to their strong sense of self-preservation."

You have to keep in mind that if your mount survives, so will you. A mule will take care of himself first and foremost. Mules can "see as much with their ears" as they can with their eyes, and they seldom can be forced beyond what they consider safe. Records demonstrate that since the mule trains started traveling the canyon in 1922, no mule has ever gone over the side. Through the years, more than eight hundred thousand mules and riders have made the trip down and up without a mishap. Undoubtedly, this is a good safety record.

Choosing mules for the Grand Canyon remuda was not a duty Clayton took lightly during his 20-plus-year tenure at the canyon. Mules had to meet his rigid standards before they were trusted to take a visitor to the bottom. Even at quality sales, like those offered by the Reese Brothers of Gallatin, Tennessee, out of five hundred or a thousand mules Clayton may have only found one good enough to use at the canyon. Clayton says, "To be used in the canyon a mule must be strong of stature and big of heart, gentle, not easily spooked by noises or the trail, and not nervous. It also needs to be a people mule, meaning it has to like people."

Even when Clayton found a mule he really liked, the mule did not start by hauling folks down to the Phantom Ranch.

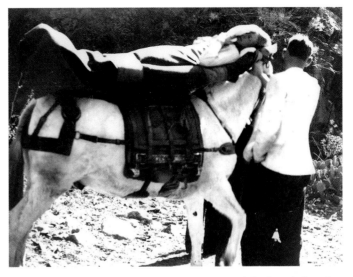

A "mule ambulance" was used to transport the sick and injured out of the canyon. Circa 1935

At the Grand Canyon, new mules generally spend a season as "rookies." Rookie mules get pack duty: hauling groceries and supplies into the canyon, and toting garbage out. Once a mule gets the hang of the pack string, he graduates to being a wrangler's mount. Ridden by a wrangler, he gets used to visitors, backpackers on the trail and all sorts of distractions. Once the mule passes this last test, he is considered safe enough to carry a dude (novice rider), at which time he is added to the passenger string.

Sherry Patterson, a wrangler for the mule operation, has been guiding mule rides at the canyon for many years. She loves to ride, loves people and loves the mules that put up with the dudes every day. She believes she has the perfect job. "You have to respect the mules and what

A Grand Canyon Scrapbook

CLOCKWISE FROM TOP RIGHT:

Men work on an emergency phone on the South Kaibab Trail, 1937.

Getting a boost up the Bright Angel Trail. Circa 1910

Harvey Girls using the "Donkey Telephone." Circa 1906

Louis Boucher and his mule, Silver Bell. Boucher was the hermit that Hermit Camp and Trail were named after. Circa 1910.

Fred Harvey mules welcome the first and only airplane to land in the canyon at Plateau Point, 1922.

CLOCKWISE FROM TOP LEFT:

Fourteen well-dressed riders pose outside the El Tovar Hotel, 1908.

New York City Mayor Fiorello LaGuardia mounts up for a mule wrangling lesson, which he greatly enjoyed, 1935.

Mules await their riders for another trip down the Canyon, 2004.

A snowbound Union Pacific work party walked to Roaring Spring and were met by the welcome sight of a string of saddle mules, 1937.

A National Park Service Ranger transports trout fry in milk cans down the Clear Creek Trail to be released in Clear Creek, 1940.

Wrangler Sherry Patterson.

they learn to tolerate," says Patterson, indicating that dude riders seldom give the wranglers any trouble. They listen and follow instructions. More often, the riders who cause problems are those who ride frequently, because they want to do things their way. "But we all have to follow the rules and there is a good reason behind everything we ask the riders to do. Otherwise, you become a hiker," says Patterson.

"I get the biggest satisfaction out of watching a totally non-rider gain confidence in the mule and relax so they can enjoy the scenery," Patterson says. "Probably my biggest thrill was taking a young deaf couple to Phantom Ranch on Christmas Eve. They were on their honeymoon. I was chosen to lead them because I didn't have a moustache like the men wranglers and they could read my lips easier. I had taken some sign language in high school so we had no trouble communicating. The whole experience was wonderful.

"I think women make good wranglers because by our very nature we are caring individuals," Patterson says. "But of course we have to command respect."

There are some general rules everyone has to abide by. Everyone weighs in and must be under two hundred pounds, including all necessary gear. No exceptions. Riders must wear hats with a brim and a stampede string. They must follow all directions of the wranglers and use "the motivator," or a crop, to make their mule keep up with the pack.

In 2004, Clayton retired as lead mule man, and Shawn Bray, an assistant wrangler since 1997, accepted the position of head wrangler. Bray is supported by Assistant Wrangler Casey Murph, who has been employed at the canyon since 1989. These men know the mule business and keep things moving smoothly and safely up and down the sheer canyon walls.

Few if any changes have taken place under the new management. Rules are rules when it comes to taking mules and the public safely in and out of the canyon. When asked what he would like prospective mule riders to know before they commit to making a canyon trek, Bray said, "I wish they could all understand this is not a short jaunt on a bridle path through the woods. This ride is not easy; it is hard and very physical." He further remarked that people are just not as tough as they used to be. Sedentary lifestyles make it hard for people who never ride at all to put in six or more hours in the saddle.

Head wrangler Shawn Bray catches a mule on a wintry Grand Canyon day.

When asked about the "fear factor," Bray said, "People are all different when it comes to the degree of fear they can handle. I suppose if a person were truly afraid of height this might be a hard ride for them at least in places. But, what causes more fear for the average rider is the size of the mules they have to ride. You see, most of these people are pilgrims [first-time riders] who know nothing about a horse, mule or donkey. They may say mule, but in their minds they see a donkey. Then when they arrive and see a corral full of our eleven hundred- to fourteen hundred-pound mules that stand fifteen hands tall, they are extremely intimidated."

However, Bray says his mules are very forgiving and they will take their riders to the bottom and back no matter how little the rider knows. The mules are so bombproof that they are very popular with the mule-riding public. Many people want to buy the mules that come off the canyon string because they have such a high safety rating.

The public also likes to ride its own horses or mules into the canyon. Bray believes this is a good thing. There is no competition between the National Park Service and the private user. Bray believes that the more private riders come and use the park the longer the park will stay open to equestrian use. His advice for riders is to condition their animals beforehand. Backyard animals or "weekend warriors" are not the best-conditioned animals to take down into the canyon. If a rider loves and respects his animal, he needs to make sure that horse or mule is in a condition to face the challenges this trail has to offer.

The north rim of the Grand Canyon rises about twelve hundred feet higher than the south rim. Most of the nineteen hundred square miles of the park are maintained as wilderness. There are three distinct sections of the park: the south rim, north rim and inner canyon. Each section has its own climate and vegetation, and gives the rider a unique experience.

According to many sources, the south ride is more strenuous, more of a "gut grabber" than the ride on the north side. It is not necessarily more beautiful; it simply has a higher thrill factor. Different mule rides traverse each canyon wall. The mules leaving from the north rim can carry twenty pounds more weight than those leaving from the south rim. However, the rest of the requirements are similar.

No matter which side you approach from, the majesty of the canyon is inescapable. If you are fearless enough to enjoy the ride to the bottom and back on a mule, so much the better. And having done this, you will have a new respect for the faithful, fun-loving animal—part donkey, part horse, and all mule.

A Grand Canyon wrangler prepares a new party of dudes for their trip down the canyon.

The Great Donkey Rescue

If an African of 4000 B.C. were to walk through his town or village today, his mind would be boggled by change. But he would find comfort in one ubiquitous similarity—the presence of donkeys performing their function as the primary beast of burden as they did before the first pyramids were constructed. Donkeys now compete with bicycles and motorized vehicles, but the dun-grey floppy-eared beasts are everywhere, transporting people, agricultural products and manufactured goods on their backs or pulling heavily laden carts as they trot along dusty trails or alongside four-lane highways.

As a Peace Corps volunteer many years ago and more recently as an international business and political consultant, whether working in a modern urban area or remote village in sub-Sahara or north Africa and the Middle East, I am most always in the presence of *Equus asinus*, that descendent of the Nubian and Somalian wild asses. As they bear their burdens alongside exhaust-belching eighteen-wheelers, I have to remind myself that the domestication of these animals marked the shift from sedentary, agrarian societies to mobile, trade-orient-

BY FRED WHITING

Fred Whiting is an international business/political consultant, spending much time in places you would not want to go on vacation. When in the United States he rides mules and fly fishes. Whiting served for ten years in the South Dakota legislature. He resides in the Black Hills of South Dakota.

ed societies. First probably domesticated in Lower Egypt, donkeys were critical to developing long-distance trade down the Nile Valley and across the deserts. From Africa they were brought to Europe by the second millennium B.C. and were carried to the New World by Christopher Columbus in 1495. The donkey has truly played a large part in the evolution of our world, and lives on today in much the same role as in the time of the pharaohs.

I have observed that, as a valuable asset in the economies of African towns and villages, donkeys are, by and large, well cared for. When I lived as a Peace Corps volunteer in the village of Birnin Kebbi, on the edge of the desert in northern Nigeria, I first observed that there are local rules concerning the treatment of donkeys. For example, in order to protect the backs of small donkeys carrying human loads, the rule was that older children and adults must ride on the haunches of the donkey rather than in the middle of its back. All donkeys were to be well fed and watered. Any person abusing a donkey would be sternly reprimanded.

Perhaps it was this donkey-ethic that recently put me in a sticky spot in the desert oasis of Siwa in Egypt. Siwa is in the northwest corner of Egypt near the Libyan border, a ten-hour dusty bus ride from either Cairo or Alexandria. Donkey carts still dominate the traffic in Siwa, hauling everything from dates (Siwa's main product) to propane tanks to burka-covered women, and are mostly commanded by teenage boys. While I was escaping the heat at a small outdoor café facing the town square, I heard some elderly men at the next table shouting at a boy across the road who was mercilessly beating his donkey. The boy paid no attention, seemingly demonstrating his machismo in front of onlookers. Perhaps inspired by the donkey ethic of Birnin Kebbi and with a natural

abhorrence for the ill-treatment of any animal, I found myself marching across the road, taking the whip from the boy's hands, breaking it into pieces and throwing it into the donkey cart. Half-expecting the locals to find insult in this reprimand by a foreigner, I was surprised (and relieved) as people up and down the road applauded. The "great donkey rescue" had succeeded, and the donkeys of Siwa could carry on their millennium-long role free from the blows of at least one small boy with a big stick.

Mule Appreciation Day
October 24

**MULE APPRECIATION DAY 1985
HON. BOB STUMP OF ARIZONA
IN THE HOUSE OF REPRESENTATIVES
THURSDAY, OCTOBER 24, 1985***

MR. STUMP: *Mr. Speaker, as we observe Mule Appreciation Day on October 24, 1985, and there is again some interest in the Army using pack mules, the following will be of interest to many.*

Its author Fred Burke, of Wickenburg, Arizona, joined the Army in 1936 as an enlisted man in the Army's 11th Horse Calvary in Presidio Monterey, California. Upon his retirement some twenty years later at Fort Huachuca, Arizona, he was retired with the last MOS of pack officer. During his career, Fred was the company commander of the 256th Quartermaster Pack Company, a part of the 10th Mountain Division and the last of our military to take mules into combat in Italy.

Fred Burke's analogy of the GI and the pack mule, origi- nally written for the Stars and Stripes *during World War II, follows:*

THE GI AND HIS PACK MULE

Now that the Army is talking about reviewing the use of Army pack mules, the close analogy between enlisted draftees and the conscription of pack mules should prove interesting reading.

Drafted GIs and mules both joined against their wills. Mules and GIs were both sent to training centers. The mules' centers were called Remount Stations. They were both physically processed with physicals and haircuts. The mules' manes and tails were cut short.

Both received immunization shots and both received a serial number. Mules got what was called a Preston brand and it was burned on their necks. Although the GI didn't get physically burned, most carried a brand in their mind for the rest of their lives at the memory of this first training.

Both had service records filled out with serial numbers, hometowns, date drafted, age and family if known. For mules, the families' names might include a mare named Miss Cookie and the father a jack donkey named Sam's Man.

Both were given uniforms at training camp. The mules received new shoes and halter. Both were given basic equipment to take recruit training with. The GI got a gun, backpack, canteen, etc. The mule got a packsaddle called a Phillips saddle, saddle pad, tarp, lash rope to tie on loads and a lead rope.

Now they were both ready to take basic training and were assigned to a training company. Both learned how to carry heavy loads over long forced marches, to bivouac in the field and live on reduced rations.

During this time, they were assigned living quarters. In the GIs case, it was called a barracks; with the mule, it was called a stable and corral. GIs had mess call three times a day; the mules only twice. The mules got grain and hay; the GIs got food that tasted about the same. When it came to cleaning their respective quarters, the mules had the best of it. The GIs had to make their own beds and scrub the barracks. The mules were fortunate to have a detail of enlisted men who cleaned the stable for them.

During recruit training, both would get blisters, sore muscles and sores from the equipment rubbing on former- ly unused spots. They got colds from field training trips. Both mules and GIs would report to the medical facilities in the morning to be placed on the sick call book.

In the mule's case, his doctor was called a veterinarian. Both received treatment and a notation as to light duty, full duty or confinement to quarters with a report back date. The sick book was a permanent record for both. They were both accused of malingering to get out of work.

In the mule's case, he learned that if he went on sick call, he got to loaf in the corral and didn't have to take a long march with a pack.

After recruit training, GIs and mules were assigned to a replacement depot for future assignments to their permanent companies. Their service record went right along with both and the serial number was their identification.

Upon arriving at their new company, both were assigned to a platoon. The mule was given a number from 1 to 50—almost the same number as in a GI's platoon. The mule's number was put on his halter and his saddle. He also got a GI haircut on his tail that told his platoon number. A one bell cut was the 1st platoon, a two bell cut was the 2nd platoon, a three bell cut was the 3rd platoon and no bells was the 4th platoon.

By now both were full-fledged, fully trained healthy individuals ready to join their comrades in defense of their country, willingly or not. From here on both were career military.

The parallel continued in love, duty, living conditions and retirement. An exception was leave time—the mules had no leave. And a GI could retire at 20 years with half pay. The mules were sold as surplus and sent to farms.

In love matters, the GI had the PX girls, the USO or Canteen girls. And of course, there was always the girl next door who would someday marry and reproduce more GIs. The mules had only the platoon "bell mare" for love. Each platoon had one and she was like a queen bee. All the mules in the platoon loved her with a fanatic passion and would follow her to death and did so on several occasions.

The mule sometimes fell in love with a local camp follower who would stray close enough to camp for him to pick up her scent. The mule would go AWOL just like the GI to spend some extra time with a sweet young thing.

Unfortunately for the mule, he was different from the GI when the subject of reproduction came up. The mule could not reproduce but he enjoyed the pleasure of trying.

During WWII at Camp Swift, Texas, a large number of mules went AWOL, and were seen enjoying the pleasure of free love among the horses in the river bottom near Bastrop, Texas. This was just prior to their going overseas with their GI counterparts to fight in the 10th Mountain Division in Italy.

In death both mules and GIs were together at times. Sadly, at times both were killed in either a minefield or by enemy artillery fire. In this case, they both had the same notation in their service record … "KIA."

*Note: There are reliable references to Mule Appreciation Day as being both October 24 and 26.

During the preparation for the big "push" in Italy by the U.S. Fifth Army, the men, mules, and armor of the 10th Mountain Division and supporting tank units moved forward, April 14, 1945, Bologna, Italy.

The Mule's Last Bray? Nay! (or Neigh!)

Mulemen and cannoneers all rolled into one, the men of Battery C, 26th Battalion, Field Artillery Replacement Center, tackled nearly impossible terrain as part of the day's work in 1942. With their guns and auxiliary equipment slung on the backs of army mules, they broke through thick forests, forded streams, and scaled mountain ranges. Their job was to go where mechanized and horse-drawn artillery couldn't go.

I recently read a book, *The Mule's Last Bray*, about how the mule served the United States faithfully in times of war. The book's premise was that the helicopter and four-wheel-drive vehicles had ended the mule's usefulness to the United States military. In addition, there have been many eulogies written and spoken on behalf of the mule, and most people believe that the mule is outdated, no longer of any use to our highly technological modern army.

But consider this: In November 2001 an eleven-member United States Army Special Forces "A-Team" disembarked from a Black Hawk helicopter, in the

BY JOHN HAUER

John Hauer is a dedicated mule lover who can never get enough information about these long-eared critters. He loves riding mules in the Sonora Desert of Arizona, on the high peaks of the Rockies and any-place between. He and his riding buddy recently started raising mules, which he says is addictive. When asked where he is from, the answer is Arizona, Utah, South Dakota, and Wyoming, all great places to ride.

dead of night, in a barren valley in southern Afghanistan. This was to be the Green Berets' most concentrated mission since the Vietnam War. The A-Team's equipment was the most technologically advanced gear ever used by ground forces. They were equipped with night-vision goggles and rifle scopes, highly accurate M-4 carbines, survival gear, explosives and satellite communications systems that would enable them to talk to aircraft overhead or to the Pentagon.

This Special Forces operation proved to be one of the army's most important missions in the special-operations ground war against the Taliban. Defense Secretary Donald Rumsfeld credited the mission with turning the tide of the war just when American forces appeared to be bogged down.

Captain Jason Amerine, a West Point graduate, was the leader of the A-Team. As the Black Hawk helicopters put down that night, campfires and robed tribesmen encircled the landing zone. The *Washington Post* quoted Amerine as saying, "I looked up and saw these heavily robed tribesmen just like you see on TV. It was almost eerie, the sight…a very kind of primitive thing. The whole meeting was coordinated down to the mule train that carried our rucksacks."

The army apparently learned something from the experience that Amerine and others had with mules in Afghanistan, because in June 2004 the army issued an updated field manual titled *Special Forces Use of Pack Animals*. Later that summer, members of the 19th Special Forces Group received training in mule packing and other equestrian skills at a training site in the mountains of Colorado. They learned to pack fifty-caliber machine guns and other heavy weapons on mules.

The army contracted with a company called Winterhawk Outfitters to train the Special Forces troops. Winterhawk, with headquarters in Silt, Colorado, trains guides and operates deer and elk hunting camps. Larry and Laura Amos, Winterhawk owners, have enjoyed their experience with the soldiers. Said Larry, "They are all aggressive young guys who are eager to learn. Where they are going their lives may well depend on the skills they learn here."

The program has been so successful that the army may contract with Winterhawk to do all of its packing training. Larry attributes the success of the program to his head packer, Bob Shellum, a retired Marine Master Gunner Sergeant with thirty years of service. "Bob understands what these guys and their mules will be up against in a combat situation. He knows how to teach the skills they will need to come out alive and uninjured," Larry said. Clearly we have not heard the mule's last bray in the military yet!

THE MULE'S BRAY IS HEARD IN FUND-RAISING AND HELPING CRIPPLED CHILDREN Another way in which the mule continues to contribute to our quality of life is the work done by the internationally famous Al Kaly Shrine Mule Train. These special mules perform in drill competition and parades throughout the nation, promoting the serious side of the Shriners' work—the nineteen Shriners Children's Hospitals and three Burn Institutes. Services at these twenty-two hospitals for children are provided without charge to the patients or their parents.

The Al Kaly Shrine Mule Team

The Al Kaly Shrine Mule Train was created more than forty years ago, in September 1957, when the army decided that the days of the mounted units had come and gone.

That afternoon, with great pride, the new owners took the mules to their new homes. During the night, over half of the animals managed to jump out of their corrals and make their way back to the stables at Fort Carson. They had not yet been exposed to the good life of an Al Kaly Shrine Mule Train mule.

Another interesting fact is that the mule train had assumed care of Hambone, the army's famous jumping mule. When he died in 1966, the army requested that he be buried at Fort Carson. The mule train furnished the plaque on his grave. An agreement was also made with Fort Carson to bury the last surviving army mule, Wind River, alongside Hambone at Fort Carson. However, when Wind River died at the age of 46, the army requested that she be stuffed and placed in the Fort Carson Museum. The mule train paid for her taxidermy. Wind River was moved later to Fort Leonard Wood, Missouri.

By 1974, the mule train had become established as a parade unit, but incentive was lacking. In order to fill this void, it was decided to form a precision drill team to compete with other shrine-mounted units; this team is the only precision mounted Shrine drill team comprised of mules.

The drill team enjoyed immediate success and began to accumulate numerous trophies, which soon exhausted all the available space in the tack room. One of the drill team members died in 1980, and through his and his wife's generosity a twelve-by-fifty-foot addition was made to the room. In honor of the team member it was named "Art's Room." The new addition provided room for more trophies and also made it possible for members to build a bar and lounge area.

Members had a trailer for the mules, but no motor power. A sum of $10,000 was approved for the purchase of a 1970 Kenworth tractor in good condition. That transaction was like getting married: The initial price was cheap but the upkeep was terrific. It was sold a few years later,

much to the relief of the membership.

After winning first place in the 1983 Imperial Parade in Denver, the mule train was invited to participate in the Tournament of Roses Parade in Pasadena. Sixty-five members, wives and guests made the trip. Being in the Rose Parade is a big chore, and includes getting up at 2 a.m. to actually enter the parade anywhere from 9 a.m. until noon. The parade route is five miles long and thousands of people pack the sidelines.

The Columbia, Tennessee mule show was another big event for the mule train. They take their mules seriously in Tennessee, and the mules received a warm welcome, especially with the drill and flag ceremonies.

At that time, the mule train became the source of mules for the Army–Air Force football games in Colorado Springs. A highlight of 1992 was the invitation from veterans of the Tenth Mountain Division to bring some mules to their reunion in Leadville, Colorado. Three riders, their wives and mules spent two days with the veterans.

THE MULE'S BRAY IS ALSO HEARD IN THE WORLD'S WORKFORCE In the United States, the mule's primary use has changed from being a beast of burden that was often unappreciated, abused and neglected to a pleasure animal that is often spoiled, pampered and loved. In other, less technologically developed countries, both mules and donkeys are still used extensively for all the work industrialized nations do with trucks, trains, planes and tractors.

The Al Kaly "Tack Room," which houses tack, clubhouse, lounge and trophy room.

The mule team hits the road regularly to participate in parades and mule-related events.

Participants were provided with authentic World War II uniforms (that did not fit), and vintage gear for the mules. When the group appeared in the parade, many veterans had tears in their eyes. Some had not seen a mule since the war. The second day they moved to Camp Hale, Colorado, home of the division. Most of the day was occupied with veterans petting the mules, taking pictures and some actually mounting the mules for old time's sake.

In 1998, the outfit performed in Branson, Missouri, and won first place in drill and parade competition. In 1999, the team performed in Dallas, Texas, and received the President's Trophy. Also in 1999, the group went to Tulsa, Oklahoma, and won second place in parade and drill competition. The team annually participates in eight to ten local parades, as well as a drill demonstration for the Pike's Peak or Bust Rodeo in nearby Colorado Springs.

For the shrine, perhaps the most gratifying result of the mule train has been the contribution by mule train members of more than four million dollars to the Intermountain Hospital for Children.

In late 1960, the mule train was selected to be the official Colorado unit in President John F. Kennedy's inaugural parade. Details of the event, now many decades in the past, are still vivid in the memories of those who made the trip. One thing that many remember was the bitter cold weather. Eight inches of snow had fallen the previous night, and a thirty-mile-an-hour wind kept the temperatures well below freezing all day long. There was an eight-hour wait before the parade started, and at the conclusion, one rider was so stiff he had to be lifted off of his mule and carried to a waiting bus.

THE MULE AT THE EARTH WALK IN MOAB, UTAH

Mules are used in many ways to give pleasure to young people. From 2001 to 2003, mules owned by John Hauer were used in the Moab, Utah, Independence Day celebrations to give short rides to more than three hundred children. Many of these kids had never before had a chance to ride a mule or horse. In the summer of 2001, thirteen inner-city kids from Denver were given an opportunity

Everyone loves a parade, and the Al Kaly mules are always ready to put on a show.

or mule. A few of the kids were experienced riders, a few were afraid of the mules and others were wide-eyed with joy and love for their new long-eared friends. One very small Navajo boy refused to get off when it was time to load the mules into the trailer. He even wanted to ride the critter inside the trailer! For a while it appeared that John and Sena would have to either adopt the little boy or give him the mule.

to ride mules on a ranch north of Moab. The kids were participating in a summer camp sponsored by Earth Walk, a nonprofit organization that "offers adventure, opportunity and growth to inner-city youth through service, art, culture and nature." The program is made available at no charge to the students' families or schools.

The executive director of Earth Walk said the mule ride "helped the organization to continue the very vital work of replacing despair with hope in the lives of the children and families we serve."

As recently as September 2004, mules were used in a 4-H Fair in Moab when John and Sena Hauer were asked to provide the community's youth with a chance to ride an equine. Many of the children who received rides had never before had the opportunity to even touch a horse

THE MULE'S BRAY IS HEARD IN ADVERTISING

The Borax Twenty Mule Team Perhaps the most enduring advertising campaign featuring mules is the U.S. Borax Company's use of the Twenty Mule Team, which became the symbol for Borax in 1891 and continues to be

Twenty-mule team on its way back to the Lila-C Mine, California. Circa 1892

MULE GOES HOLLYWOOD

HOLLYWOOD, May 23, 1949 (UPI)—Hollywood, amid much pomp and ceremony and braying of animals (two-legged as well as the other kind), held its first screen test for a mule today. It was a Missouri product that snagged the movie contract.

The studio shelled out $450 to fly her to Hollywood for the screen test, and the way she breezed through it had eight other mule hopefuls standing around with their ears drooping. They hailed from New Mexico, Rhode Island, Texas, Colorado, North Carolina, Tennessee, Mexico and California. But it was clear from the beginning "Miss Missouri" had an "in."

"She has appeal," beamed Producer Robert Arthur, forgetting that's one thing mules DON'T have. "Look at those long eyelashes —and that photogenic face."

Francis did, indeed, have appeal and a great personality. She was flown to numerous places to "meet people" and fan mail poured in, in appreciation of making her acquaintance.

Years later Donald O'Connor would remember his experience with Francis.

O'Connor swore off any future involvement with the animal a full 25 years ago.

"I quit in 1955 because I frankly didn't want to be identified with the mule anymore," he admitted. "I mean when you've made six pictures, and the mule still gets more fan mail than you do, you start wondering. I thought it was hurting my career. But I was wrong. The Francis pictures and the musicals I did earlier were

totally different entities. And the Francis movies made more money than any of my other pictures."

Don't be surprised in scanning a television screen today if you note a talking mule with the gravelly voice of Chill Wills in casual conversation with a youngish Donald O'Connor.

of borax. The load had to be hauled 165 miles up and out of Death Valley, over the steep Panamint Mountains and across the desert to the nearest railroad junction at Mojave. The twenty-day round trip started at 190 feet below sea level and climbed to an elevation of two thousand feet before it was over.

Built in Mojave for nine hundred dollars each, the wagons balanced strength and capacity to carry the heavy load of borax ore. Each wagon, which carried ten tons, had to grind through sand and gravel and hold together up and down steep mountain grades. Iron tires–eight inches wide and one inch thick–encased the seven-foot-high rear wheels and five-foot-high front wheels. The split-oak spokes measured five-and-one-half inches wide at the hub. The wagon beds were sixteen feet long, four feet wide and six feet deep. Empty, each wagon weighed 7,800 pounds. Two loaded wagons plus the water tank made a total load of 73,200 pounds, or thirty-six tons.

used today. The Borax Twenty Mule Team is one of the most memorable icons of the American West, and of the pioneers who transformed its mineral wealth into a foundation of modern industry throughout the world. Today, that team is the symbol of a visionary company that has become a global supplier of products and service.

The saga of the Twenty Mule Team began more than a century ago in the arid deserts of California's Death Valley. J.W. S. Perry and a young mule skinner named Ed Stiles thought of hitching ten two-mule teams together to form a one-hundred-foot-long, twenty-mule team to haul a load

Between 1883 and 1889, the twenty-mule teams hauled more than twenty million pounds of borax out of the valley. A loaded team traveled an average of only seventeen miles a day and made camp in the desert at night.

During this time not a single animal was lost, nor did a single wagon break down—a testament to the ingenuity of the designers and builders and the stamina of the men and mules.

Swinging the team around a curve on a mountain pass tested both driver and team; one mistake could mean death for all. As the team started around a sharp curve, the chain that ran from the front of the wagon between the pairs of mules tended to be pulled into a straight line between the lead mules and the wagon. To keep the chain going around the curve and not pull the team straight over the edge, some of the mules had to jump the chain and pull at an angle away from the curve. These mules–the pointers, sixth and eighth pairs–would step along sideways until the corner had been turned. Swinging a curve successfully was an awesome demonstration of training and teamwork.

Maneuvering the team across the rugged desert was only part of the mule skinner's job. He also had to serve as a practical veterinarian and mechanic, caring

When fully loaded these two borax wagons, plus a water tank, weighed 36 tons.

for any sick or injured animals and repairing the wagons along the way. Characteristically, these mule skinners were solitary men with short tempers, accustomed to enduring extreme hardships. For their efforts, mule skinners earned from $100 to $120 per month–very high wages for the time.

First used in 1891 and registered in 1894, the Twenty Mule Team symbol became the trademark of the Pacific Coast Borax Company–and, in turn, of Borax–and its many industrial and household products.

Mules and the BBD&O Agency Mules are being used in advertising even as this book goes to press. In September 2004, John and Sena Hauer were contacted by a location scout for one of the world's largest advertising agencies (BBD&O) and asked to provide three pack mules with full packs to be used in magazine advertisements for the 2005 Dodge Power Wagon.

The big Dodge truck and the pack mules were taken to a rugged site on a cliff overlooking the Colorado River near Moab, Utah. For seven hours, eight advertising professionals took photographs of the mules jumping up a ledge behind the truck, walking behind the truck and carrying their cargo up the side of the red rock cliff.

It appeared to the two mule wranglers that the photographs were intended to show that the mules can carry very large, heavy loads in very rough and steep terrain and that the Dodge Power Wagon is just as tough as the mules. It was obvious to the wranglers that the mules could go places the truck couldn't, but that undoubtedly won't be the point of the advertisement.

Numerous companies have used the mule's brawn to help demonstrate the toughness of their products. For example, one synthetic leather company uses a takeoff on mule hide, and a pickup truck–mounted hoist uses "mule" in its name. A roofing company refers to one of its products as mule hide roofing, and Wells Lamont uses a sketch of a mule head in their logo along with the slogan, "STUBBORN ABOUT QUALITY." A motorcycle manufacturer calls its rugged four-wheel-drive hauling vehicle The Mule.

MULES IN THE MODERN GERMAN ARMY

According to an article in the November 2004 issue of *Western Mule*, mules play an important role in today's German Army. They constitute a "special force for transport problems in difficult mountain areas," according to field veterinarian, Dr. W. Noreisch. He explained that there are conditions in the mountains that make helicopter missions impossible, but "our mules work always, no matter if it rains, snows or how hard the wind blows. Our unit can't be replaced by anything. No other means of transportation has ever been so reliable as our mules," he said.

For his unit "a mule is ten times better than a horse," Noreisch said. "Mules can walk much better on rocky trails than horses. They can carry more in a load due to their straight backs. These animals don't need as much food as the horses for the same work. They hardly ever suffer from colic. They are resistant to extreme cold and hot weather. They have extremely hard hooves. Mules are very interested in everything."

A mule in the German Army is used for hard military active service for about twenty years. Noreisch explained that when the mule is discharged from the army it "provides satisfying services for another twenty years as a private mount." The army assumes responsibility for finding the retiring mule a good civilian home and reports that it has been very successful in finding loving homes for them.

Pat McNamara's "Mule Store" is a colorful 42-page catalog that offers an amazing selection of serious and frivolous products for mule lovers. Pat's mule, Sara, is used to take her catalogs and smaller items to the post office which is two miles from Pat's home in North Prairie, Wisconsin. Pat refers to Sara as The Official Mule Store Open Air Transport Vehicle.

We asked Pat why she chose a mule for this important job and she responded: "Why do I prefer mules? Their intelligence, strength, endurance, personality and perserverance never cease to amaze me. The fact that man is unable to totally dominate the mule and that the mule is able to take care of himself 'just fine thank you very much' without our help is a real plus. Also the kind, honest and giving folks that are in the long-ear world are second to none. It's impossible to have a big ego and a mule at the

A good-looking mule was used on the cover and inside a catalog recently published by "Cattle Kate," a western clothing company. The mule certainly gave the catalog a distinctive and unique look. (Editors' note: You can get a Cattle Kate catalog by calling (800) 332-5283. The current catalog may be muleless, but you can bet it will feature clothing that will look good on you the next time you ride your mule.)

Pat and Sara, "The Official Mule Store Open Air Transport Vehicle," after another successful mail drop at their local post office.

same time. I guess that sums it up ... they're an 'ego buster with a sense of humor.' Ya just can't beat that!"

For a copy of The Mule Store catalog, call toll-free 1-877-654-6853.

THE MULE'S BRAY IS HEARD IN ACADEMIA

Central Missouri State University athletic teams are now known as the Mules. The university was formerly the state Normal School, and the teams were known as the Normals. In 1921, the school became a college, and a contest was held among the students to choose a new name for their teams. John Thomason's entry, the Mules, was chosen over 79 other suggestions, including skunks and hippopotamuses.

In 1974, the university held a similar competition and the women's teams were named the Jennies. Contest winner, Cynthia Almaguer, told the contest judges, incorrectly, "The reason I picked the name (Jennies) is because of the obvious feminine kinship of the jenny to our mule mascot. It is a fact that a mule is a descendant of a female donkey—the jenny."

Graduate Sam Smiser, an expert mule producer and promoter, donated the university's current mascot, Abbedale. The university's student newspaper is *The Muleskinner*.

Central Missouri State University's mule mascot, Abbedale, and trainer Lawrence Chaney.

Mo the Mule, CMSU's offical mascot.

LIVESTOCK ENCYCLOPEDIA

The following information is taken from the 1914 LIVE STOCK: A CYCLOPEDIA FOR THE FARMER AND STOCK OWNER, by A.H. Baker, M.D., V.S., founder and for twenty-seven years dean and professor of theory and practice of veterinary medicine. Published by Inter-Collegiate Press, Kansas City, Missouri, 1914.

The wild ass is said to have been indigenous to Arabia Deserta, and the countries that formed the Babylonian Empire. Those now found in the northern region of India are said to be so fleet, in the hill country, that no horse can overtake them.

ANTIQUITY OF THE MULE

Mules were used and much prized from a remote antiquity, and are mentioned both in sacred and profane history. They were introduced into the chariot races in the seventieth Olympiad, or about five hundred years before the Christian era. And in the time of the Romans, Q. Axius, a Roman Senator, paid four-hundred thousand sesterces, or more than thirteen thousand dollars, for a male ass (for the stud); and he also states that the best female asses were worth a like sum to breed sides. When we compute the difference in value between money then and now, the price was greater than that currently paid for the most celebrated racing and trotting horses.

The Knight (one of George Washington's jacks) was of a moderate size, clean limbered, great activity, the fire and ferocity of a tiger, a dark brown, nearly black color, white belly and muzzle; could only be managed by one groom, and that always at considerable personal risk. Knight lived to a great age.

His mules were all active, spirited, and serviceable; and from stout mares attained considerable size.

The longevity of the mule is proverbial. It was a common saying during the Civil War that "mules never died;" they might sometimes be knocked over by a shot, but if one ever died a natural death the army wags refused to credit or record the fact. Pliny gives an account of one, taken from Grecian history, that was eighty years old; and though past labor, followed others, that were carrying materials with which to build the Temple of Minerva at Athens, and seemed to wish to assist them; which so pleased the people, that they ordered he should have free egress to the grain market.

A gentleman in my neighborhood had owned a very large mule for about fourteen years that cannot be less than twenty-eight years old. He informed me a few days later that he could not perceive the least failure in him, and would not exchange him for any farm horse in the country. And I am just informed, from a source entitled to perfect confidence, that a highly respectable gentleman and eminent agriculturist, near Centerville, on the eastern shore of Maryland, owns a mule that is thirty-five years old, as capable of labor as at any former period.

It is beyond dispute that mules will continue to labor for at least double the period of the usefulness of the horse. They endure extreme heat better, but are pinched with cold.

Weight for weight, they will draw a heavier load; and for the reason that they take little notice of what is going on about them, do not fret and seldom scare. As pack animals, they are far superior to the horse; while, in sure-footedness and freedom from disease, no farm animal, except the goat, can compete with them.

The mule will work strenuously for a kind master. Nevertheless, he must have a master, one firm and yet kind. The mule, as some of our readers probably know, has a most perfect means of offense and defense, namely, his heels.

THE HISTORY OF MULES COMES FULL CIRCLE

BY SENA HAUER

R.C. Bradley has seen the value of mules come full circle in his long lifetime. He's seen their popularity rise and fall, and he's fully pleased to see mules once again be the prized possessions they were in his youth.

"Mules have been in my life since I can remember," says Bradley, who was born in 1925 in Oklahoma. "I used to run all the way home from school when it was gathering time so I could get on the wagon seat and hold the lines of Jack and Dan, our mules. Not that I was needed, but it sure made me feel important to hold the lines of that big team while my dad and the neighbor gathered corn and threw it on the wagon."

Bradley remembers the importance of mules when he was young, because they powered

The "Go Devil" sled cultivator and "The Scratcher" or spring tooth harrow.

all the farm equipment. "When I was nine years old I remember that dad got what we called a 'Go Devil.' Some called them a sled cultivator; it was the only piece of equipment that we had that included a seat. With this new equipment, I no longer had to run to keep up with the mules."

In 1936 Bradley was eleven and old enough to operate a piece of equipment called "The Scratcher." "Some called it a spring tooth," says Bradley, "and I worked with it and the mules for my dad until I went into the Marine Corps in 1942."

Thoughts about mules didn't stray too far from Bradley's mind while he was in the service, and in 1946, just as soon as he returned from duty, he got back into business. "I traded for and bought every mule I could find. I got several old mares and a mammoth jack called Dexter."

Over the years he amassed a rather large herd, but the popularity of mules began to decline. "That was the dying end of the mule. Everyone was selling their mules for tractors," said Bradley. In addition, while the popularity of horses remained strong during that time, mules

had a bad reputation due to poor breeding. "If a mare didn't throw a good horse colt, you bred her to a jack, and that's why we had so many outlaw mules." That factor, along with the advance of tractors, doomed the mule industry. He sold out to a government program that sent the animals overseas, and it marked the beginning of a sad era for mules in the United States.

"In 1948 or '49, a man by the name of Willis Grumbine from Kansas, along with another buyer whose name I don't recall, came through buying mules for the government. They were doing this under the Marshall Plan, also known as the Lend-Lease Act, where the government was sending the animals to Belgium and France because the people there had eaten their stock during World War II.

"I sold them all of my mules for $85 each," says Bradley. The mule buyers left his place with two trailer loads, or about forty-four mules. The French and Belgian people were supposed to use the mules to farm with, according to Bradley, "but you know what happened ... They ate 'em."

Using the proceeds from his mule sell-off, Bradley got enough money to move to Kansas and "go to work in the oil patches," which he did for a couple of decades. It would be twenty-five years before he got another mule; he'd gone back to wheat farming and had a place to keep the critters, and he was excited to see the quality of mules that were finally being produced. Thus began Bradley's latest era as a mule buyer, seller and trader.

It's no wonder that Bradley would continue to have mules throughout his life. He's a mule man through and through, and he'll tell you why: "They take care of themselves. My vet bill is half of what it would be for a horse. Mules won't overeat; ninety-nine percent of them won't founder on water or feed. They have a strictly business point of view, and they're smarter than most people."

Bradley now lives in Caballo, New Mexico, on his place called Mule Hill. "I still have mules today, and I still love to look at good mules." He acknowledges that, "Mules have had a hard role." And pondering their return to popularity, he says, "That sounds good. They're coming back."

Required Reading

I just read a book that I believe should be required reading for everyone currently under the age of sixty and for students in all future high school social studies classes. The author, Lonny Thiel, interviewed seventy-eight elderly people over a three-year period starting in 2007. Every one of those people had worked with mules when they were growing up.

Reading this book will give people an understanding and appreciation for the hard work (by both people and mules) that was required to provide the basis for the comparatively luxurious lives that most Americans lead today.

Although this book deals with people living on farms, many of those living in cities and small towns were working just as hard to make ends meet, and the country as a whole was fighting a war against Hitler and his tyrannical allies. The period is part of our history of which we should be knowledgeable and proud. Most of the men and women interviewed by the author worked on farms from age seven to eighteen and then served in the Armed Forces, many in active combat in World War II and or Korea. Many of those interviewed grew up with seven or more siblings.

Statements from the author in the forward and the introduction:

"Of the 78 people I interviewed for mule stories, I can only recall one of them talking about having a veterinarian treat a mule. The biggest surprise to me from the interviews was the number of people who started working mules as early as seven or eight years old.

"I wrote this book as a voice for Missouri farm mules from the 1930s and 1940s—a voice for more than 245,000 incredibly hard-working, resilient, versatile equine survivors who possessed 'a keen intelligence that in many incidents seem to be a sense of humor.

"There were 300,000 mules in Missouri in 1930. Where there was a mule, there was a story."

John Hammond's story is pretty typical of the life led by farm kids in the 1930s and '40s. He was born in 1928 and

That Son of a Gun Had Sense *by Lon Thiele. To order a copy, write to Lon at: PO Box 884, Poplar Bluff, MO 63902.*

had four brothers and four sisters. Like most other young men in that era, he served in the US Army. Below are some excerpts from his interview:

"Dad wouldn't have anything but a mule."

"Us boys started plowing when we were seven or eight years old. Because the mules would turn the plow, we'd just follow them ole mules all day long. They could tell time better than a human being. When it got noon at the end row closest to the house, they'd stop. That's the way of us boys could tell that it was time to go in for dinner. We'd get our butts whipped if we rode them mules. My dad said them mules work too. We walked them to the house."

"We (boys) all worked one field. We would follow each other. Dad would be working nearby clearing new ground but he was never very far from us. He kept an eye on us and made sure we done stuff right. If we didn't do it right, he would take a brush to our hind ends. He told you how to do it, and that's the way you better do it. Back in them days you didn't disobey your parents."

"You walk 14 hours a day with a breaking plow. Your legs get tired. My mom used to come in my bedroom and rub down my legs with alcohol. Back then we were in the depression. We didn't have a choice. You either work, or you didn't eat."

"You had to get up at 4 o'clock every morning. You worked from when you couldn't see, to when you couldn't see, and you never got done with your work. Didn't make any difference if you were sick; there wasn't no doctors. Our mom and dad doctored us. They done the best they could."

Hammond lied about his age and went into the Army at age seventeen and spent four years overseas. After being discharged from the service, he worked at Fisher Body for five years, then worked at Balls Brothers glass company for thirty-nine years. He and his wife Barbara were married for fifty-four years.

The Natural Superiority of Mules

MULE MATTERS

Using Mules for Packing

A pack mule calmly crosses a mountain stream with an uneven but well-balanced and secure cargo.

The pack mule is one of the most reliable animals for use in the packing/outfitting industry. A mule is content to be part of a string of animals and let the lead mule or horse do all of the thinking. String mules don't try to be in the lead and they don't try to keep going around the animal in front of them. They have a smooth gait, too. Of course, to reach this utopian vision, you must have animals that are familiar with one another and have been working together. There is nothing like a string of mules that has been working together for years. You can look back at your string, their heads all at about the same level and those big, beautiful ears are flopping with every step. The mules—and you—are completely content!

BY STEVEN RICHARDS

Steven Richards, who believes he was "born with the innate need to wrap his legs around a mount and ride," was forbidden to ride his Grandpa's fillies until they were two years old. Imagine Grandpa's surprise when they were broke at one year! Richards has been able to fulfill his love of riding in one of the most beautiful places in the world, the Rocky Mountains around Cody, Wyoming. He has hunted, packed, done professional guiding and outfitting, and ridden for fun. His favorite mounts are two look-alike palomino mules.

The ideal mule for packing is a draft cross, specifically, a Belgian mare crossed with a mammoth jack. Belgian draft horses seem to be the most docile of the draft breeds, and the mammoth donkeys are the most docile of donkeys. The draft side gives the mule bigger, more solid bones, and their quiet nature helps them deal with "rattley" loads that have the potential to startle. Another important characteristic of a good pack mule is the size and shape of its withers: it should have well-defined, substantial withers. This helps stabilize the load and keeps it from getting knocked off center.

Some people like a shorter mule so they don't have to reach so far when lifting a load. There are many good mules to be had in that category. The main things to look for are the withers and how quiet the animals are. Are they easy to handle? Do they kick or strike with their feet? Do they startle easily or think they see ghosts in the rocks or trees? Generally speaking, mules that are eight or older are better than the young ones, as they've managed to mature out of the "kid" stage of their lives and are ready to settle down and work.

I have owned several mules that only packed, but I want my mules to serve both functions: riding and packing. It makes good sense. If something happens to your riding mule, then you have an alternate riding mount to get you back to civilization. Some mules are not as suitable as riding mounts as they are pack animals, but when you are deep in the wilderness, even those mules seem like the best thing you ever sat on.

One time I was on an elk hunt with a group. The hunt was successful, and we were loaded with the camp equipment as well as all of the elk meat. We had made arrangements with a friend to meet us on a mountain road to take the equipment and meat home so we could run the pack string down free of their burden. The day was bitter cold and snowing with a strong, biting wind. We were late getting to our rendezvous, and the lights from the pickup truck in the distance were a welcome sight.

As luck would have it, there wasn't a tree or post with-in a mile of the rendezvous point, so one of us had to hold the pack string while two of us unloaded the mules and loaded the trucks. Just as we unloaded the last panniers from the last pack animal, something spooked the string and they exploded into the night. The only animal I had was the pack mule I was holding. Luckily, this pack mule was also a well-trained riding mule. The downside is that I knew I'd have to ride a packsaddle all the way back to the ranch.

A good pack mule will not object to packing sharp or smelly objects. Elk hides and horns are a real test of a pack mule's tolerance.

Anybody who has had the experience of riding a pack-saddle knows they aren't built for riding comfort. After sending the pickup down the mountain, I jumped on my pack mule and rode off into the night, hoping to run into my string of lost animals. After about an hour of freezing temperatures, a lumpy riding saddle, and uncomfortable rump, I came to a line fence and a group of saddled pack animals and the saddle mount. Although I was frozen to the bone, I was able to gather up the string and had an uneventful ride the rest of the way home. This is a perfect example of why it's a good idea that your pack animal also be trained as a riding mule!

This pack mule is loaded using the Decker packing system.

PACK EQUIPMENT Many people just starting out in packing ask which is better: packing sawbuck style or with a Decker packing system. The best packers will learn both ways, as each has its pluses and minuses. You can pack everything on a sawbuck that you can pack on a Decker, and vice versa. I suggest that you learn to pack according to the standard of your area. That way, if you run into trouble on the trail and someone else comes along, he can help you since he will be familiar with the technique. If you are in an area where no one else packs and you want to get started, then I suggest packing saw-buck style, unless you think your loads would be better served by the Decker packing system.

The sawbuck system has been around since the time of Genghis Khan. Many packers take great pride in knowing various kinds of knots, which can be quite confusing and discouraging to beginners. Packing can be as simple as buckling a top pack on a set of panniers and buckling a cinch, or even just hanging the panniers on the packsaddle.

The first thing a packer needs to do is fit the pack-saddle bars to the back of the animal that is being packed. If you have a packsaddle with wooden bars, the bars need to be shaped to fit your animal. To do this, apply flour or carpenter's chalk to the animal's back. After taking the harness off the pack tree, carefully set the tree on the mule's back, lifting it off to see where the chalk or flour remains. Take a wood rasp and file off all high spots on the tree then set the saddle on the mule's back again. Continue to reapply and rasp the saddle until you get an even application of chalk or flour. This will ensure that you have an even fit. Refasten your harness to the saddle and fit it to the mule. Make sure that the breast collar and the britchin' are not too tight. You should be able to put a flat hand between the front shoulder and the breast collar. The britchin' should just bump the rear leg in its fullest stride. The newer, adjustable-bar packsaddles seem to be the best answer to an even fit on a variety of animals. The bars are on a hinge and swing to fit each animal.

Some packsaddles have an adjustment in the center of the arch to accommodate a wider back or mutton with-ers. This way the bars spread better across the back. Also, these bars are made from a high-impact type of plastic and are stronger and safer for the pack animal.

Besides leather, there are many new materials that are far superior and stronger than leather, such as bio-thane and beta. They do not rot or mildew and offer one thousand pounds of tensile strength. One of the greatest advantages is that these two materials stay flexible down to fifty degrees below zero. These materials work well in the wet and cold regions of the country or in areas with high humidity. Some packers put a skirting made of leather on the bars of the packsaddle, but it makes the bars too long and will usually rub the hair off around the animal's hip area.

Since most people spend a lot of time on their riding pad, it is just as important to pay close attention to the pack pad. Most packers will use a thick felt pad with extra length, but those types seem to rub the hair off where the sharp edge of the felt comes into contact with the mule. The stiffness of the material also wears the hair off where the load is being carried. Usually there is no permanent damage, but the best way to get the cushion between the load and the back of the mule is to use a quality fleece pad with a felt pad on top of that. That eliminates most of the hair breakage and provides adequate cushion.

MANTIES, PACK COVERS AND PANNIERS A mantie is a piece of canvas or similar material that is somewhere around eight feet by eight feet square. It is used with the Decker system in bundling up the loads. A three-eighths-inch rope about thirty-three feet long is used to tie up the bundled load by using a series of half hitches divided in thirds along the bundle. A pack cover, which is also sometimes called a mantie, is a seven-foot-by-eight-foot piece of canvas or other material thrown over the top pack and panniers. It is tied down by a half-inch-diameter lash rope that is thirty-five to fifty-five feet long, and it has a lash cinch tied on one end. Panniers are bags made of leather, canvas or nylon. Boxes made of rawhide, wood, plastic, aluminum or steel are also used. They are made with loops on the back so they can be looped over the cross-bucks of the sawbuck saddle.

BALANCE Balance and equal weight are two of the most important parts of having loads ride successfully. Put the heavy items of your load next to your mule inside the pannier or mantied load with the lighter items resting on the outside of the bag. Try to make the loads as equal as possible from front to back. Remember that packing is three-dimensional. Where most packers get into trouble is at the end of packing, when they have all the panniers loaded and can't find anywhere else to put things. They end up putting them on the top of their load. The loads become far too high, heavy and bulky. As the animal is walking up the trail, the top pack begins swaying back and forth. As it sways, it will eventually shift to one side or the other.

When it shifts to one side, it then makes that side heavier, throwing off the balance and then turning the saddle. When traveling down the trail, you can also run into trees or rocks that will bounce the panniers off balance. An important detail is that when you put on the panniers, check to see if they are hanging evenly on both sides. Examine the mule from the back to see if the bottoms of the panniers are even. If they are balanced correctly, they should be hanging equally and you should have a trouble-free journey.

Another method, used well in Decker packing, is to rock the load by grabbing the bottom of the mantied load or pannier, lifting and letting go. The mule's skin is loose, and the load will rock and then settle. If the load settles to one side, then it is too heavy on that side and an adjustment needs to be made. Add or subtract weight to balance it. You can also raise or lower the opposite side until the load centers after rocking it.

It is also important to know the physical condition of your mule and your equipment. A fat and out-of-condition mule will lose weight quickly at first, and the latigos and cinches will soon become loose. Even if your mule is in good condition and all of your equipment is new, new leather and cinches all stretch. It is always a good idea to put on and adjust your packsaddle and take it out empty a couple of times before you go on a pack trip so that all components have had an opportunity to stretch.

If you follow these basic guidelines, you should be ready to hit the trail and enjoy a great pack trip with few problems.

THE COLORADO MULE RIDERS

BY BEN TENNISON

Ben Tennison is the editor/chief of *Western Mule Magazine*. He is a dedicated mule trainer, and a member of the Colorado Mule Riders.

Good mules, good men, golden aspen and breathtaking views just may be a perfect formula for the successful existence of any organization.

It certainly has worked for the Colorado Mule Riders (CMR) for nearly thirty years. Many organizations come and go these days, but it's standing room only to get a chance to experience the ride of a lifetime with the famous CMR.

In the summer of 1976, a group of riders were discussing where they might go with their mules. Dave Frank, Jim Frank and Gale Fortney suggested that an annual all-mule trail ride be held in different parts of the state of Colorado. In those meetings the name "CMR" arrived. John Ladd prepared the incorporation papers and the Colorado Mule Riders became official.

The CMR today has a membership of thirty-five riders. Any member has a first right to participate in the annual fall ride that begins on the third Saturday in September each year and lasts for five days. If a member cannot participate in the ride, a non-member may take his place. Riders often choose to bring their own mules but they can rent a mule at a reasonable fee. The accommodations are always first class. A rider has nothing more to worry about than saddling up a mule for the day's ride. However, gaining a bit of weight from five-star meals for five days could be another worry.

The first ride was held at Lost Valley Ranch, approximately sixty miles west of Colorado Springs. Lost Valley provided all those things that the CMR thought would be required such as location, lodging, food, facilities for the mules and a place where they could go and enjoy themselves.

Today the CMR relies on the Colorado Dude Ranch Association for details on guest ranches. The CMR has developed a great rapport with this group of guest ranchers, and the ranches look forward to the arrival of the mules and their riders.

The mule riders come from all walks of life, and from throughout the United States and Canada. Occupations are left at home on a Colorado Mule Ride. Each year, there are usually from one to half a dozen new riders on the ride. First-time riders are called mavericks, and one of the rides during the week consists of travel to a high mountain

In addition to the annual ride, participants enjoy events such as the keyhole race and cattle penning.

where maverick and empty saddle ceremonies are performed. The maverick ceremony is to welcome those first-time riders and to give them a glimpse of the sprit of the CMR, and the empty saddle ceremony remembers those who have passed on.

To become eligible for membership, you must have participated in two rides and you must then be nominated by a member. The membership votes on the nominees. If you think you would like to participate in a Colorado Mule Ride, you may fill out an application and proceed from there. An application can be obtained by calling Gale Fortney at (719) 596-5248. There are just a few riding regulations given out before the year's ride begins to help maintain order and safety for the riders. On the regulation list are these instructions: "This is a fun ride, leave your business affairs and worries at home!" If you feel you can do this, we welcome you to come spend time in the company of the CMR family.

Saddles and Mules

BY GARRY MCCLINTOCK

Garry McClintock is a well-known and highly respected saddle maker who lives in Descanso, California.

Mules have variously shaped backs, as do horses. The shape of the mule's back depends on the shape of its dam's back. The back of the jack is rather flat, as compared to the horse, which has more "rock" or sway to its back.

Another characteristic of mules and jacks is that they are what are called "easy keepers," which means that it takes very little feed for them to stay fat. If mules are not ridden very often, they may get too heavy.

If you are lucky enough to have a saddle and it just happens to stay on your mule, ride the heck out of it, and if that means an hour or so in an arena a few times a week, life is good. However, if you get out on the trail quite a bit, and notice that the ears of your mule seem to have gotten a little closer than when you started and your reins are suddenly much too long, then quickly find a good place to quietly dismount in a way that your saddle does not roll under your mule when you try to get off. Your cinch will be loose, and your saddle will have slid forward. Anybody who has ridden much will know what kind of a wreck this can cause.

The photograph on the left shows a mule tree sitting nicely on a mule's back. On the right, the bars do not fit properly, the back of the bar is in the air and causes too much of the weight to be carried in the front.

Don't simply run out and buy a britchin' or a crupper to solve the sliding problem. Either item will help, but take a little deeper look at what is going on here so you can deal with this, as it comes up with different animals in different situations.

In the above scenario, the first thing that happened was the saddle slid forward. Why did that happen? The saddle was probably built for a horse, which means that the bars of the saddletree were built to accommodate the sway that is in a horse's back, instead of the flatness of the mule's back. Picture the rockers on a rocking chair and you will understand what I mean. You can see this on your mule if you will place your saddle on his back without any padding or cinches and take a look at how it rocks back and forth. Do not put the saddle too far forward on his shoulder blade or it will not work, and neither will he. The back will settle a little when you ride, so do this before and after you ride in order to get a bet-

ter understanding. There is less bearing surface to evenly distribute your weight over the bar surface as it sits on the back, and the tree or saddle will skid along more easily, and usually move forward. A saddle with mule bars is different because the bars are built to have less "rock" in them and are consequently flatter than the bars built for a horse.

A mule can also have a back with pronounced withers, like a Thoroughbred, or be mutton withered like a burly Quarter Horse, depending on what the mule's dam was like. What this means to a saddlemaker relates to the angle to which the flatter bars are set. We can still use Thoroughbred bars at ninety degrees, semi-Quarter Horse bars at ninety-two degrees, or a full Quarter Horse angle at ninety-five degrees on the mules, just as we do on horses. Generally, the bars for mules are set to a semi-Quarter Horse angle, with a little more separation between the bars, like six-and-one-quarter to six-and-one-half inches of width, which accommodates the more fleshy or heavier wither area. The big, wide, flat-back mules need a full Quarter Horse bar angle with seven inches of width between the bars. The backs of mules are just as different as are those of horses; they are generally flatter like the jack that fathered them.

The other thing that needs to be considered is where the cinch will be located in relation to the size and shape of the belly of the mule. A saddle can have the front cinch far forward in a full position, back to the middle of the seat in a center-fire position or anyplace in between. This is where fat can get in the way.

To understand this a little better, place your saddle on your mule where it is supposed to be, back behind the shoulder blade and not on it. Now take a look at where the ring that holds the latigo is located. A full position, or Spanish rig, is under the horn or a little forward of the horn. This is about as far forward as you can get it. Some mules require the cinch here, because their belly fat will push it there anyway. The problem is that you may gall the mule as he moves and rubs against the cinch and/or the buckle. A neoprene cinch can solve the rubbing, but that material is slippery and in other positions can move more easily than a stranded cinch. If this happens on your mule, and the rigging position is more toward the middle of the saddle and consequently the belly, a saddlemaker can move the position of the ring to a full position. Otherwise, the saddle will continue to slide forward to where the cinch wants to come to a rest, in the little hollow spot just behind the front legs. This will vary depending on the conformation.

The rigging position should be placed directly above this hollow spot to help keep the saddle in place. The saddle may still slide forward, up onto the shoulder blade, but this will minimize the movement. This is when you need a crupper, or better yet, a britchin', because it can hold the cinch as well as the saddle, and a britchin' adds class to the long ears. Any rigging position that places the cinch on the downhill slide of the belly will only cause it to move to where it will stop. If you are lucky and have an animal that is more hound gutted, the cinch will either move back toward the tail or stay where you put it and not move. A breast collar is an easy solution.

Over the years I have had an opportunity to spend time with some of the ranchers of Baja, California, where they are just now getting roads and pickup trucks. These hardy mountain folk have used mules and donkeys since Cortez first settled the country, and I mean literally. This is a steep, rough and sparse desert, and their stock will go where the feed is; rounding them up can get interesting. These are the true Californians who still use the center-fire saddle effectively. They place the cinch right in the middle of the belly and crank it down. The cinch is only twelve or maybe fifteen strands wide, and they put it on tight and keep it there.

If you were to watch riders come off of some of those hillsides, you would not believe they could do it, let alone keep their saddle in place. But sure enough, with a center-fire saddle and no crupper, britchin' or breast collar, the saddle stays in place. I think the difference is the fat. Those mules are all muscle and have backbones and withers to help keep the saddles from sliding around. I often use a center-fire saddle on my mule, and without a britchin' the cinch still slides. In my opinion, the center-fire position is the best place for the cinch, because it pulls from both ends of the saddle, which evens the pressure on the bars and back, and the cinch pull is around the belly and not the heart and lungs.

Even though the center-fire position may be theoretically better, it is bound to cause a wreck if it slides. In today's world, your best bet is still the seven-eighths double rig. The back cinch should be used equally as tight or tighter than the front cinch. If you do not tighten it, you might as well leave it home. Tighten it up in a round pen at first in case the mule needs time to get used to it. Let him buck if he needs to; he will get the hang of it without you on his back. Make sure you have a strap between the two cinches, so they cannot move away from each other, forward or back. Besides keeping the back cinch out of the flank, it will keep the front one off of the leg or shoulder. This should help to keep the saddle from moving.

Your best bet is a lot of wet saddle blankets and a little experimentation. Padding can often make a bad situation better; get off your animal once in a while and loosen the cinches and let the back breathe. If the saddle is too tight, it can burn his back even if it does fit him well. If you have dry spots, pad around them and see if you can make a better fit. It is hard to go out and buy a new saddle simply because your trainer says to. Seek the advice of those who have been there; they can help. In the end, it is up to you.

Fitting saddles to mules continues to be a dilemma. Mules' backs are generally flatter than horses, and saddles with flatter bars are better for their backs, but all are different and need individual attention. Do what you can, but be safe. White spots (caused by bruising) happen, but they are not the end of the world. If they happen to you and you think your mule is less valuable, let me know—I am always in the market for a good mule.

Things to Do with Your Mule

A List of Major Shows and Mule Events Across the Country

BY SUE COLE

Jake Clark's Mule Days, Ralston, Wyoming, Father's Day weekend annually. Show and select saddle mule auction. www.saddlemule.com

Tennessee Mule Sales. Reese Brother Mule Co., Gallatin, Tennessee, promotes annual mule sales in Westmoreland, Tennessee. Large numbers of mules with buyers and sellers attending from all across the country. 615/452-2478 or 615/452-2544 www.reesemules.com

Mule Day, Columbia, Tennessee, early April each year. A large gathering of mules and mule people with a very large non-motorized parade, saddle, gaited and draft mule shows, mule races, craft festival and much, much more. www.muleday.com

Annual Great Celebration Mule & Donkey Show, Shelbyville, Tennessee, mid-summer. Miniature donkey show, draft and saddle mule show, vendors. Hundreds of quality mules and donkeys from all across the nation gather for this three-day event. www.twhnc.com

Mule Days held annually Memorial Day weekend in beautiful Bishop, California. 800-522-1555 or 619-873-6351.

Montana Mule Days, Hamilton, Montana. Montana's largest donkey and mule show, mid-June. www.montanamuledays.com

Winnemucca, Nevada Mule Race & Show, early June annually. Pari-mutuel and Endurance Races, Mule Show and Draft Horse Driving events. www.muleshow.com

Pari-mutuel Races, Mule Show and Draft Horse Challenge, Winnemucca, Nevada, early June annually. www.mule-drafthorse-show.com

Clark County Mule Festival, Kahoka, Missouri. Mule Show and rodeo, vendors, trail rides. Mid-September annually, 28th Annual in 2013. Mid-September annually. www.clarkcountymulefestival.com

Hells Canyon Mule Days, Enterprise, Oregon, always the weekend after Labor Day. 888-323-3271 www.hellscanyonmuledays.com

Horse Progress Days, mid-summer, held in different eastern state locations annually. Equipment demonstrations using draft mules and horses. www.horseprogressdays.com

Ozark Mule Days, Ozark, Missouri, held Labor Day weekend annually. Mule and donkey classes for young

and old. Lots of fun classes for exhibitors and spectators.
417-343-9412
www.ozarkmuledays.com

Iowa Donkey and Mule Society State Show and Futurity, Held annually in the fall. Futurity, performance and donkey classes.
www.idmmms.ws

Idaho State Draft Horse and Mule International Show held mid-September in Sandpoint, Idaho.
www.idahodrafthorseshow.com

International Mule Jump, held annually in Pea Ridge, Arkansas. Mule Jumping Capital of the World.
www.pearidgemulejump.com

National Championship Chuckwagon Races, Clinton, Arkansas. Labor Day weekend. Exciting spills and thrills as chuckwagon racers from across the country gather together to claim national championship titles. Snowy River Race, mule races, trail rides, bronc fanning.
www.chuckwagonraces.com

Annual Wagon Train, Lovelock, Nevada, travels the old California Trail across the forty-mile desert route from Lovelock to Fallon, Nevada. Early September.
775-867-3590

Delmarva Coon Hunters, Powellville, Maryland, annual show, mid-October. 410-835-8327

National Western Stock Show, Rodeo, Mule, Donkey and Horse Show, Denver, Colorado. Mid-January annually. www.nationalwestern.com

Donkey and Mule Show, Houston, Texas. Mid-March annually, held in conjunction with the Houston Livestock Show and Rodeo.
www.rodeohouston.com

Mule Mania Mule Show, Dayton, Washington. Mid-July annually. Mule and Donkey Show, workshops, antique auction, tack sale. 208-816-8682
www.mulemaniadayton.com

Jody Kelso Select Mule Sale, Murray, Kentucky. Mule preview, quality saddle and draft mules. 270-293-0691
www.kelsomules.net

Pennsylvania Mule Sales, Lancaster County, Pennsylvania. Weanling to aged mules—riding and draft type. Winter months. 717-354-6431

Cameron Mule Co. Mules & Mountains trail ride and clinics. Summer/fall annually. 406-369-5190.
www.MuleTrainer.com

To learn more about these and other mule events across the country subscribe to MULES AND MORE magazine.

Mules and More, Inc.
P O Box 460, Bland, MO 65014
Email: mules@socket.net
www.mulesandmore.com

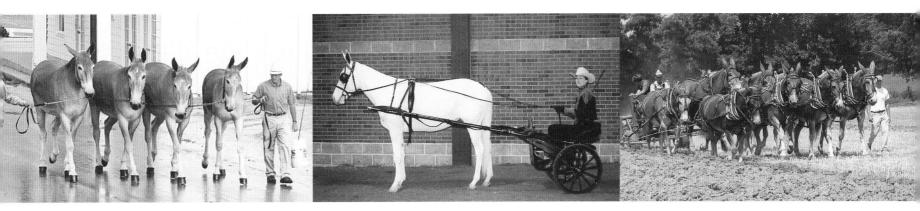

Canyon Trail Rides

BY SENA HAUER

OPPOSITE: *Mules and horses take riders into Bryce Canyon National Park.*

Sena Hauer is editor of this book. She is a former newspaper editor and author of the book *Beautiful America's UTAH*, part of a series published by the Beautiful America Publishing Company. She is the wife of John Hauer. Sena's backcountry trail rides take beginners and experienced riders on trails traveled by John Wayne, Billy Crystal, Ben Johnson, Paul Hogan, and other movie stars who chose the beautiful canyon country along the Colorado River north of Moab, Utah, to film their movies.

Pete Mangum and one of his hard-working mules.

For more than thirty years, one family has been providing trail rides into Bryce and Zion national parks in Utah and at Arizona's north rim of the Grand Canyon. Pete and Keela Mangum, their three children and families plus a host of wranglers take thousands of riders into the depths of these majestic national parks each year from spring to fall. Throughout their three-plus decades of providing horseback tours, the profile of their herd has been changing: the ears on their equines are getting longer!

Paul "Pete" Mangum, of Tropic, Utah, started Canyon Trail Rides in 1973 when he purchased the trail-riding concession at Bryce and Zion. Ten years later he purchased the business on the north rim. "We started out with three mules," recalls Mangum, "and now we have 180 head." Another seventy horses round out his herd, but mules are strictly used on the north rim, per a federal requirement that prohibits concessionaires from using anything but mules for commercial trips into the Grand Canyon.

"Mules are better for this type of work," says Mangum. "Mules won't hurt themselves, and they can see their hind feet," a trait that gives them added insurance in taking the right step on steep canyon trails. Mangum notes that

A wrangler briefs dudes about their ride into Bryce Canyon National Park just before dropping over the rim.

mules' longevity has been a plus in maintaining a herd for dudes year after year. The oldest mule he used was forty-seven.

Mangum also appreciates the willing attitude of mules to perform day after day carrying unskilled riders on difficult terrain. "A mule gets better all day long every day he's used, whereas a horse will tend to get better for a while and then become tired and cross," said Mangum. "Also, a mule will do his work every day on half the feed of a horse." Mangum has found that he has to use almost no medicines to keep mules healthy throughout the season, but he has to doctor the horses quite often because they contract ailments.

The Union Pacific Railroad actually started offering horseback tours into the parks back in 1925 as part of the company's efforts to develop tourism around the parks. The Mangum family has continued this tradition, guiding riders from all over the world, including the Prince of Thailand, the U.S. Secretary of the Interior and staff from *National Geographic* magazine.

The Mangums also offer a seven-day adventure called the Red Rock Ride, wherein groups ride off the beaten path to places that can be seen only on foot or astride in Zion and Bryce Canyon national parks and in the Grand Staircase–Escalante National Monument. The route follows trails used by cattle rustlers and outlaws such as Butch Cassidy and the Sundance Kid. Participants see prehistoric Indian petroglyphs, pristine slot canyons, clear creeks and renowned rock formations.

Guests on this ride may choose to ride horses or mules. Pete reports that by the third day most of the horse riders have switched to mules.

The event is fully managed by the Mangums and catered by Houston's Trails End, Inc., of Kanab, Utah.

MULES AND THE BACK COUNTRY HORSEMEN OF AMERICA

The U.S. Forest Service and commercial outfitters have used mules for years to pack supplies, equipment and personnel into the backcountry. However, during the past decade, there has been a dramatic increase in the number of mules used as both riding and pack stock among outdoor recreation enthusiasts. Currently, one of the larger mule-user groups is the Back Country Horsemen of America (BCHA).

This nationwide volunteer service organization was created in the early 1970s to counter the growing trend toward restrictions on horse and mule use in the backcountry. Currently, the BCHA has a membership of over fourteen thousand. Chapters can be found in most western states, and there is a growing presence in the southeastern United States.

The mission of the organization is to work cooperatively with the U.S. Forest Service, the Bureau of Land Management, the National Park Service and other land-management agencies to ensure that public lands remain open to recreational stock use. The organization educates users of the backcountry about protecting the heritage of backcountry stock use. The name was chosen because it signified an interest in much more than wilderness; members are interested in perpetuating recreational stock use on all public lands.

The BCHA also has a strong educational component that emphasizes practical conservation techniques designed to minimize recreational equine impacts on natural areas. Members believe that continued horse use, in harmony with the capacity of public lands, is in the best interest of the majority of Americans. Members offer their time and equipment to government agencies for such tasks as packing out trash, clearing, building and improving trails, building trailhead facilities and assisting in planning strategies that will benefit the public.

Another strength is an extensive volunteer program. BCHA members have contributed nearly two million dollars annually in donated services to public land agencies. Much of this support has involved the use of mules for both riding and packing. Stocking fish, providing fire support, and transporting supplies and building materials into remote backcountry areas for the Forest Service has been done on the backs of mules. In their effort to clean up the outdoors, BCHA volunteers have packed out everything from tin cans to World War II bombs.

ARIZONA RIDING

BY DIANE LOVETT

Diane Lovett is one of the founders of the Caballos Del Sol Benefit Trail Ride. She has been a mule rider for more than a dozen years.

The Caballos Del Sol Benefit Trail Ride celebrated its eleventh annual ride in March 2004. Over the past eleven years, this event has given away all of its proceeds to local charities. To date, more than ninety thousand dollars have been donated.

Central Arizona is an area with diverse vegetation, mountains and rolling hills. There isn't a lot of green to get in your eyes. The hills are covered with mostly mesquite, ironwood trees, prickly pear and other species of small cactus, a few rattlesnakes and lots of rocks. The scenery is awesome and the weather almost perfect, year-round. It would be better, of course, if you could take some of the summer temperatures (90-110 degrees) and move them over to some of the winter days (30-50 degrees), but all in all, we ride our mules all year.

In the early days of the trail ride, the only mule to participate was mine. This was when mules were not as popular as they are now, and until the riders had ridden a few rides with Ruby and me, they frequently asked why I would want to ride a mule. After knowing Ruby and watching her, many people learned that a mule can be a great trail leader, riding companion, friend and protector.

Each year, more and more mules have appeared on the ride. This past March, at least 10 of the 115 riders were mounted on mules.

Mules are great on large trail rides such as ours. They camp easily, handle five continuous days of trail riding well, don't get jumpy as many horses do, and manage rocks easily. Also, they don't need to have water at every stop, they can take the challenges of steep climbs without stress to them or their riders and, if it turns hot, they don't get themselves in a sweat, drink too much water or need a veterinarian. So, if you do not know what to expect on a trail ride, you do know your mule can handle whatever comes up.

The annual Caballos Del Sol Trail Ride welcomes mules; organizers understand the need for a good animal. The ride also welcomes mule riders (and, of course, horse riders) and invites them to enjoy good trails, good food, good entertainment, good dancing and an all-around fine time spent camping with your critter and meeting many people.

Any place in Arizona is a good place for mule riding, with plenty of challenges and great riding weather. I have ridden my mule down the Grand Canyon, into Supai Canyon, in Monument Valley and into Canyon de Chelly, as well as in the desert around Phoenix, Tucson and Wickenburg. The mule adapts well to all of Arizona's varied terrain.

Gymkhana & Roping Mules

Loren Basham on Hoosier Daddy, clearing the hurdles at Camp Verde, Arizona.

The little gray mule entered the arena gate, turned, looked at the pattern and took off. The rider sat in the saddle and hung on. Blue ran the pattern, whether it was through poles, barrels, a keyhole or hurdles, and there was no need for the rider to guide him. Gymkhana mules quickly learn what is expected of them. Not all of them can anticipate like Blue. Blazin' Blue has taught three families how to run—the Hawleys, Higginses and Bashams.

Gymkhana mules have to have a true desire to run; it can't be forced. The good gymkhana mules enjoy the run, the patterns and the crowds. When choosing a gymkhana mule, you should look for certain characteristics: a big heart, a big hip, a large gaskin muscle and a height between 14.1 and 15 hands. It doesn't take a very large mule to run gymkhana events. A big heart means the

BY LOREN BASHAM
The Basham family's list of accomplishments is impressive. For example, Cori Basham was the 2001 North America Saddle Mule Association (NASMA) Reserve Champion Youth Rider, and Loren won the All-Around Championship at the 2001 Jake Clark Mule Days in Cody, Wyoming. Cole Basham is the world's most relaxed trail rider, and Lenice Basham is the mule photographer for *Mules and More* magazine. Also, Loren is a top-notch mule trainer.

desire to go, the will to please and a desire to win. You can have the fastest mule in the world, but if it doesn't have the desire, the mule will never be a winner.

Gymkhana events include barrels, poles, hurdles, keyhole, flags and pylon alley. The mules run against a timer, and the mule with the fastest time is the winner. For many people, the timer is the best judge. There are no opinions, no partiality and no wondering what the judge does or doesn't like. It is a competition in the truest sense—one mule against others, and the fastest one wins. It's a good place for children to start competing. The children and mules can go at a pace they're comfortable with. There isn't anyone else in the arena to have to worry about, and they know how well they did against everyone else. They don't leave the ring wondering what they did right or wrong, as they might in a western pleasure or trail class.

THE ROPING MULE Team roping with a mule goes by the same principles as team roping with a horse. There is a header and a heeler. It's a race against time; the fastest catch wins. The biggest difference between roping with a horse and roping with a top-notch roping mule is that the mule will outlast the horse. At any practice roping, a horse will use its energy quickly, needing time between runs to cool off. At the same practice roping, the mule will conserve its energy between runs, neither heaving nor sweating.

We look for the same characteristics in a good roping mule as we do in a good running mule. A heeling mule

should be between 14.1 and 15 hands, whereas a heading mule can be bigger. Mules seem to catch on quickly to team roping, and they love the chase. Roping gives many mules something new to think about. After spending hours in the arena practicing for pleasure classes or mulemanship, Sugar Gee, my daughter's mule, finds extra energy to chase a steer out of the chute. It is amazing to watch a laid-back mule lay her ears flat and chase a steer.

MY FAMILY'S MULES My family has an eclectic list of mule experiences and enjoyments. Every member has a different mule activity he or she enjoys most. Even vacations are planned around the family's mules. Cole, my son, enjoys trail riding more than just about any other activity.

Al Barraza, Riverside, California, running the barrels at Camp Verde, Arizona

94

*Loren Basham and
Jessie roping in
Oklahoma City, Oklahoma.*

*Cole Basham
on Jessie*

*Cori Basham with
Sugar Gee*

Cole's favorite hobby is picking up turtles along the trail and taking them back to camp. He started riding not long after he was born. He rode in the saddle with his mom and would sleep most of the time. He continued to sleep in the saddle even after he moved to his own mule, Blue. At only ten years of age, he had thousands of hours in the saddle. One of his greatest accomplishments has been getting to ride the same trails John Wayne rode in Utah.

Cori, my eighteen-year-old daughter, enjoys showing. She loves the practice, the competition and the wins. She shows a seventeen-year-old mule, Sugar Gee, who will run gymkhana, perform in English classes and ride western. Sugar Gee excels at pole bending. Cori's greatest thrill is showing against horses. To her, it's a big deal to win in a class of mules, but it's a really big deal to win in a class of horses. Cori also shows in local hunter/jumper horse shows. At her first show, the horse people weren't the least bit concerned when we pulled in with our trailer, except insofar as our mule braying might distract their horses. They lacked even a sense of curiosity. During Cori's first class, the whole attitude changed. The horse owners started to pay attention when Cori and Sugar Gee won the jumping classes. They weren't happy—but they were respectful of the mule.

My wife Lenice enjoys trail riding on a mule named Tammy. The quiet, the serenity and the trail can make any day a great day for her.

For me, my favorite activity is any mule activity. As long as I'm in the saddle, I'm satisfied. My mule, Jessie, is a top-notch roping mule, and we also run gymkhana events.

The World's First Mountain Bike/Mule Challenge

And the Winner is ...

BY JANET LOWE

Janet Lowe is a freelance writer who lives in Moab, Utah. She was recently introduced to mules, having kept a healthy distance from equines most of her life. When her travels took her to Morocco in North Africa, she had an opportunity to see how other parts of the world utilize donkeys and mules. Her poetry has appeared in *The Saturday Evening Post, Puerto del Sol, Earth's Daughters, New Letters* and a variety of anthologies. She has contributed to a number of Fodor's Travel Publications guidebooks including *Guide to the National Parks of the West, Gold Guide to Utah, Compass Guide to Utah, Gold Guide to the Rocky Mountains*, and *Escape to Nature without Roughing It*. She no longer has to take tranquillizers to ride mules.

The Slickrock Bike Trail in Moab is one of America's most gnarly mountain bike routes. Twelve miles of sandstone "dunes" stretch across the horizon. Near-perpendicular drops are challenges for cyclists, who struggle to keep their bicycles from doing "endos," or falling end over end. Just as it sounds, in an endo the back wheel of the bike flips over the cyclist's head and can leave the rider in a bloody heap on the rock. It is not just every once in a while that a rider encounters these hair-raising drops on the smooth sandstone terrain—it's more like a twelve-mile roller-coaster ride on a bicycle. Only the truly gonzo cyclists or the truly crazy tackle this trail.

One sunny, fall day I decided to go see what was happening out at the Slickrock Trail. It's always exciting to see a rider scale the rock and come down the other side unharmed. This particular day, however, it was even more exciting because the cyclists were sharing the trail with mules. Mules, you say, on a world-famous mountain bike trail? Mules, you say, in the mountain biking capital of the world, Moab, Utah? Yep, mules!

The occasion was the annual Moab Fat Tire Festival, and the event was an exhibition challenge between mountain bikes and mules. Since cyclists often share trails with horses and mules in the Canyonlands area, John Hauer, Moab's official Mule Man, organized the event hoping to foster cooperation between the two different kinds of saddles that dominate many of the trails. A good-natured challenge where mountain bikers were willing to be embarrassed by a mule would surely be the beginning of a beautiful relationship. Which mode of transportation could offer the most stability when scaling the smooth rock surface? Which rider could better avoid an "endo?" Which transport mode was less likely to break down in the backcountry?

Readers of this book will not be surprised to learn that the mules always prevailed—well, almost always prevailed—in this contest. There was one time when Honeybee, John's favorite mule, stared down at a perpendicular drop, looked back at her faithful rider and owner as if to say "You, sir, may be a fool, but I am certainly not," and refused to move. Of course, this "failure" only proves the higher intelligence of the mule over the bike rider who zipped down the steep slope without hesitation but ended up tangled in his cycle at the bottom.

Mules definitely excelled in the area of climbing up. Five-foot ledges created

Barefoot mules and mountain bikes have great traction on the type of sandstone known as slickrock. Equines wearing steel shoes are what put the "slick" in the stone's name.

a nearly impossible barrier for the bike riders unless they cheated by dismounting and carrying their bikes over the ledge. Honeybee and Johnny Reb, another of John's mules, didn't even blink their long eyelashes or wiggle their luxurious ears at the little jump. In fact, after hopping up, they stood calmly at the top watching while the cyclists brutalized themselves and their equipment as they tried to negotiate the ledge. Finally, the cyclists hoisted their bikes upon their shoulders and walked up the cliff. Now that's not what I call reliable transportation!

The deep red sand of this high desert area didn't trouble the mules either. While the bicycles came to an abrupt halt when attempting to move through the sand, the mules waltzed through while grabbing bites to eat from a nearby juniper.

As far as reliability on the trail, well, you be the judge. Bicycles suffer from flat tires, broken chains, bent frames, failed brakes and general mechanical breakdowns that can leave their riders miles from the nearest road, let alone bike mechanic. Mules will outlast a cyclist any day with their exceptional talent for going without water and with their food handily located on nearby trees or shrubs. A rider is likely to get worn out before the mule is worn out, and I have yet to meet a mountain biker who preferred a bite of rabbit brush to his or her high-protein, two-dollar energy bar!

And speaking of riders getting worn out, have you ever seen mountain bike riders after a twelve-mile jaunt on the Slickrock Bike Trail? They are hot, sweaty, dirty, dehydrated, cranky and generally a little bloody. Their bikes need repairs, and their spandex outfits are torn. A cowboy atop his mule is still sporting his clean, starched white shirt, and his hat is still jauntily poised atop his head. His mule is thinking, "What's next? Let's bag a peak, okay?"

The Rest of the Story:
An Interview with Jody Foss

BY JOHN HAUER

Jody and Mavis enjoy the wide open spaces of Catlow Valley, Oregon.

Jody Foss has twice crossed the western part of the United States, a total of seven thousand miles, on a mule. Foss recounts her adventures in two books, *Mules Across the Great Wide Open*, and *In the Company of Mules*. Jody's sister accompanied her on the first trip. Her second adventure was solo. This interview with Foss was conducted in 2002.

Jody, did you grow up with horses and/or mules?

I longed for a horse since the day I was born, like most other little girls. When I was thirteen, my friend Laurie Weed and I were lucky enough to become the caretakers of two wonderful Welsh ponies who had lived most of their lives on the desert out in Apple Valley, California. I still remember it like it was yesterday when we went out with our dads in a rented truck and trailer and picked up Sarah and Star. From that day on, we could be found riding the fire roads and trails above our town of La Cañada. Our parents let us have the ponies as long as we covered the costs, so Laurie and I started a Birthday Pony business. Moms and dads in station wagons packed to the brim with kids drove up our road to the corral on the edge of the Angeles National Forest, and we entertained the children with rides and a tour of our tack room and stalls.

In the tack room we built a miniature living room for a little black-and-white rat named Stanley who wandered in one day and stayed. When we called his name, he would come up out of his hole next to his tiny mailbox and sit on a little chair I made in my dad's shop. The children had a chance to see how we picked the ponies' feet with a hoof pick, how we brushed them, and what we fed them. Only once did a little kid pee on our saddle pads! Laurie and I would plan for months for the big Honolulu Days parade in Montrose, California, and more often than not, we'd win a prize.

It was a tearful day after high school when we gave Sarah and Star to two younger girls. Those ponies provid-

The perfect mule? Jody says, "Not too tall; a molly; a grey like Mavis with a sweet disposition; always ready to go; young so they will be around for the rest of my life!"

ed us with a chance to be on our own in the mountains and even though it was a lot of responsibility having and caring for them, we loved every minute of it, and we both have mules or horses today.

Before you got acquainted with mules, what was your general impression of these long-eared critters?

My dad always loved the mountains and my mom was a Hollywood girl. When they married, Dad made sure that Mom became a mountain girl. With a group of eight adults and ten kids, we packed out of Bishop with a mule train. We rode horses, and I remember once my horse jumped off the trail into a lake! The mules were so steadfast and sweet. I loved their eyes, how they held such intelligence and a look I didn't see as much in the horses; of course I loved horses too. Those weeks I spent in the high country with my own pack train? Well, it was just about as close to heaven as I could imagine. We all enjoyed fishing for trout and hiking around, but I could most often be found with the mules, making sure they had enough water, and I would bring treats to them in the pocket of my jacket. Those commercial pack trains provide families with such a rich experience!

The answer to the question is this: I've always loved mules. Interestingly enough, I still have my original copy of *Brighty of the Grand Canyon* by Marguerite Henry, and that book provided me with hours of dreaming about that free little donkey, running up and down the trails of the canyon. I love to look at the colorful illustration on the first page, by Wesley Dennis, and see my name written in pencil. I guess I always knew what I wanted out of life. An open trail and a donkey or mule to enjoy it with, just like Brighty and the old miner. Funny how some things just stick!

Why did you choose to ride a mule on your cross-country trips instead of a horse or an all-terrain vehicle?

We started out on our first trip from Park City, Utah, to Spokane, Washington, with a bunch of green-broke Appaloosas. My horse Cowboy was smart enough and really walked out. My sister's horse went lame in Wyoming and she had to walk the whole way. Sarah Jane, our white mule, packed our gear. Everything we needed to learn, Sarah Jane taught us. She was calm as a cucumber under any circumstance. When the horse ran off after a bee sting and disappeared into the State of Montana, Sarah just stood calmly by and shook her head. We could see that she always thought it out before making a move. That mule walked twelve hundred miles with us all the way to Spokane. In a bar up in Montana, we flipped quarters for her to see who would keep her once the long journey to Spokane ended. I was the lucky one; flipped four heads in a row, and for twenty-seven years that mule and I rode the West.

How did your mule adventures affect your later life?

Sarah Jane found me my husband, gave me my own personal career, kept me in the country, taught me how to laugh at myself and carried me to the top of the Continental Divide, the Pacific Crest and the Sierra Nevada Mountains. She always gave me an excuse to go home when it was time to part company—"I've got to go feed the mules"—and introduced me to friends all over the country. I created several slide shows about my travels with the mules and presented them all over Japan one year, so in a way, the mules helped me get to Japan.

In Tomales, California, where I have lived for more than fourteen years now, I am known as the Mule Lady. Who could ask for a more complimentary title? And we've ridden the northern California beaches with the wind blowing in our hair, enough to make any worry disappear. Because of the mules, my husband Charlie and I bought a beautiful ranch up in Oregon that backs up to Bureau of Land Management land, so we can ride to Idaho on dirt roads if we want, grow our own hay and enjoy the life that the mules have led us to.

For me, I have always had a mule to hug, since the time I was twenty-one years old and first set my eyes on the young Sarah, as we headed out from Utah with a bag of grain and sleeping bags. Now there is Juanita Jo, a wild mule from eastern Oregon; Nadine, a fancy line-back dun from Tennessee; Brighty, a California girl; Mavis, from Spokane; Reba, who was given to me on a six hundred-mile trip from Bend, Oregon, to Virginia City, Nevada; Buddy and Chester, our only john mules; an adopted donkey named Olivia Lavender; and a horse we hope to breed to a jack someday soon. I heard a little saying that "a truly happy person is one who can enjoy the scenery on a detour." The mules have taught me the joy of slowing down and keeping my eyes open to the beautiful world around me.

How do your horse-riding friends react to your mule riding?

Most are a little jealous at the end of the day, since the mules are so smooth to ride it isn't half as tiring. Others wonder if I don't want a faster steed. The mules are steady and know how to pick their pace.

What would constitute a perfect mule for you? (Size, sex, color, disposition, age, etc.)

Not too tall; a molly; a grey like Mavis with a sweet disposition; always ready to go; young so they will be around for the rest of my life!

What would you tell a horse-riding or non-riding friend who was considering buying a mule?

What previous experience with humans has the mule had? Does the mule look you in the eye, and can you pick up the mule's feet? How about hauling in a trailer? Everything depends on the person who will be caring for the mule: they are so smart they can size you up and decide for themselves if you have what it takes.

Remember, every mule loves a good scratching or brushing. Take the time to groom your new friend, and also remember, no one takes the time like you do. This will create a bond between the two of you. I personally don't like to see a mule kept alone; like people, it is nice to have a little company.

Where would you like to go if you take another epic mule ride?

I would like to leave from our ranch in eastern Oregon and ride to Idaho. From the back gate, there are dirt roads all the way. It really doesn't matter where I go. It's getting out the gate and down the road that matters. And then, anywhere I travel on my mule is magic.

How did a mule help you find your husband?

There's a fellow named Jack Elliott who plays guitar and loves mules, trucks and big old wooden boats. He met Charlie Parker at the boatyard in Sausalito when Charlie used to work down there on the *Wanderbird*, a historic pilot schooner. Jack brought Charlie up to Tomales to meet Sara Jane, and a week later Charlie called me back and said he noticed my fences needed mending. What else could a woman want? We got married two years later on the mules. Sarah and Brighty were bridesmaids, and Mavis almost knocked me off on a tree when she saw all those people in folding chairs!

If you only have a day or two to ride, what do you consider to be an ideal ride?

I would have to say the Pacific Crest Trail in Oregon by the high mountain lakes along the crest. Or maybe a day on the Crest Trail, and a day on a deserted Oregon beach.

Mules in Mounted Shooting

BY MARLENE QUIRING

Cowboy mounted shooting as a competitive sport was founded in 1991 by Jim Rodgers of Phoenix, Arizona. The first shooting competition was held in February 1992 at the Ben Avery shooting range near Phoenix with three contestants. Since then mounted shooting has grown steadily so that the Association [CMSA] now has more than 100 local clubs in four countries and over 12,000 members. Entries in the World Championships now are in the hundreds. The organization sanctions over 500 events annually and pays out more than $700,000 in prize money per year. There is also the Mounted Shooters of America. This organization continues to add affiliate clubs all across the United States, as well as Canada which presently has clubs in Alberta, British Columbia, Saskatchewan and Manitoba.

Cowboy mounted shooting typically involves shooting 10 targets on a set course with two single action .45 colt revolvers while maneuvering and turning your chosen mount at a full gallop. It's an adrenalin-packed sport that is drawing a lot of competitors. There are levels for all riders so you compete at your own skill level.

Competing at the Prairie Mountain Shoot at Rumsey, Alberta. Photo courtesy: Charles Gremp Photography.

Cam Fleury, from High River in southern Alberta Canada, is certainly a man who loves his mules; and now also mounted shooting. Cam recalls that he has ridden horses ever since he could walk. While studying in Oklahoma to become a farrier he got his first exposure to working with mules, but didn't get a chance to own one until much later.

Cam's employment was centered on working with horses, as a full time farrier and also as a guide and outfitter. He mainly worked with Quarter horses and he used them in team roping, his favorite hobby at the time. After his initial introduction to mules in the States, Cam became further intrigued with them after observing their hardiness and ability to travel so well in the mountains. With the bug to own a mule never leaving him, several years ago Cam bought his first mule, Jazzie. Together Cam and Jazzie stacked up a pretty good portfolio of various working jobs, including packing posts and wire for the grazing association, doctoring yearlings, dragging calves to the branding fire, leading pack strings and just a few

Cam and Jazzie show their versatility in the Shotgun event. In this class, five targets are shot at with a .45 colt revolver, then a barrel turn for home—reins are thrown away and there are two more targets that you shoot at with a double barrel coach gun. Cam says Jazzie does really well in this event as she is very honest and runs straight in the rundown.

years ago, Cam added driving to fifteen-year-old Jazzie's list of duties. Cam affectionately describes Jazzie as his "go to mule." Now, cowboy mounted shooting has also been added to their list of accomplishments.

Jazzie has placed at many competitions since Cam started using her in mounted shooting and in 2012, they got a first in the 3D Level at the competitions during the Ponoka Stampede. In the fall of 2012, Cam and Jazzie travelled to Nampa, Idaho, to shoot in the Western States Shooting Association Finals. "Jazzie performed very well, but I let my nerves get the better of me and missed a few too many targets to place. Even so, we got a lot of compliments and after a particularly nice run, a much respected competitor and rancher from Oregon, asked if I would be willing to sell my mule. That's about as good a compliment as you can get – as good as winning a buckle in my book."

Cam has also started competing with his younger mule, five-year-old Lace. Cam bought Lace as a two-year-old in Kalispel, Montana, and started riding her at three. Thinking he wanted to use her for mounted shooting and realizing that it might be a bit much with trying to train her in the sport while still learning it himself, Cam contacted world champion mounted shooter, Kenda Lenseigne to see if she would be willing to take Lace in training. Thinking that Kendra would probably not be interested in training a mule, he was pleasantly surprised

when Kenda said she would take on Lace as long as Cam realized that she had never worked with a mule before.

Kenda Lenseigne is a highly respected riding instructor and horse trainer, who trains half the year in Washington and the other half in Arizona. She has won numerous world and national championships in mounted shooting and is the holder of eight world records. She is one of Cowboy Mounted Shooting's most renowned competitors. In 2009, Kenda became the first woman in CMSA history to win the Overall at a world championship, beating all of the men and women to claim this prestigious title. Just six months later, in April 2010, she again made history by becoming the first woman to win the Overall at the championship again.

After training Cam Fleury's mule Lace, for mounted shooting, Kenda has a whole new outlook on mules. "Although I have been training mounted shooting horses for over a decade, "Lace" was my first mounted shooting mule project. I started her the same as I do all of my horses, slowly, in a building block program that emphasizes confidence, trust and understanding. Lace took to the sport better than I first anticipated and became one of my favorite students to date. I grew to enjoy her so much that it was difficult to give her back to her owner when she graduated. She is extremely athletic, willing, and so personable it's hard to imagine anyone not falling in love with her.

Lace has opened up a whole new perspective in my world as a trainer, and has emphasized the importance of reading and adjusting to the needs of an animal while communicating something new to them. When once I didn't have much of an opinion on these long-eared equines, now I am a big fan. I would find no greater accomplishment than to take a mule to the peak of the winner's circle in a horse dominated sport."

In July, 2012, Cam brought Lace home from the States and directly into competitions culminating in a clean round and their first prize money at the Wildrose Mounted Shooting Association Finals in September. Cam states that "Lace is the most athletic mule I've had and the best equine I have ever ridden. We have a good connection and the potential is limitless." Cam has set his goal at competing on Lace at the Cowboy Mounted Shooting Association's World Championship in Amarillo, Texas.

in his area competing with a mule in mounted shooting, but if he has his way, others will soon be checking out these long-eared hybrids. Cam has found the people in mounted shooting to be very supportive of new Shooters and of the mules. Now with goal-oriented riders like Cam, mules like Jazzie and Lace, and high caliber trainers like Kenda Lenseigne, we will definitely be seeing more mules in mounted shooting and in the winner's circle in this exciting, challenging and fast growing sport.

Marlene Quiring lives with her husband, five mules, two horses, and a few cats on an acreage near Ponoka, Alberta. Retired from raising mules, Marlene is still active in the Alberta Donkey and Mule Club and is still passionate about longears. You can reach her at marlenequiring@hotmail.com

www.cowboymountedshooting.com
www.canadianmountedshooters.ca
www.kendalenseigne.com

Cam and Lace, the mule trained by Kenda Lenseigne, competing at Prairie Mountain Shoot in Rumsey, Alberta in 2012. Photo courtesy: Christa Paterson

Cam only rides mules now, having slowly replaced his horses with them. In case he needs more mules to compete with, Cam has started to raise his own, having purchased a Mammoth Jack and crossing him with Appendix Quarter Horse mares. Cam has not yet found anyone else

In this photograph, which was taken in 1917, Old Blooth was acting the part of a make-believe school bus. The kids on the bus were (back to front) Walter Hilderbrand, Laverna (last name not available) and Grace Hilderbrand. Cleda Hilderbrand is standing by the mule/bus.

The kids were living on a wheat ranch a few miles from Washko, Oregon. The mule was raised by Cleda's father, George Hilderbrand.

The photos of these kids were provided by Cleda's daughter, Sharon Lynn. (See pages 106 and 162.)

The Natural Superiority of Mules

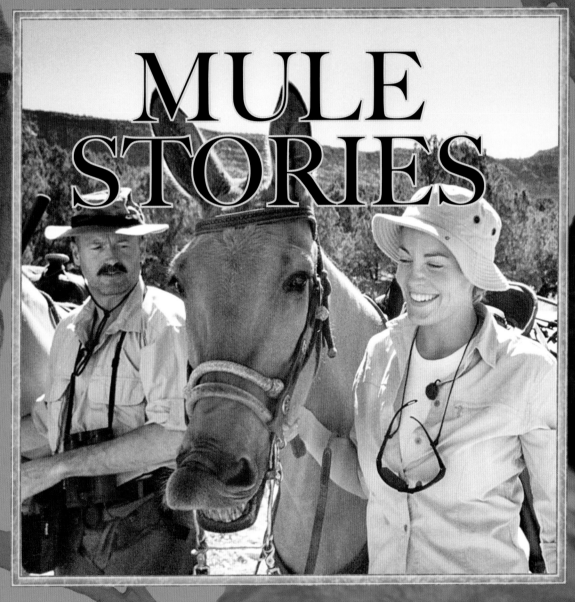

MULE STORIES

Laverna and Cleda Hilderbrand have converted Old Booth to what they called a "tail a phone." The photograph was taken in 1917 and was obviously the prototype for the very first portable telephone. Those girls certainly had a lot of fun and imagination.

The Mule and the One-Armed Bandit

When it comes to performance mules, one of the most well-known is Moe, the mule that world famous rodeo entertainer John Payne, The One-Armed Bandit, rides in his show.

John and Moe met for the first time in Ada, Oklahoma, at the mule sale in 2007. Moe was almost thirteen years old.

Moe got along well with the buffalo, who are some of his fellow performers.

John lost an arm in a brutal accident in 1973 and is known as the One-Armed Bandit in his award-winning rodeo specialty show. Photos courtesy Bink Picard.

John saw the shear ability of the mule. Therefore Moe has secured his place in The One-Armed Bandit's specialty act. John especially appreciates the mule on those rainy nights when the ramp is slick and muddy.

Moe has been featured in the largest rodeos across in North America the past five years.

John says, "There is nothing like a good mule, but you'll wear out a new pickup trying to find one."

Four Mules I Have Known

OLD SARGE

My first mule experience, or should I say my first "education by mule," was with Old Sarge. Sarge was an army mule, and although no one knew much about his background, he wore a U.S. brand. Sarge also fit the type used by the military. He was a good-sized mule, but not of draft-horse type. He was dark brown with a lighter brown muzzle. Sarge could have been among one of the last groups of pack animals used by the army after World War II. Animal units were considered obsolete and were mustered out of Fort Carson, Colorado, in 1956. Somehow, Sarge came to Wyoming and went into a pack string of an outfitter who ran a hunting camp on the Greybull River west of Meteetsee, Wyoming.

In the fall of 1962, my hunting partner and I made arrangements for a weekend elk hunt out of this outfitter's camp. Two of the guides were friends of mine, and they made us a deal since our outing was scheduled between hunts by regular, out-of-state clients. Although we were without riding or pack stock, my friends promised to help us pack out if we got an elk.

The hunt went well. My partner killed a big, club-horned bull on a steep, rocky slope several miles above camp. We field-dressed and quartered the animal and then returned to camp to get a pack animal to haul out the meat. The guides gave us Sarge.

With the mule in tow, we headed back up-country to get the elk. Sarge was a perfect gentleman. He led well, stood patiently while we put two of the elk quarters in canvas bags, hoisted the loads up and hooked the straps on his packsaddle. Sarge seemed oblivious to the dead elk, the weight, the rough terrain and

BY AL SAMMONS

Al Sammons is a mule owner who lives in Riverton, Wyoming. Sammons grew up on a working cattle ranch in western South Dakota where as a kid he spent a good amount of time in the saddle riding ranch horses. He moved to Wyoming and has spent nearly forty years riding and packing in the backcountry of the Cowboy State. Sammons acquired his first mule in 1982 and has been an avid mule advocate ever since. In addition to his riding activities, Sammons has been an active member of the Back Country Horsemen of America (BCHA) at the local, state and national levels. He served as national chairman of the fourteen thousand-member organization from 2001 to 2003. The BCHA is an organization of recreational equine users with chapters in nineteen states whose mission is to keep public lands open for recreational saddle and pack stock use. Sammons is a past member of the Wyoming State Trails Council and has served on numerous committees with the U.S. Forest Service, BLM and county public lands agencies. He has also been involved with driving events and historic wagon trains. He owns a petroleum marketing business in Riverton.

the two greenhorns who were packing him. The trip back to camp was without incident.

Since it was still early in the day and with half an elk to go, we started back for a second load. But then the whole climate changed. Sarge "sullied up" and refused to go anywhere. Only after we put a chin chain on his lead rope and one of us used a willow switch could we get the old mule to move. It was a struggle the entire way back to the kill site.

Sarge refused to let us load him. We finally had to short tie him to a big tree at the bottom of the slope and pack the meat to him. Even then, I had to blindfold Sarge with my jacket and hobble his front feet in order to accomplish this.

Eventually, we got him packed and back to camp. The minute we arrived, he stood quietly and let us unload. When we turned him loose in the corral, he rolled, shook himself and went about his business.

I've often thought about the experience with Sarge and have come to several conclusions. First, Sarge was an old, experienced mule who knew what work was all about. One trip on the trail with a heavy load was fine, but don't ask him to make a second trip! Sarge figured his work was done after the first trip and that was it. Now that I have been around more mules, I realize that sometimes you simply can't understand why they do as they do. It's not that they are unpredictable, they just have minds of their own and will not hesitate to use them!

RED POLLY AND THE WHITE STRIPE

I have a fine-looking, blood-bay molly that I call Red Polly. Her dam was a good-sized Quarter Horse and her sire was a mammoth jack. Consequently, Polly has size and athletic ability, and has developed into a fine saddle mule with good cow sense.

A neighbor asked me last spring if I would help him move his herd of Longhorn cattle a few miles to a set of corrals that had wider alleys and chutes. The larger facilities could better accommodate this breed of cattle with their wide horn spreads. The Longhorns were to be loaded in semi trucks and hauled to summer pasture.

At first, the drive was tough. The old cows were reluctant to leave the pasture, where they had been fed all winter. Some would break back at the slightest opportunity, so the cowboys had to be quick about heading them off and turning them back into the bunch. To compound matters, most of the cows had calves that tended to become separated from their mothers. Because the calves wanted to stop and bawl, we had to keep pushing them on—whooping and hollering—or the whole drive would stall.

Red Polly in the Washakie Wilderness, Wyoming.

Red Polly did really well for her first time with cattle. It didn't take long for her to almost anticipate the moves of the "cut backs." She seemed to know what to do when an errant cow had to be chased back to the herd, and she wasn't nervous about the whole noisy affair.

We had to drive the herd several miles down a blacktop county road that had the usual markings—yellow stripes down the center and a white line along the edge next to the shoulder. At first we were able to keep the cattle in the ditch, but some of the cows soon crossed over and eventually covered the entire road.

The notorious Paddy Murphy with his owner, Butch Sammons. Paddy is a classy riding mule, but a real nuisance around camp.

When I started to cross the highway, Polly would have no part of it. I "over and undered" her with my reins and spurred her hard several times to no avail. She would go as far as the white stripe on the asphalt and that was it. Finally, we came to a turn-in that ran to a neighbor's place and, without hesitation, Polly moved out onto the blacktop. She crossed the yellow stripe but as soon as I got her to the white line on the far side, she refused.

Then I realized what was happening. I keep my mules on irrigated pasture here in Wyoming and often use temporary, white-tape electric fencing. Polly had associated the white stripe on the highway with the white electric fence tape, and even though it was on the ground, she was not going to cross it.

From then on, whenever I needed to move on or off the asphalt, or cross the highway, I merely found a spot without a white stripe, where Red Polly could cross without trepidation.

PADDY MURPHY AND THE NAKED LADY

Mules are much more alert than their horse counterparts. Leave a gate or barn door open, and a mule will be the first to spot the opportunity for food or mischief. Mules are also inquisitive, which can sometimes lead to trouble. A few years ago, my mules spotted a porcupine waddling across the pasture and proceeded to check out the slow-moving creature. Had it been a dog or cat, the race for safety would have been on, but flight is not the porcupine's strong suit. Needless to say, I spent several hours pulling quills out of the muzzles of two of my mules—not an easy task.

Some mules, like some people, always seem to get in trouble. As a matter of fact, a friend of mine has a big black mule named Trouble, a handle that fits him well. But perhaps the biggest pest, nuisance, troublemaker, character-of-a-mule that I know is Paddy Murphy, a bay saddle mule owned by my brother Butch Sammons, of Lovell, Wyoming.

Several summers ago, Butch, two of our doctor friends and I went on a fishing trip in the Beartooth Mountains just south of the Montana state line. Rather than pack in, we drove our rigs to a fairly remote spot, set up our camp and then rode out daily to fish the multitude of high alpine lakes in the area. Our camp spot had plenty of wood, water and grass, so when we got in from the day's foray, we would merely hobble the animals and turn them out to graze. Just before dark we would take the stock string to water and put them on a high line for the night.

We had the area to ourselves except for a sheep outfit that was camped several hundred yards below us. The herders who watched the band of six hundred to seven hundred head of lambs and ewes were a young couple from back east that had signed on with the sheep company for a summer adventure. Their camp consisted of a traditional sheep wagon and a supply trailer for various odds and ends. A pair of large, white Great Pyrenees dogs helped to protect them from the coyotes. In addition, the herders kept a couple of old horses picketed near the wagon, which they rode only when necessary.

The first day went without incident. Our horses and mules were content to graze and stay put in the meadow adjacent to camp. However, on the second day, curiosity got the better of Paddy, who proceeded to check out the sheep wagon. The two herders were gone at the time, so the mule had free rein to look around. In short order, Paddy was into the dishes of food that had been set out for the dogs. We happened to notice his absence from the rest of our animals and soon located Paddy sampling the dog chow.

The next afternoon, while our backs were turned, Paddy again visited the wagon. This time the young lady herder was at home, and after some yelling and waving of arms she was able to chase Paddy off and also get our attention. We made a quick capture, and Paddy went to the high line.

Things were fine for the next couple of days, but then came the finale. On our last afternoon in camp, Paddy slipped his hobbles and, with better mobility, decided to make a final visit to the neighbors. The day was quite warm, so the female herder had decided to take a bath in a large washtub behind the sheep wagon, out of sight of prying eyes. Paddy trotted around the wagon at about the time the young lady was lathered up. She let out a yell and threw her bar of soap. Paddy spun and somehow got mixed up in the clothesline that held the towels and clean clothing. Garments and modesty coverings were soon scattered across the pasture.

Hearing all the fuss, we realized the mule was causing trouble, so Butch went off in hot pursuit. A few minutes later, and a bit red-faced, he returned with the errant mule.

The next morning, the young woman walked up to our camp and presented Butch and Paddy Murphy with a sack of dog food. As she scratched the mule's nose, her words were, "You're a good mule, but maybe you should eat at home so I can at least have time to take a bath."

MULES AND MOOSE

Naturalists say that elephants have great memories. I think the same can be said for mules. My brother Butch Sammons relates the following story about his saddle-mule Clyde.

Clyde is a big, sixteen-hand sorrel mule that can really travel. He has sort of a rolling single-foot gait, and the only equines that can keep up with him on the trail are those of the gaited walking and trotting breeds.

Several years ago, Butch and Clyde were headed down a trail up in the Shoshone River country of Wyoming. The trail was good, so Butch was pushing Clyde right along. They busted around a little patch of timber and practically ran head-on into a good-sized bull moose. The moose went one way, Clyde the other. Butch claims that it took him half a mile to get Clyde settled down and an hour to coax him back up the trail past where they crashed with the moose.

A year or so later, Butch was up the same trail with Clyde and when they got to the spot of the moose encounter, the mule remembered. He got wall-eyed and snorty, and Butch had a devil of a time trying to get him past the spot.

Mountains and Mules:
A Profile of Brad Cameron

*"Everything
I do is for
the mule."*
—BRAD CAMERON

*Trainer Brad Cameron
communicates quietly
with Red Hot, one of
his mules.*

BY MARY S. CORNING

**A writer and photographer, Mary S.
Corning lives in the foothills of the
Oregon Coast Range.**

Brad Cameron was raised in the mountains of Montana. The family business of packing involved using both horses and mules, and at the age of fifteen he started training his first saddle mule. In high school, he began breaking horses for a neighboring ranch. These horses could get really wild. It was an early lesson in staying ahead of things in order to stay out of trouble. He followed the only experience he knew, the concepts passed down through generations.

As he continued to work with mules and horses, he began to see differences between them. The mule colts he was riding never seemed to get as bothered as the horses. It appeared the mules had a little something extra, and Cameron was intrigued.

Over the years it became more and more clear to Cameron that mules were quite different from horses. He used mules in the mountains, not only for outfitting but also for the U.S. Forest Service, and while doing so he developed a deeper respect and understanding for them. This respect would be the foundation for his life's work.

While Cameron was working on a ranch outside of Bozeman, Montana, he observed and admired the horsemanship skills of his co-workers, so he began applying to his mule much of what he saw. He was determined to show the mule as a worthy counterpart.

As he did so, Cameron noticed that mules seemed to possess a high level of awareness—if a mule he was training could be convinced it was in his best interest to perform, the possibilities were very fruitful. He saw in mules a primal instinct to excel, and that motivated Cameron to refine his mulemanship.

One very sensitive mule, Annie, made this new way of thinking very clear to Cameron. Annie took Cameron to his first show, where she earned the Reserve High Point Performance Award. She later went on to teach a lesson in her own high points.

Annie never really lost the need to buck, and some time later she pitched Cameron off a mountainside. This incident inspired him to search for answers, rather than a new mule. He called upon his good friend Roland Moore for insight. Moore told him of a man named Buck Brannaman who was giving horsemanship clinics. Much of what Brannaman taught about horses echoed Cameron's own beliefs about his mules. By now Cameron was committed to learning all he could to incorporate his mule experience with quality horsemanship. He began to study diligently the concepts presented to him.

"I knew these were things I had to learn and I set out to do just that," said Cameron.

The philosophy and understanding of mutual respect, combined with natural responsiveness, inspired Cameron.

Through this method he was compelled to achieve a successful partnership with his lifelong friend, the mule.

Partnership meant understanding how things worked and why. It was no longer enough to focus on the outcome. Cameron knew there was more to mules' ways of thinking. It was time to see what lay at the core of their behavior.

Visiting with wild horses in the Nevada desert. Their curiosity led to some close encounters.

This opened a channel to the mules that he had not yet explored. In order to find pieces that fit, it meant using the mules' natural instincts rather than force. Once he began to understand this, Cameron learned that force was not the mule's way of life, it was man's way. Instead, mules learn from the release of pressure. This was, and still is, the most valuable lesson of all.

Could it be that people's most common belief in training the mule is the complete opposite of what is effective? If so, wouldn't that say a lot for the mule's ability to exist in an alternative environment? This would explain in great detail why mules were so misunderstood, and why so few historically were used for riding.

At the heart of this enlightenment came a sense of responsibility toward the mule. This meant that Cameron would no longer do what he had always done. He was going to have to dig deep and once again let the mule show him a better path.

His guide for this part of the journey was Annie. It didn't take long for this intuitive mule to respond to the positive reinforcement. Soon she realized that Cameron followed the path of least resistance. Through reconfirming it in every situation, and being consistent, Cameron and Annie developed trust. Once Annie was assured

During one of his clinics, Cameron works a colt from the ground and then from the back of his mule, Cowboy Bar.

that things would work out, she could focus her sensitivity on the task at hand. All of this started shaping up, and it was easy to see the improvement.

The folks at the local mule club could hardly believe it. They had seen Annie in her earlier stages and could appreciate the changes she made. The truth of the matter was that Cameron had made the greatest changes of all. Annie was just telling the story.

After seeing the evolution take place, people began asking questions. Cameron, however, ran into difficulties trying to explain his method, so he broke it down into steps people could understand. He developed a course based on using less force to produce more gain, one that headed off trouble from the very beginning.

This process starts on the ground before riders mount their mules. Combined with Brannaman's influence and Cameron's own ideas for the mule, Cameron developed basic ground exercises designed to build communication. These techniques use a light touch and the ability to direct the mule without using excessive force. Once this understanding is developed on the ground, it is much easier to establish it in the saddle. By employing the concept of releasing pressure for what is desirable, and focusing on positive reinforcement, success is more easily achieved.

The success of Cameron's techniques became known in the mule world, and a clinician was born. At first Cameron hesitated at the prospects of teaching as a career; his life's ambition was to work with mules. He tried to deny what was inevitable, but he felt a responsibility to teach people, which in turn could help a lot of mules. His efforts would also dispel old beliefs about the mule's mind. He would be able to help develop in others the respect and appreciation he had felt his entire life.

To begin with, Cameron's clinics were set up over three-day weekends. Each one began with a colt class that would establish the fundamentals used throughout the clinic. Cameron knew that if mules and people got a good start, their futures would be much more promising. This also enabled those in the mulemanship class to see firsthand the benefits of groundwork. Within those three days, mule colts in the clinic achieved an understanding of what would be asked of them from the riders, and then they were ridden for the first time.

Much of the work took place in a herd environment, with several colts in the round pen. This gave the mules a sense of security. Once the riders had safely mounted, Cameron helped them teach their mules to make smooth transitions through the gaits–a very important part of advancement because that promotes balance and softness.

Through his own experience, Cameron knew the athletic ability of the mule. He taught refinement and timing, and the mules understood this perfectly. The challenge was in teaching the riders. Using his own mule as an example, Cameron inspired students to reach higher levels. Higher levels of sensitivity, awareness, and understanding were possible not only for the mules, but also for the students.

It has been said that there is nothing more powerful than an idea whose time has come. Cameron knew the time had come for a better understanding of mules. He had confidence that mules would help teach the lessons, just as they had throughout his life. But it would be up to him to facilitate understanding and to encourage people to think in a more abstract way. He wanted to enable people to explore alternative methods, rather than rely on old forceful tactics.

One thing is certain, and certainly true with a mule: Force begets force. All the bigger bits, sharper spurs and mechanical devices only serve to harden the mule. Unless Cameron could change the relationship between rider and mule, there would be no possibility for sensitivity and understanding, just a bigger brace between the two who had begun in pursuit of partnership. The mules' innate ability to survive had taken them this far. Those who could benefit most from Cameron's ideas would be the people who appreciated the mule's strength, so he set out to reach these people.

Cameron still lives in the mountains of Montana. Traveling the country nine months out of each year,

he offers tools that encourage, rather than discourage, responsiveness. He has produced many helpful videos to reinforce the concepts he teaches in his clinics. He continues to study under Buck Brannaman, and realizes that the opportunities to learn are infinite.

Although Cameron has an exceedingly busy schedule, he will still, at the first opportunity, take a string of mules up into the hills and light a fire to "burn some coffee."

Cameron works a green mule
sorting cattle at a livestock sale.

There is no place on earth where he feels a stronger sense of belonging than in the mountains with his mules. It was here that the journey began, and it is here that it will continue to expand.

Not a day goes by that Cameron doesn't appreciate all that the mule has given to him.

"Everything I do is for the mule," says Cameron. "Very few people realize the personal sacrifice that is made to commit to something like this. But it's my life, it's what I do, because the mule deserves it!"

116

HASTEEN BI' JHA NEEZ LITSO —The Man with the Sorrel Mule

BY ERIC ATENE

Eric Atene was born and raised in southeastern Utah near Navajo Mountain. At a very young age he was sent to Shonto Boarding School and then to Monument Valley High School. In 2003 Atene earned a Bachelor of Science degree from Northern Arizona University in parks and recreation management. He is an adult educator, employed by the Utah Navajo Development Council. Atene says his strength comes from riding and exploring the uncharted canyon country and from his grandfather's teachings and stories.

My grandfather's name is Buck Navajo, Sr., and he is about eighty-nine years old. He herds sheep every day on the Rainbow Plateau near Navajo Mountain in southern Utah. To him, there is no such thing as a holiday or a day off from herding sheep. He rides his mule every day to tend his sheep even in rain or snow. Every day is a good day to ride, and there are no bad days when he is riding his mule.

In his younger days, all of his relatives knew him as Hasteen Bi' Jha Neez Litso (The Man with the Sorrel Mule). He often guided backcountry hikers to Rainbow Bridge National Monument with his mules. His pack mules would travel through the rugged terrain on the historic Rainbow Trail and still manage to arrive back home in a single day. He was also known as an avid horseman. During his younger days, he must have gone through at least ten new saddles, and his iron grazing bits were worn down to thin mouthpieces.

The last time I saw my grandfather's old sorrel mule was about two years ago. The mule must have been about forty years old, and had been retired for ten years. My grandfather has two mules in his corral at home now. One brown, blaze-faced mule, now about twenty-six years old, has a bad saddle sore from having been ridden since she was five years old. The other mule, a bay, is about twenty years old and strong as a three-year-old. For some reason, this mule is always nervous and scared even though my grandfather rides her every day. This mule will only allow my grandfather to get near her without a fuss. I have named this bay mule Ricochet because she will bounce off things left and right. If you are not careful, you will be walking home.

My grandfather's animal stories are always interesting and fun to listen to, and in the process I have acquired much traditional knowledge. I have also developed a mutual understanding for animals. There are many stories in the Navajo culture about plant life, insects, birds and animals. The elders say that the environment is an essential part of our survival and existence today. Our environment can nurture us by allowing us to live in harmony if we observe it and take care of it.

All the stories are passed down from generation to generation, through oral history. These stories are also considered sacred and should only be shared with people who have a deep understanding and appreciation for life. Another point that our elders emphasize is that people should dedicate their lives to animals in order to gain respect for themselves and the animals. Our elders also recommend that you should learn from animals and you can teach yourself in the same manner.

The story I am going to share with you is one of my grandfather's favorites. It is about the animal kingdom. In Navajo beliefs, all living things have a purpose on earth. Animal stories are very important to learn, because they help us identify who we are and where we come from as a society. Moreover, animals keep us in balance with nature.

My grandfather says that when the Creator made all of the animal kingdom on this land, the Creator was left with a small piece of sacred material in his hands. The Creator then asked all the spirit people to gather and asked what they would contribute. Each spirit person then gave the Creator his or her special gift so that this particular animal would be made different from other animals. All the spirit people's contributions resulted in an extraordinary animal, with long ears, a smooth muscular body, a mind capable of sensing a person's mood and an attitude and instincts enabling it to survive with split-second decision-making. This animal also walked with a smooth gait and its every movement was elegant. This special animal became what is known today as the mule. It was agreed among the spirit people and the Creator that the mule would overcome any obstacle in its life. One of the mule's special powers would allow it to easily adapt to any harsh living condition. The mule can also survive without food and water longer than the horse by conserving energy. All this is made possible with the gifts from the spirit people and the Creator.

My grandfather concluded that he prefers mules to horses any day, anytime and anywhere.

No Halters Necessary

BY CAROL LUCAS
WHITESIDE
Carol Lucas Whiteside lives in Roanoke, Virginia.

*Around Town
Judy Brown spent
the first part of her
life as part of a wagon
train for VisionQuest.*

My husband Bob has always loved mules. Although he never owned one, he always kept a horse or two. He said he felt sorry for mules because "they got a bad rap. America was built by mules, and they never seem to get the credit they deserve, or any pleasure; they just work." When we were married in 1981, I remember thinking, "This mule thing will pass!" Well, it never did, and when we retired in 1987, we became serious in our quest for a saddle mule.

Bob's back isn't what it used to be, and for our mountainous terrain in Virginia, he wanted the smooth ride of a racking mule. Our research took us throughout several states until we came full circle to the mule farm of Mr. Yeatts, just an hour south of us in Gretna, Virginia. Thinking we should breed our racking mare, we visited Mr. Yeatts's farm primarily to see his breeding jacks. There, among the yearlings, was a mule colt out of a Tennessee Walking Horse mare. We bought the colt, named him Spencer and began his training. We learned many things about mules from Spencer; he taught us not to be in a hurry, that mutual trust is the key, how to listen and to be patient. Mule people have learned that just because you are an experienced horseman does not mean you know mules. I'm sure I will spend the rest of my life learning about our long-eared friends.

When we started out, we weren't aware of the saddle mule organizations, magazines, and mule events. Now our annual July vacation is driving nine hours to central Tennessee for the Great Celebration Mule Show in Shelbyville. There is so much to see, gifts to buy, hundreds of mules to visit, reunions with mule friends and new friends to meet. Above all, we always appreciate the work accomplished by everyone.

The 1994 Celebration is where we first saw her—the mule of Bob's dreams. A ten-year-old girl was riding her in the sidesaddle and gaited classes. The following September, when the mule became available for purchase, we drove six hours back into southern Tennessee, and since we had just seen her a few months earlier, Bob and I felt comfortable about bringing the trailer with us.

We learned that this fifteen-hand chestnut molly mule had been purchased from the VisionQuest wagon train. (VisionQuest is an alternative to incarceration for troubled juveniles.) Her particular wagon train traveled round-trip from Georgia to Pennsylvania. This was her third trip, and she was only six years old! We decided to call her "Around Town Judy Brown."

Mules need to have good eyes: big, wide, clear and alert. Judy's

Whitney came to the Whiteside family after plowing tobacco fields for many years.

eyes are so deep that you feel you can reach her soul. She is the most affectionate equine that I have ever been around. It is truly unnecessary to put a halter on her, especially for grooming. We work on all of her hooves and groom her endlessly as she rotates around us, moving to where she wants to be groomed next. From her VisionQuest experiences, Judy has literally "been there and done that." Riding her is the definition of pure pleasure. Our motto is: "If Judy won't do it, it can't be done!" I often ask Bob how it feels to be riding the safest (and smoothest) animal around.

By now Spencer had completed some time with Jack Shelton, a Walking Horse trainer in Gretna. I had obviously inherited a wonderfully gaited mule, but because I was raised and educated as a hunter/jumper rider, I don't have an interest in the smooth racking gait like Bob does. We concluded that Spencer was racking too well for me to ruin with my "hunt seat," so we decided to sell him and look for a new mount.

Wow! Imagine being able to purchase any equine that you wish. My mind raced: Did I want that black Percheron that I begged for as a child? Or did I really want a seventeen-hand Warmblood that would jump anything you put before her? No, I'm afraid mules are now in my blood; I must have been kicked in the heart because mules are there to stay. We talked to everyone, everywhere. Eventually I made the decision for a big (sixteen-plus hand) molly mule. Even though she would be large, we thought she should be talented, athletic and not too drafty. Since I did not plan on showing in halter classes, my view of conformation meant the physical ability to maneuver a tough trail safely. I discovered that I was drawn to a dark mule, whether black, dark bay or black-brown. Age didn't matter, although I really did not want another youngster that couldn't be ridden immediately. Most importantly, she needed to have those eyes, plenty of heart and lots of personality.

Of course, I called Randy, from whom we had purchased Judy, and described the mule I wanted. He had

These days, Judy and Whitney enjoy the finer things in life.

just received an eleven-year-old mule of that description. She had been plowing tobacco fields for years, but was nice to ride under saddle, but he said, she "wasn't a looker." She had white harness scar marks and was too fat. He sent us a video of her, so once again we prepared the trailer for the twelve-hour journey to Tennessee and back. When we arrived, it took about ten minutes to say "sold" (after all, I did have to ride her), and within twenty minutes we were headed home with my new mule, whom I named Whitney.

I only dreamed of finding a mule as sweet and affectionate as Judy. Now we have two in our barn. No halters are needed—just be prepared to do a lot of grooming, because they both dearly love attention. Each spring I give the girls a full body clip without having to tie them, and they think the wet/dry vacuum is just a loud, personal massage machine. They love these instruments of pleasure (the clippers and vacuum), which is a good thing considering how much they both adore dust baths.

We can't complain about their hygiene habits either; they always go to the same spots in the pasture where the manure accumulates like neat little tepees. Around the

barnyard, both girls actually back up to the manure cart! They are also almost potty trained while traveling, Bob and I simply walk them to their manure cart on the way to the trailer, thus planting the idea of "last call" before loading—and it works. We then just point them toward the trailer and they walk right in.

Approaching Whitney is easy anywhere. She always comes to me. Every day when I bring the mules in from the pasture, Whitney will stay by the fence while I walk around her to mount. I ride her home bareback with only a halter, although it is not necessary, just a common-sense precaution. Judy always follows. When picnicking out on the trail I drop Whitney's bridle across the saddle for her to graze; the problem is keeping her out of our space and the food! During forest trail maintenance, Bob handles the overhead work on Judy as I trim the trail from the ground because Whitney follows like a shadow, no strings attached.

Judy and Whitney have paid their dues by working hard for people all of their lives. Now they are our very willing partners, traveling many trails, and have yet to refuse anything asked of them. Perhaps we should have called them "Safe and Sound." Our mule passion is satisfied, as we feel their constant love and appreciation. Bob and I feel that we have created a mule home equivalent to a five-star resort for our girls, where no halters are necessary!

Mule Mail

In my ongoing love affair with mules, I have met many people who have shared my devotion to our long-eared friends. None have touched me more than the correspondence I have had with Mr. Gentile, a man of the earth whose simple words somehow cut to the essence of what it means to bond with a one-of-a-kind mule.

Mr. Hauer,

It was nice of you to write and call me. After talking with you, it brought back of lot of good times. I started thinking about my past. It again brought back a lot of good times. I lost my dad in 1977. He was my buddy, pal and friend. I think of him often. My dad taught me everything about cattle and horses that I know. He taught me how to take care of cattle and livestock in general. We did all of our own vet work. My dad also taught me how to cut up meat. My dad owned butchers' markets and we did all of our butchering. My dad taught me that you break animals with kindness a lot better than doing it the wrong way. I have bought what he told me all of my life.

He also taught me how to work with animals that are hurt some way or another. As I said, my dad had meat markets where he taught me how to cut meats and deal with people. I learned to treat people like you want to be treated, and in time they will treat you as good. That goes for mules also.

One day my dad sent me to the cattle sale to buy some number-one hogs to butcher. My dad would take one week out of the month to make sausage. ... He had people that would come 180 miles to buy his sausage. The people that did their shopping with him were real close to him.

When he passed away everyone that had stores closed for his funeral. That really made me feel good. Dad was all the time helping others. I never will forget one month he sent me to buy some hogs to butcher that week for his sausage. Well, when I pulled up to the cattle sale, I saw a large black mule in the back of a man's truck. So I walked over there and asked the man was the mule for sale and how much would he take for the mule. The man replied that if I could put a halter on him he would sell me the mule for $60. So I went back to my truck and got an old halter and rope lead. I went back over to where the mule was and climbed up on the side of the truck. I showed the mule the halter and patted him on his neck and head. The mule looked at me, as if to say "When are you going to put that halter on me and get me out of the truck?" So I put the halter on that mule, and asked the man to back down into the ditch so I could unload the mule. The man replied, "When you get him out, he's all yours."

So I got into the truck and led the mule off the truck. The man told me that the mule had been on a South Dakota ranch and had never had anyone try to get the mule up out of the land. The man could not believe I could handle that mule. So I led the mule over to my cattle truck and tied him up on the side of the trailer. I got out a curry brush and brushed him down. All the time I was talking to the mule and calming him down so he would load up good. I led him to the back of the trailer and put the lead over his neck; the mule looked at me and went right into the trailer. I put some hay in the trailer and closed him up in the front.

I then went into the sale and bought the hogs my dad had sent me to buy. After the sale I backed up to the loading dock. While I was loading up the hogs, the man that I had bought the mule from came over to me and gave me back the money that I had paid for the mule. The man also told me that he had brought the mule to be butchered for dog food. So, in essence, I saved the mule.

After the man gave me back my money, he said, "You have a job on my ranch if you want it." But I did not take up his offer, because my dad needed me more at that time. So when I got back home and was unloading the hogs, my dad came out and told me I had done a good job buying the hogs that we needed. My dad then looked in the front of the trailer and asked me if I was going to break the mule to rope off of and hunt off of. I said "Yes sir." So my dad did not say anything more about the mule.

After unloading the mule, I walked him over to the wash rack and gave him a good bath. After leaving him to dry, I looked back and saw the mule braying. He looked like a large hunk of black gold. While the mule was drying I went and got the shears. When I turned them on it spooked him, so I just laid them down while they were running, and then I walked back to the truck and turned on the radio on a country channel. The mule started calming right down. I got my hoof trimmers and went over to him and cut his hooves. He would let me do anything I wanted to do with his legs or hooves. After that he let me cut his mane and tail. It took me approximately two hours handling him, before he trusted me all the way.

From that day until now I have had a longing for mules. If I find myself sad or down I just go back to thinking about the good times that I had with that mule. If Black Jack knew that something was not safe, he would balk, and then when it was safe, he would go back to doing his job. After old Black Jack was too old to work, I would load him up and he and I would go riding in the woods. Then I would bring him back and unsaddle him, and he would go to his stall and wait for me to come and comb him down and feed him.

One day I went out to feed him, and Black Jack was dead. So I loaded him up for one more ride to the woods. When I got to a spot where he liked to graze, I unloaded him and dug him a grave. After burying Black Jack, I put a cross on his grave, saying—"What a Hell of a Mule."

Thanks for your time and thanks for calling me.
Your friend,
Michael A. Gentile

RAILROAD TRACK WIDTHS

NOTE: We can't confirm this is true ... but it sure is humorous!

The United States standard railroad gauge (distance between the rails) is 4 feet, 8.5 inches. That's an exceedingly odd number.

Why was that gauge used? Because that's the way they built them in England, and English expatriates built the United States railroads.

Why did the English build them like that? Because the first rail lines were built by the same people who built the pre-railroad tramways, and that's the gauge they used.

Why did THEY use that gauge then? Because the people who built the tramways used the same jigs and tools that they used for building wagons, which used that wheel spacing.

Okay! Why did the wagons have that particular odd wheel spacing? Well, if they tried to use any other spacing, the wagon wheels would break on some of the old, long-distance roads in England, because that's the spacing of the wheel ruts.

So who built those old rutted roads? Imperial Rome built the first long-distance roads in Europe (and England) for their legions. The roads have been used ever since.

And the ruts in the roads? Roman war chariots formed the initial ruts, which everyone else had to match for fear of destroying their wagon wheels. Since the chariots were made for Imperial Rome, they were all alike in the matter of wheel spacing.

The United States standard railroad gauge of 4 feet, 8.5 inches is derived from the original specifications for an Imperial Roman war chariot. And bureaucracies live forever.

So the next time you are handed a specification and wonder what horse's ass came up with it, you may be exactly right, because the Imperial Roman army chariots were made just wide enough to accommodate the back ends of two war horses or mules.

Now the twist to the story

When you see a space shuttle sitting on its launch pad, there are two big booster rockets attached to the sides of the main fuel tank. These are solid rocket boosters, or SRBs. The SRBs are made by Thiokol at their factory at Utah. The engineers who designed the SRBs would have preferred to make them a bit fatter, but the SRBs had to be shipped by train from the factory to the launch site. The railroad line from the factory happens to run through a tunnel in the mountains. The SRBs had to fit through that tunnel. The tunnel is slightly wider than the railroad track, and the railroad track, as you now know, is about as wide as two horses' behinds.

So, a major space shuttle design feature of what is arguably the world's most advanced transportation system was determined over two thousand years ago by the width of a horse's ass. ... and you thought being a HORSE'S ASS wasn't important!

—AUTHOR UNKNOWN

Pete

I own an eight-year-old red dun john named Pete. He stands 14.3 hands and is out of a double-bred Jackie B Quarter Horse mare. We have been together in the backcountry many times in Colorado, Wyoming and Utah. He is a joy to ride and a great pack animal. In the summer of 2001, Pete was at my farm in Coalville, Utah, in an eighty-acre pasture with four mares and four other mules. He was one of those "take charge" animals who considered himself responsible for all the mares, and he had the nicks, bite marks, and bare patches to prove it.

He was the one who always came to you in the open pasture or at the gate when you appeared on the scene. A piece of baling twine was enough to bring him in and if you left without him, he would walk the fence and let out a twenty-decibel bray that would cause the neighbors to think he was being slaughtered. Pete had a thing going with one of the mares, a three-year-old sorrel and white paint. He was never far from her in the pasture. She, of course, could not care less about him.

In July of that year my son Mike, who is a big game outfitter, called me and said he had leased a place for fall elk hunts in the high mountain country of southern Utah. He invited me to go along with him to scout the land. Early one morning, Mike and I left Coalville with two mules and camp gear for the three hundred-mile trip to the Summit Mountain area. I took Pete and considered taking the paint mare for Mike, but decided instead to take Maggie, a big, stout molly with plenty of go and experience. By early evening we were on the mountain and had selected a campsite. Our camp was at 9,500 feet in the kind of country you dream about in winter months–steep, rugged terrain with heavy stands of pine, scattered patches of aspen, high open meadows, grass to the mid-calf, and water everywhere. We had an idyllic spot all to ourselves, shared only with wildlife and a relatively small band of sheep grazing about four miles to the

BY GRANT MACFARLANE

Grant Macfarlane is an attorney and rancher who has been involved with cattle, horses and mules for many years. For the past decade his interest has focused on mules, which he uses in his ranching endeavors and for recreational purposes.

east. After a Dutch oven dinner, we shared memories of times past under a bright mantle of stars and the light of a near-full moon. We planned to get an early start in the morning.

We were up at daylight, fed and watered the mules, fixed breakfast, and then brought Pete and Maggie over to the trailer, where we loaded the gear for the day's ride. Pete had not had a good night. The ground where he had been tied looked like it had been plowed, and he had touched only part of the flake of hay left for him the night before. He did, however, stand quietly at the trailer next to Maggie with no apparent urgency to get

Pete in action.

going. I finished with the tack and gear and slipped on the headstall with a snaffle bit, and a mecate with the loose end wound around the saddle horn. I was ready to go except for locking the truck, putting the halter and lead rope in the saddlebag, and snugging up the cinch.

Mike was still loading gear and Maggie didn't have a bridle on yet. I took a few steps to the truck to lock the door. Mike reminded me that Pete was not tied, but I promptly replied with confidence that he "wasn't going anywhere." At that moment Pete simply did a 180-degree turn in his tracks and started down the ridge at a brisk trot. I was sure that he would pause to graze or simply go a few yards, find himself alone, and then return to the other mule. He did neither. It was as if he had a destination of his own and limited time to get there. He was leaving town! I wasted no time getting after him, but in my chaps, boots and spurs, I was no match for his pace. By the time Maggie was ready to go, I was well down the ridge and Pete was out of sight. We tracked him along the open ridgeline for about three-quarters of a mile. At the place where we last saw his track, the ridge dropped off on three sides into heavy stands of pine. Pete was gone.

As the reality of his disappearance sank in, my first reaction was irritation at myself for having left him untied. Next I was annoyed at Pete for leaving us. However, I knew that he would find an open meadow, pause and graze, and that at worst, our expedition would only be delayed for a few hours. Wrong! The canyon that he dropped into was heavily forested with thick undergrowth and tall grass. Tracking is certainly not my forte; and here the tracker is handicapped by heavy ground cover and a lack of established trails that a mule might travel along.

Summit Creek Canyon is primitive and there are no roads. We rode Maggie all day long, but never caught sight of Pete or found another track that we were sure was his. By the end of the day my frustration had turned to concern that the rein was down off his neck and that Pete was "hung up" somewhere. This was plausible, given the density of the forest, the steepness of the terrain, and the amount of deadfall. Also disturbing was that he had taken with him my best saddle, a Capriola given to me by my wife twenty years before, and camera equipment with an expensive three hundred-mm lens, altogether an investment of several thousand dollars.

Fortunately, he had a full saddle britchin' and breast collar, but he would lose girth as time went on; he was sure to roll the first chance he got, and the cinch wasn't tight. Would the saddle stay on top of him?

Mike and Maggie.

At the end of the first day's search it was obvious that we needed help. I contacted a friend in St. George who referred me to his son Vern, who was well connected in the area and knew people who were familiar with the country where Pete was last seen. Vern dropped everything and spent the next two days searching with us. He brought along his horse and recruited two friends, another horse and an ATV. Meanwhile, we got the word out. Mike contacted landowners and livestock people with property and stock in the area. We reported the lost animal to the Iron County Sheriff's Office and to the Parowan City Police. We visited with the Brianhead town marshal. The Parowan Café posted a "lost" notice at the cash register. We drove over to the sheep camp located east of our campsite and visited with the herder and the owner of the sheep.

The word was out in Iron County. As might be expected, we began hearing stories of other lost horses in this part of the country. In one case, the horse had never been found. Another story we heard more than once told of a horse that took off with full gear, got ledged up and was found dead a year or so later with the saddle still on the body.

We theorized that if Pete wasn't hung up he might do one of about six things: 1) Return to our campsite. 2) Travel generally downhill and when he hit the bottom of the canyon, go down and out the canyon. 3) Find an open meadow with water and hang out for a while. 4) Answer and come to the whinny of a herd-bound search horse traveling through the country. 5) Find the sheepherder's horses and stay with them, or 6) Go down the dirt road that provided access to the property. None of these theories proved out, and at the end of three days of search on horseback, ATV, and foot, we were empty-handed.

We concluded that Pete was likely close to where he was last seen, but hung up, or that he was a long way from the campsite. At the end of the third day of searching, we loaded up Maggie and made the three hundred-mile trip heading north to Coalville. I had an engagement the next day, after which I planned to either stand by the phone for a while, or load up fresh animals and go south again.

When I ended my Monday afternoon meeting, there were two messages on my cell phone. The first was a message from a deputy sheriff in Cedar City who reported that a motorist had seen Pete on the Brianhead road, and, being alarmed that a rider may still be in the forest, had caught the mule, tied him to a tree and then called the sheriff's office. The second was a message from Mike who had heard from a friend in Iron County that Pete had been caught. I promptly called the sheriff's office and talked to the deputy who had called me. He told me the mule was tied near the scout camp on the Brianhead road. He would get off work in about three hours and would hook up his trailer to go get the mule.

I appreciated this generous offer so much that I hesitated to suggest an alternative, but as soon as I hung up the phone I knew that I needed to call him back. I had him back on the phone in minutes and told him the mule was likely tied by the mecate and that he would certainly break the headstall. He wouldn't be there in three more hours. I told him that he was carrying a saddle that had sentimental value and camera equipment of significant monetary value and that I would be very happy to pay someone to go up and retrieve the equipment as soon as possible. He said he would see what he could do. As it turned out, he called the Parowan City Police and one of their officers drove up the Brianhead road, located the mule and took the saddle and gear off, leaving the mule tied. The officer then went back to get a trailer for the mule, but by the time he had returned, the headstall was broken and hanging to the tree and Pete was off again. It was later that evening before the sheriff's deputy called to tell me that the saddle and gear had been retrieved, but that Pete was gone again.

Bright and early the next morning I loaded up the Paint mare and headed south toward Brianhead. On the way down I stopped for a few moments at a packsaddle shop in Spanish Fork. When I got back to the truck, there was another message on my cell phone. I returned this call and it was another Iron County Deputy Sheriff who lived in Parowan. He told me that Pete had been found in a valley several miles from where he was last seen near the scout camp. He said a truck driver had seen the mule traveling along a remote county road in a sweat and at a brisk pace as though he had some place important to be. It must have been obvious that he was not a local animal. The truck driver called a friend on his cell phone who knew immediately that this must be the lost animal that had been so widely reported. When the driver got out of his truck, the mule came to him. He took off his shirt and put it around the mule's neck and held him while his friend hooked up a horse trailer and drove over to the scene. The friend then hauled the mule into Parowan and left him with a deputy sheriff who had a set of corrals. It was this deputy who called me the next day.

When I drove into the corrals at the deputy's ranch, the Paint mare had her head out the feed door and whinnied. Although Pete was not in sight at that moment, he immediately responded with a loud bray. He was pacing the fence when we got to him with a halter and lead rope. I led him to the side of the trailer where he put his head up and nuzzled the Paint for several moments. He then completely settled down. I loaded him and the two traveled side-by-side back to Coalville.

Pete had traveled alone from our campsite on the mountaintop through rough, roadless terrain for a distance of at least ten miles to the place where he got onto the Brianhead road and was found by the first motorist. After breaking loose from that point he traveled alone at least another ten miles over rough mountain terrain, including another high ridge line, and from there down into the next valley. When first seen in that valley, he was still moving out at a fast walk. In looking at the map I could see that his route of travel was on a direct course back to Coalville.

I will always believe that he was on his way home to the Paint mare. He knew where he was going, but he probably did not know (or care) that it was a three hundred-mile trip. He had been gone more than four days and nights. It had rained hard every night. The saddle required some repair at the local saddle shop, and the camera went back to the manufacturer for repairs. One of Mike's clients took a trophy bull elk in the Summit Mountain area that same year. Altogether, it was a heartwarming experience for Mike and me.

Pete makes friends a bit closer to home.

THE MULE TRADE

BY BRETT JOHNSON

Brett Johnson is a cash commodity broker in Clovis, New Mexico. His office is located on Main Street in a building that his great grandfather built in 1929. The street is paved with brick, and his great-grandfather supervised the laying of the bricks. His grandfather's job was to water the mules and horses that pulled the wagons used to carry the bricks to the site. Johnson owns three mules and two broodmares and raises mules. He and his son, Rio, are avid hunters and trail riders but admit that killing a deer is the least important thing about the hunt. The best part is being able to camp, ride their mules and enjoy the mountains of New Mexico.

This story was told to me by my grandfather, a dentist/cowboy in Clovis, New Mexico, so I pass it on as the truth.

About thirty-five miles west of Clovis is a beautiful spring with many cottonwood trees around it. This was the headquarters for the Hart Ranch. My grandfather worked for Mr. Hart on the ranch until his parents gave him the choice of becoming a preacher, a doctor or dentist. He figured being a dentist would be the easiest of the three and spent thirty years in a profession he hated. During this time, he always owned and traded horses, and he roped off of horses until one day he almost lost a finger. He decided that if he was to continue to feed his family, he had better not rope anymore, because a dentist without a finger is not a very good dentist.

The story was told to me as follows: Mr. Hart was a fine horseman/mule man and a trader. He was known to have a preference for roan horses and mules. He happened to come through Portales, New Mexico, and stopped at a friend's house for a visit. Mr. Hart stayed until almost nightfall, ate supper with them and had a good visit. As he was leaving, he noticed that his friend had a beautiful roan mule. His friend told Mr. Hart that a little kid rode the mule from Elida, New Mexico, headed to Clovis to sell the mule. Mr. Hart's friend bought the mule and saved the boy the trip to Clovis. Mr. Hart inquired if he planned on keeping the mule or selling him.

"Everything is for sale," he said, "so I guess I'd sell that mule."

"Does he buck?" asked Mr. Hart.

The friend replied, "Like I said, the kid wasn't but twelve or thirteen who rode up on him and no bigger than nothin'."

A trade was made, and Mr. Hart told him he would send a cowboy over to fetch the mule sometime. Hart himself had to leave the country for a few days, so he dispatched his cowboy and told him to go pick up the mule and ride him back to the ranch. When Hart returned from his trip, the first thing he did was to ask his head cowboy about the mule. The cowboy told him the mule bucked everyone at the ranch off except the cook, and the only reason he didn't buck the cook off was because he wouldn't get on him!

As you can imagine, Hart got mad, so he got in his car and headed to Portales to have a talk with his so-called friend. When his friend answered the door, he called him a damn liar and thief and said that was the last time he would ever buy anything from him!

His friend quietly asked him what was wrong and he told him, "You told me that mule didn't buck and he has bucked off every single cowboy on the ranch!"

"Now hold up," his friend said." I didn't tell you the mule wouldn't buck. You asked me if the mule would buck and I told you a little ol' button of a kid rode up on him who wasn't but twelve or thirteen years old. I just left out the part that that was the ride-nest kid I ever saw in my life!"

My grandfather then told me that Mr. Hart had out-traded his friend some years earlier on another horse deal, and his old buddy was just getting even by selling him a buckin' mule!

Brett Johnson's great-grandfather in his work wagon sometime in the early 1900s after arriving in Clovis, New Mexico.

Strayhorse Ranch

BY TROY COOKE

Troy Cooke owns and operates the Strayhorse Ranch in northern Arizona. He is also a rodeo competitor.

The Strayhorse Ranch is located about thirty miles south of Alpine, Arizona, in the Blue Range primitive area. The ranch, which I purchased in 1994, encompasses twenty-seven thousand acres and is about twenty miles in breadth. The country is a little rough, with high timber and eighty percent slopes throughout.

After I bought the ranch, I started working cattle with ranch horses, as I have always done. It takes thirty straight days of hard riding to gather our cattle during the spring and fall roundups. After a year of having the horses go down, get chewed up and spit out by the tough country, I decided to try some mules. My brother had an old hunting mule named Rocky, so I tried him out. I figured that with a name like Rocky he was bound to do well in the rocks. Even though he was just an old hunting mule, he worked better than all the ranch horses, so I decided to start looking for and buying good mules. Instantly, my life became easier.

Since I began using mules to work cattle on the ranch, I have been able to travel twice as far in a day. The mules are able to cover much more country at a faster pace than my horses could. They are also more sure-footed and make the days go by more quickly and safely.

We use Catahula dogs to find and hold the cattle, and we use mules to find the dogs and bring the cattle out to the shipping pens. Most of our ranch trails are narrow, single-file, and steep, and they have cross-running creeks. We bring the cattle out, brand, rope, sort, and work them with mules.

I have had several different mules over the years, but the ones that will never leave my ranch are Arnie, Jake, Jobe, Kay and Hondo. Arnie, a 16.2-hand bay, was one of the first mules I started using on the ranch. Arnie had bucked off most

Mules are a family affair at Strayhorse Ranch. Left to right are Canyon, Cougar, Troy, and Cieneca. The mules' names are Kay 2 and Jobe.

the prettiest big mule I have owned. She is now my top mule, and I could run the ranch with her alone. Hondo is a16-hand buckskin that we raised from a foal; he still thinks he is a baby. He loves to help me work. When I'm building fence he will pull the pliers from my pocket and hand them to me. Hondo is a good overall mule for trail riding and hunting; he can really cover the country.

It may sound like the mules solved all my problems, but with the good mules came the good stories to tell. When I first started using Hondo, he wasn't too sure whether he liked cows. One day I was trying to get a fourteen hundred-pound Brangus bull out of the winter pasture and move him to the spring range. He did not want to leave, so Hondo and I decided we were going to force him to move. After a few charges that almost knocked Hondo out of his shoes, Hondo decided that he would turn and run every time the bull turned and looked at him. We finally got the bull, but Hondo was never the same. Ten years later, Hondo still spins away every time a cow looks at him. To top it all off, for some reason, the calves like to mother up to Hondo. I guess they think he looks like their mom.

The other day I was bringing out some cows, and the mother cow in front decided to turn around and give Hondo a good look. As if on cue, he spun around and headed back down the trail. The calf decided that he wanted Hondo, and of course the mother cow followed the calf. I tried to stop Hondo (who thought he was being chased by a big monster calf), and the mother cow

of his previous owners, so I was able to pick him up pretty cheaply. Arnie and I came to an understanding—quickly. He could buck off the saddle and anything I had tied to it every morning, but he could never buck me off. I walked him first thing in the morning for a mile or so before I got on. I would stop walking him and look him straight in the eye and say, "Arnie, are you ready yet?" and sometimes the look he gave me would be no, so we would walk on. After I got on Arnie, I could dismount a hundred times and he would never move. Overall, he became one heck of a ranch mule. Arnie is now retired and spends his days in the pasture.

Jake, a 15.2-hand sorrel, was my best cow mule. I always told people I could get a cow out of the top of a tree with Jake if I had to. Jobe is a 16-hand black, with an outstanding personality. He is one of the gentlest mules I have ever owned. He excels at working cattle, or anything else you want to do with him. Kay, a 16.1-hand grulla, is followed close behind bellowing. After about a mile, I stopped Hondo and gathered the cows, and we were on our way out again. Even though Hondo has his quirks, I wouldn't trade him for three ranch horses.

I have had several really intelligent mules over the years, but the smartest mule I ever owned was Apache. One day, I was loading my horses in the trailer to head off to a rodeo, and I had three loaded and went to get the fourth. When I returned, Apache had loaded himself in the last stall of the trailer and was all set to head off. As it turned out I probably should have taken him that day, because my bulldogging horse didn't work very well. I have always told people that I can teach a mule in three days what it takes a horse three weeks to learn.

We also had some trouble with the ranch employees, who showed up with their "trail" horses. It didn't take long to convince them that they couldn't beat a good mule. Over the years, as we eliminated the horses, the employees seemed to improve. Don't get me wrong; we still like a good horse or two to pack with. It is not uncommon for us to be riding mules and packing salt and fence supplies with horses.

Helping out neighboring ranchers was always a fun experience. I would show up with my mule, and they would laugh and make jokes. By the end of the day they would all be trying to buy my mule. Most of my neighbors' ranches have terrain similar to mine. It didn't take long to convince most of them to use mules to work their cattle.

My mules have saved me several times on the ranch. I tend to ride longer days than I should, and I am always getting caught in the dark. I just give my mules their heads, and they follow the trail right out to the road. My wife has experienced this with me a few times.

The first few years working at the ranch, my wife was a lot of help to me. However, I think I pushed her to the limit one Thanksgiving Day. We moved cattle until dark, and there was no moon. I couldn't see my hand in front of my face, and a flashlight was useless. I told my wife to just drop the reins and hold on. It was like riding a roll-er-coaster. I didn't know when my mule was going to hit a switchback or start downhill. By the time we got out, my wife was ready to kill me, but was forever grateful to her mule. That was the day she became a mule believer.

My neighbor Ron Robertson, a retired Wyoming cowboy, was one of my longtime ranch hands. He had two good horses: Benny, a blue roan, and Fawn, a bay. These were two of the best ranch horses I have seen. When Benny died from a freak accident, Ron decided to purchase a big mule named Ruth. She was part draft horse, but was real catty in the mountains.

One time we were moving eight bulls out of some rough country. I think Ron was wishing he was riding Benny, but Ruth was doing fine. I happened to be on Hondo that day, so we were having trouble. These bulls were not the gentle kind, and I still don't understand why all eight were together in one bunch with no cows. That might explain why my calf crop isn't up to par! We were having a heck of a time getting these bulls out. Every time a bull would turn on us, Hondo would spin around and run past Ruth. Ruth didn't know whether to keep after the bulls or run after Hondo. Because of her size, Ruth practically blocked the narrow trail, and it was all Hondo could do to get by her. I thought she might serve as a roadblock, but Hondo still managed to get by her and away from the "monsters." Ruth wasn't bred for working cows, but I bet she could have pulled all eight of them out of that canyon in a wagon. By the end of the day, we managed to move all the bulls out. Ron continued to ride Ruth, and we used Fawn to pack with. She became our favorite pack animal. The point of this story is that I turned one more horse rancher into a mule rancher.

The Strayhorse Ranch has given me a great ranching experience. Over the years, my father and brothers have all decided that ranching in this country is for young men on mules. My sisters and mother Mickey are all a part of this ranch and have been a great help keeping it going over the years. They were also good at sending up friends to help in their absence. The problem was that most of their friends didn't know how to ride or work cattle. Luckily, I have a few good mules that make good babysitters. One time, one of the friends rode half a day without his stirrup. I asked what happened to it, and he said he thought he lost it. It took me a couple of hours to find it. My mules are so used to having inexperienced riders that nothing bothers them. By the end of the day, this friend had lost his saddlebags, coat, and one rein. He lost almost everything but the mule!

Occasionally, the Forest Service would send up some of its employees to ride. One time, a biologist and a couple of range managers came up. I decided to take them on a little longer ride than usual to show them some different country. By the time we took our lunch break, their poor horses were tired, and my mule was barely warmed up. Actually, I think my mule was wondering why we were having such an easy day. The riders were pretty tired and sore, too; one had ridden under a tree and scraped half the skin off his back. Lunch was another experience. I had several of my Catahula cow dogs along for the ride. We were all sitting around having lunch when I noticed the biologist making his sandwich. First, he pulled his bread out of a Tupperware container. The bread was as nice as if you had just pulled it out of the bag. Then he proceeded to put on all the fixings from other containers, and when he was finished it was the best-looking sandwich I had ever seen. He then rested it on his knee and reached into his saddlebags for some chips. Right then, one of my dogs grabbed the sandwich and gobbled it down in two bites. I was about to die laughing until I realized the biologist was not amused. I gave him my smashed-up sandwich and went without lunch, but it was worth every hungry moment.

I am a rodeo cowboy as well as a rancher. I wrestle steers and rope calves, but on horseback. Although I am a mule man, I have to draw the line somewhere. It's not that I don't think I could compete on a mule, I just think a good Quarter Horse is a little faster and better for rodeo events. In the back of my mind I have always thought it would be great to show up at a big rodeo and win on a mule. My biggest problem would be training a mule to steer wrestle. Mules are smarter than horses, and I think a mule might decide not to run by the steer once I get off its back. I am a little worried that a mule might give me a little kick for good measure as it goes by. I think I will keep my good mules out of the arena and on the trails, where they excel.

I have owned the Strayhorse Ranch for ten years, and more than ever I swear by mules. I continue to use Catahula dogs and mules to work the cattle, and still keep a good horse or two for packing. I hope my two sons and daughter will continue the legacy of using mules on the Strayhorse Ranch.

SADDLE HAPPY

BY MARY VON KOCH

Mary von Koch works for the Bureau of Land Management in Moab, Utah. She enjoys looking at the red rock scenery from the saddle of her bicycle or her mule, Ruthie.

I just knew that I would be saddle sore the first time that Sharon Northrup, my buddy in outdoor adventures, invited me to join her for a mule ride. I was a beginner, having only been on a horse two or three times in my life. I was really excited to learn but had little confidence in my ability to make a mule do what I wanted. We would be riding on the ranch where Sharon boards her mule, Mary. The ranch is located along the shore of the Colorado River about twenty-two miles from Moab.

From all of the available mules on the ranch Sharon selected Chocolate, a mule she said would be safe for a beginner. She was definitely safe—at her own pace. We were generally fifty yards or more behind the rest of the group. Nevertheless, it was an impressive ride around the ranch. It was a warm summer evening as we climbed up onto Locomotive Rock just in time to see the setting sun focus light on the red fluted rocks of Fisher Towers, a distinctive backdrop for several John Ford films and, currently, car commercials. Samantha, a recent newcomer to Moab, expressed it best: "This is like riding in a scene from Bonanza." Waking up the

following morning, I was happily surprised to discover that I was not sore after all.

The reason, I concluded, was that time on a bicycle saddle is not unlike doing time on a mule saddle. For the past several years, I have been riding my mountain bike around Moab during the week and going on a longer ride each weekend. I can't help but be impressed every time I climb up the La Sal Mountain Loop Road—a four thousand-foot elevation gain—and realize that, while most people get to see the view down into Castle Valley from their car, I have gotten up there under my own power! I build up miles and saddle time through the spring and summer to ride in the Grand Valley Centurion race at the end of August.

I hadn't ridden a mule more than a couple of times when I was complimented for the way that I instinctively react in mule-riding situations. I had not made the connection until I rode my bike to Hurrah Pass, one of Moab's popular mountain-biking trails. The way that I hold my body and shift my weight while riding my bike on the steep pitches seems to work for riding mules as well.

It was a pleasant surprise when I was invited to join a group on a three-day mule ride on Navajo Mountain. Ruthie was the mule selected for me to ride. We fit well together. We both are small, petite and spunky. On this trip, Ruthie started to teach me characteristics inherent in mules, thus ending my mental catalog of similarities between biking and

mule riding. The climb to the top was on a very steep and rugged road. When Ruthie got tired, she just stopped and would not budge until she was rested and ready to go. This behavior undoubtedly led to the saying "stubborn as a mule," but she seemed to know her limits and was also aware that we ultimately needed to move on. The places where we stopped allowed me to take pictures of other people in our group as well as pictures of the spectacular view developing below us as we went up.

On the return day, part of the group had gone ahead of Ruthie and me and was out of sight. At an intersection, Ruthie wanted to take a side trail. I was hesitant since I could see the mule tracks continuing on the main trail. We took the side trail, which turned out to be the same shortcut that we had taken on the way up. Smart mule!

On another trip, this one in the San Rafael Swell, I was again riding Ruthie. When we came to a steep and rocky-ledged outcrop, the guide, who was riding a horse, led the group down a route that Ruthie did not like. She found a better way that was used by the people behind us. It is quite a treat to let Ruthie pick the route. In contrast, my mountain bike gets me to some interesting places, but I have to make all the decisions myself.

Mary von Koch rides a number of mules, including this trusty mount, Ruthie.

Meeting Mules at Home and in Nepal

I grew up in Texas, where everybody who owned a couple of acres had horses; no one had a mule. Everyone knew the saying "stubborn as a mule." Who would want to put their time and money into an animal that was going to cause more trouble than it was worth? I kept this attitude for about twenty years, until I was offered my first ride on a mule.

I thought I was going to be in for a struggle. A mule was not going to want to run, not going to keep up with the rest, would bite, and dig her heels into the ground and not move a step. But what I discovered was something altogether different.

The mule I rode that day was eager to get out of the barn. She was energetic and more responsive than any horse I had ever ridden. Never dawdling, my mule stepped over logs and rocks, ducked under branches, and walked across streams. She went anywhere I asked her to, and I was absolutely amazed. Sure-footed, my mule climbed rocky trails that would have been difficult on foot. She didn't worry about heights, and she walked near cliff edges. She knew where to place each foot and would sidestep barbed wire or rocks in her way. I had never experienced anything like this.

And then I remembered the way horses seemed to fight you when you asked them to do certain things; I had remembered the way horses would jump at the slightest movement. A horse could stumble over obstacles, not seeing a piece of wire on the path or a hole in the ground. Any sound or unexpected move could send a horse into a panic. This creature, however, was different. My mule used her enormous eyes and large, impressive ears to take in every bit of scenery around her. She located and avoided obstacles. At unexpected sounds or movements, she would tilt her ear or turn her head. She was calm, which made me feel calm, too.

A few weeks later, a friend took me to the mountains to show off his mules in action. Compared with a horse that was on the same ride, these mules were majestic steeds. They took the rocky, uneven steps in perfect stride, unlike the

BY LAURIE COLLINS

Laurie Collins is a Texas girl living in Utah who loves the outdoors and the arts. She loves the mountains, desert, ocean, travel, film, theater, art, music, dance, and yoga. She makes a living writing grants.

horse that jumped, tripped, and slipped up and down the trail. The mules took slow and precise steps, even on incredibly steep terrain and talus slopes. I never felt like I was in danger. In fact, I felt safer on mule-back than I would have on my own two feet. After this trip, I became a die-hard mule fan.

Now, I wonder why people ride horses at all—they're skittish and clumsy. I'll take my rides on the steadfast mule instead.

My newfound admiration of mules was broadened a few years later when I went on a trip to Nepal. I was surprised and delighted to find trains of mules ferrying supplies in the foothills of the Khumbu. I expected to see a more exotic creature in the Himalayas, some kind of shorthaired yak, camel or llama. It made me smile and actually feel a bit more at home when I noticed the familiar old mule passing me on the trail.

Although I know mules are sure-footed, I was still amazed that I never saw a mule lose its footing, stumble or fall in this demanding Nepalese terrain. These weren't trails; they were more like rocky ladders. Steep and slick from recent rain, eroded by centuries of use, these routes between the small villages of the Himalayan foothills were extreme. Huge cliffs banked some of the paths, and other paths had been laid with stones to resemble stairs. However, the stones had become shifted by time, weather and travel so that the footpath resembled streams of jumbled rocks, out of balance and ready to tumble down the steep trail onto the trekkers below.

Perfectly poised and undoubtedly happy, the Nepalese mules carried their loads with ease and grace. I never saw a mule miss a step, kick a stone out of place or even stop to rest.

I also never witnessed a mule train driver yell at his team or hit them with switches as he drove them forward—a common tactic with yaks at higher elevations. These mules seemed to know exactly where they were headed, and they usually kept their owner gasping for air and scrambling quickly over ledges to keep up with their

swift pace. I saw mules loaded with rice, wood, dung, Snickers bars, soft drinks and even Western-style toilets (for tourist accommodations in the mountains). The animals wore bells around their necks, so I usually heard the mule trains before I saw them.

Imagine twenty-five mules, each with a different soft, high-pitched cowbell hanging around its neck, sauntering down the trail. It sounded like a chorus of church bells at times. The mules usually wore exotic-looking saddle blankets, crude saddlebags, and homemade rope, but like the mules we have in the United States, they are dependable, strong and fast.

No mountains in America equal the steep, rugged foothills of Nepal. Nowhere in America do people traverse hundreds of miles on foot to provide their families with food, clothing, and building supplies. In Nepal, some villagers rely on their own two feet and a very strong back to supply friends and family. Many more depend on a sure-footed, friendly animal that can carry a larger load and handle the terrain with ease: the mule.

SUV Moroccan Style:
The Role of Donkeys and Mules in Morocco

A Moroccan boy adds a little weight to this donkey's burden.

At first light in Marrakech, Morocco, I heard the dawn Islamic call to prayer, or the *fajr*. The chant, the full text of which stretches on for about five minutes, drifted across the city and through the window of my son's apartment. I was in a jet lag haze that was the result of a 26-hour journey from Moab, Utah, to northern Africa, but I was still struck by the elegance of the prayer. The second sound I heard, and the sound I would hear just after the *fajr* every morning for the month I was there, was the clip-clop of donkeys and mules as merchants, farmers, and builders transported their wares through the busy streets of Marrakech.

Donkeys and mules are as much a part of the daily flow of traffic in downtown Marrakech as taxis are in New York City or sport utility vehicles are anywhere in America. There is no "donkey lane." They are in the stream of traffic navigating the roundabouts and jockeying for position in the rich stew of traffic that includes bicycles, scooters, motorcycles, petit taxis, Coca-Cola trucks, horse-drawn carriages, buses, and all manner of cars. Through this busy stream of traffic pedestrians weave and wind as they play "dodge car" (or "dodge donkey") while trying to make their way across streets without benefit of traffic lights or rules. Though traumatic for Western tourists, somehow it all works.

BY JANET LOWE

It is common to find donkey-drawn carts as part of the traffic flow in urban centers of Morocco. This one is stuck in a traffic jam during rush hour in Marrakech, Morocco.

mules and donkeys. The oil ran off the stone and into the bottom of the basin where it was absorbed by straw mats. Once the olives were crushed and the mats saturated, they were removed and put into a hand-powered press; thus the term "cold press olive oil." The oil flowed across bare ground into deep holes dug into the earth. The olive tanks were lined only with years of olive oil residue. When the oil was in tanks, the owners came and transferred it to plastic bottles, which were loaded into impossibly tiny carts tugged by impossibly tiny donkeys. Children stood by the side of the road and sold it by the bottle, or the oil made its way to the souks—or shops—in nearby cities.

For Americans, the sight of a donkey or mule in the mix of street traffic is a bit unnerving. But in Morocco, donkeys and mules are the equivalent of pickup trucks in the United States. In fact, the farther you travel from the cities, the fewer cars and more equines you see. Fortunate Berber women have a donkey to carry heavy loads along muddy country roads. If not, the women are carrying the loads on bended backs, even as their husbands or sons walk alongside them. A lucky woman has a donkey outfitted with two large wicker baskets that fit like saddlebags on either side of the animal.

Donkeys and mules are also used in the absence of electricity in rural villages. Walking along a dirt road through the Berber community of Ourika Valley at the foot of the Atlas Mountains, I encountered a rustic olive mill. An ancient stone building housed two large stone basins. In the center of the basin was a massive stone wheel that, when turned, crushed the freshly harvested olives, releasing their oil. Powering this great stone were

These same heavily loaded and unbalanced pyramids of olive oil, coffee beans, flour, olives, oranges, cinder block, rocks, flowers, or any type of product you can imagine (and some you cannot imagine) share not only the city streets of Marrakech, but also the narrow maze of lanes that connect the old city or medina. The medina is populated by hundreds of souks interconnected by narrow alleys and pathways. Some are no more than six or eight feet wide; others stretch to the generous expanse of ten or twelve feet. In America, most of these roads would qualify as nothing more than sidewalks.

The medina is the heartbeat of any Moroccan city. Each day, thousands of local pedestrians do their shopping for food and household goods. Sharing the narrow pathways with the crowds are bicycles, motor scooters and, of course, donkey-drawn carts hauling freight. Tourists quickly learn to dart away from the rushing carts as the drivers shout and whip the donkeys through the clogged alleys. One day, while I was exploring the souks, I saw a galloping donkey being whipped into a speeding frenzy by an angry old Marrakech man. In order to avoid

This donkey is owned by one of the few families that live in the ancient Kasbah Ait Benhaddou near Ourazazate, Morocco. His shade covered home is just outside the family's front door.

being trampled by the donkey and run over by the cart, I had to flatten myself like a spider against the ancient red walls of the medina. Although I managed to get my body parts clear of the roadway, the load in the cart snagged my bag. The sudden hook was strong enough to flip me sideways and perpendicular to the wall. The driver didn't as much as slow down and look back to see if I was still standing. He probably didn't even know that I almost ended up under the wooden wheels of his cart. Clearly, in Marrakech, donkeys have the right of way!

Donkeys may have the right of way on crowded streets in the maze of pathways in medinas throughout Morocco, but they have few rights of any other kind anywhere else in the country. They are truly considered beasts of burden. In fact, the Koran specifically speaks to the purpose of equines: "And [He made] horses and mules and asses that you might ride upon them and as an ornament."

They carry loads that would seem to break their small backs. They are whipped and shoved and driven. Never once did I see a person lovingly scratch his or her animal's long ears, give it a treat, or even offer a simple word of kindness.

SPANA, the Society for Protection of Animals Abroad, seeks to correct some of the mistreatment of animals in Morocco. Tourists have often been troubled by the condition of the caleche (carriage) horses and mules in Marrakech, and the mules working in the tourist industry in the Middle and High Atlas Mountains. Working with local authorities, SPANA devised a method of inspection for each caleche equine. Every six months, the animals are inspected and their hooves marked indicating when the next checkup is due. In severe cases of neglect or abuse, SPANA has the right to remove an equine from the street. This is only done as a last resort, however, as the owners need their animals to make a living in this very poor developing nation. SPANA helps treat more than one hundred thousand animals, including dogs, cats, camels, horses, mules and donkeys.

While in Morocco, I made the acquaintance of an Englishwoman who lives in the farmland in the shadow of the Atlas Mountains. She is locally known as the "Donkey Lady" because she rescues donkeys from the streets of Marrakech. I was able to spend time scratching the ears of the clean, happy, muscular donkeys that plow her fields and eat like royalty. When I asked the owner if I could take pictures of her donkeys, her reply was "ask them." I leaned into the ears of the beautiful Moroccan donkeys, scratched their fuzzy coats, told them they were beautiful and asked if they minded if I took their photos.

Happily for me, they all said yes.

Mule Antlers

W inter snows lay heavy in our small valley, set like a white jewel at the 8,700-foot level in the mountains west of Denver. For our two mules, Ruby and Chester, the deep snows were but a small hindrance as they enjoyed chasing each other in short, mad dashes, throwing the dry snow about them in clouds.

The Front Range of the Rocky Mountains is also home to large herds of elk, with a number of bachelor bulls yarding up in our bit of winter heaven. It was a common sight for them to greet me in the early morning darkness as I made my way to the mule barn to throw flakes of alfalfa and grass hay to our mules. They always hoped that hay leavings would come their way to supplement the taste of dry summer timothy from our meadows, and their hopes were often answered.

The mules did not seem to mind the close presence of the heavy antlered elk. As for the elk, they seemed intrigued by these large-eared critters, which looked in profile like cow elk, but smelled entirely different. Chester, a beautiful chestnut john who stood about sixteen hands, would often trot back and forth along his side of the wooden corral fence, while an equally giddy bull would move in kind on the other side. Both of these grand animals would be tossing their heads, ears forward, obviously wishing they could get a bit closer.

The bulls were never aggressive, but would often put their heads down and shake their many-tined antlers in mock battle as Chester or Ruby looked on with interest. Chester, I am certain, wished he had his own pair of antlers to shake.

One bright mid-morning, a particularly friendly elk came a bit closer to the fence than the rest of the herd, and Chester decided to grab life by the horns,

BY STEVE RUSH

Steve Rush lives on the Uncompahgre Plateau outside of Ridgeway, Colorado, with his Apache mule Ruby. Rush has been involved with mules for the last twenty-odd years (some years more odd than others) and is of the opinion that mules have taught him far more than he has passed on to them. Rush is still on a learning curve with life and mules, and looks forward to many years of each. Ruby was used in her early life to work cows on an Indian reservation near Yuma, Arizona. At near 30 years of age, and a diminutive 13.2 hands, she is still fast on her feet, but is satisfied now with moving deer and coyotes out of her corral.

138

Chester appears not to take any notice of the bull elk, but soon swings around to check out those gorgeous antlers.

Chester is now imagining how antlers might look on a big handsome mule.

so to speak. With a long reach across the top rail, he took a deep, full-bodied bite on a brow tine of the bull elk. If you have ever had your mule or horse take hold of you or something you were holding, you know what it must feel like to be trapped in a vise.

Chester, who easily had a five hundred- to six hundred- pound advantage over the six hundred- or so pound elk, roped in the surprised wapiti tightly, his bright eyes aglow

with delight at finally achieving his goal of having antlers. These were his, by gosh, and he wanted them on his side of the fence!

The bull's eyes bulged with surprise; he dropped to his knees and bellowed a cry so pitiful that the other elk quickly trotted up to see what was happening. Chester would not relinquish his hold. Like a hooked deep-sea marlin, the elk bobbed up, crow-hopped sideways, and dropped once more to his knees. The sharp crack of the two-by-six fence boards foretold a chapter I was not ready to watch. I hurrahed and waved my arms while taking the short walk toward the battling duo, and Chester obligingly dropped his grip on the brow tine. The poor bull elk fell back toward his buddies, who had moved off when they saw me coming. He lost his balance, and tumbled flat out on the snowy ground.

I wondered how the local game warden would take my story of the reason I came to have a broken-necked elk in my meadow. The elk quickly regained his feet, however, and as quickly as any terrified animal could leave the scene, he ran through the milling elk herd in a straight line to the dark timber. The crash of broken spruce limbs told me he never slowed as long as he was within earshot. Chester gave a long braying farewell to his new "friend," causing the frightened elk to move on even more quickly.

Needless to say, and much to Chester's chagrin, the bulls that remained no longer played near the other side of the fence, though he continued to entice them. And I must admit that I was happy not to continually replace broken fence, which would have been the sure result of future encounters. I am certain, though, that to this day that mule-bitten bull elk steers a wide path around anything that looks remotely like a tall, long-eared cow elk!

Long Ears and Running Walks: The Gaited Mule

BY DAN AADLAND, PHD
Dan Aadland is the author of eight books including *The Complete Trail Horse* and *In Trace of TR: A Montana Hunter's Journey*. With his wife Emily he has raised Tennessee Walking Horses since 1980, recently adding gaited mules to their ranch in south-central Montana. A lifelong packer, Dan offers clinics and workshops on improving backcountry skills for equines and their riders. His website is http://my.montana.net/draa.

On recent trail rides you may have seen mules that cruise along at a speed that should indicate a stiff trot or even a lope, yet the rider's body scarcely moves—it simply glides along as if it were on a conveyer belt. The mule's head nods up and down in rhythm, and if you can hear the animal's footfalls the sound is of four distinct beats, rattled off in four-four time. You're watching a type of mule that's mushrooming in popularity because of his endurance, smoothness, and ease for the rider. You're watching a gaited mule.

The term "gaited" is a bit of a misnomer, since all equines have gaits. Most will perform three, the ordinary walk (four-beat, right front, left rear, left front, right rear), the trot (two-beat diagonal, left front and right rear hitting simultaneously, then right front and left rear), and the canter or lope (three beats, depending on lead, outside rear leg, followed by inside hind leg and outside foreleg hitting together, then inside foreleg striking, then suspension).

But "gaited" has come to refer to equines that have a cer-

A young Tennessee Walker mule on his first ride. Photo courtesy Dan Aadland.

tain genetic gift, an intermediate gait substituting for the trot. Since the trot is a two-beat gait, it's invariably rougher than the walk, though many mules perform it with tolerable comfort. The running walk (same footfall as the regular walk, but speeded up, four even beats), the foxtrot (a broken trot), and the amble (a broken pace) are among the gaits that substitute four distinct footfalls in place of the two-beat trot. The result is the sort of magic-carpet smoothness you witnessed when you saw the gaited mule glide by.

There's nothing new or unnatural about gaited equines. Early cave paintings show horses with footfalls that indicate an amble. The Romans devised cruel hobbles designed to force their Barb horses into the smooth gaits they'd witnessed among the horses native to the people they conquered. In England it's said that virtually all horses under saddle until the 1700s were gaited. Chaucer refers to "ambling horses" in *The Canterbury Tales*.

From Mongolia to Iceland to South America and to the United States, wherever civilization outstripped road-building, thus requiring people to stay in the saddle rather than ride on the seats of buggies, gaited horses ruled. When Theodore Roosevelt went west to become a cowboy and rancher he remarked that the ordinary gait of the western cow pony was a running walk, a foxtrot, or a single-foot. Lee Ziegler, in her book *Easy Gaited Horses* identifies more than 70 gaited breeds world-wide. Among the most common in America are the Tennessee Walking Horse, the American Saddlebred, the Missouri Foxtrotter, the Icelandic, the Peruvian Paso, and the Paso Fino. A certain percentage of Morgans still show single-footing gaits, and early Appaloosas were gaited. (I recommend Ziegler's book as a guide to the subtle differences between the various smooth gaits.)

The obvious route to producing mules that share these smooth-traveling, ground-covering gaits is to breed jacks to mares of gaited breeds. Sometimes it works, and sometimes it doesn't. The resulting mule may indeed perform

a running walk, a foxtrot, or an amble, but it's not a sure thing. However, the mule is likely to show an improved ordinary walk in any case, a walk that features longer steps with overstride. The rear foot in the walk reaches up forward of the track left by the front foot on the same side. The result is a longer gait that eats up the miles.

The good news is that among donkeys, just as among horses, there are certain individuals with the genetic gift we're looking for. When my wife Emily and I decided to add mules to our Tennessee Walking Horse breeding operation we looked for a gaited jack and found one on the farm of the

Bubba (registered as Bud) is a naturally gaited jack shown here in early training. Photo courtesy Dan Aadland.

late Bill Moore of Tennessee. We'd learned in our research that a jack with natural gaits was far more likely to sire mules with the way of going we desired. Emphasizing good disposition, bone, and naturalness of gait, we'd bred

Tennessee Walker Horse mule foal. Photo courtesy Emily Aadland.

over the years an outstanding array of Tennessee Walking Horse broodmares. We were confident they'd hold up their half of the bargain.

"Bubba" (registered as Bud with the American Gaited Mule Association) came to our Montana ranch on a wintry December day, no doubt thinking he'd been exiled to Siberia. Travis Young, our trainer at the time, quickly started him under saddle, finding him intelligent and willing. The jack exhibited a running walk, amble, and foxtrot, moving from one to another freely.

Breeding was another issue. Bubba was very cautious of the mares, and they considered him a creature from outer space. Luckily, we were well equipped to collect semen and inseminate artificially. We purchased a sweet jenny to act as a decoy, and Bubba was soon trained to mount a phantom and allow collection.

Size is hard to predict. This Tennessee Walker mule is 16.3 hands at age four; her dam was 15.2 and her sire was a standard jack. Photo courtesy Dan Aadland.

The results of our first breedings were gratifying. Our seasoned broodmares didn't seem to notice the long ears of their new foals, and gaitedness was definitely present from the beginning. Some foals hit a running-walk from the very beginning. Others trotted, but walked with the free-wheeling overstride that promised a gait would be present.

Familiarity with gaited horses is definitely an asset when working with gaited mules under saddle. Like Tennessee Walking Horses, most are multi-gaited. The secret to building on natural gaited genetics is to be aware of footfalls. Assuming the mule is well broke in the impulsion department, keep him in a walk, gradually speeding up but not letting him break into a trot. Listen for four separate footfalls, even if they're not evenly spaced. If his head keeps nodding, he's probably walking. If he breaks into a trot your body will tell you, and the nodding will probably stop. Collect him back into a fast walk.

Keep him at the top end of his walk and you'll eventually find a foxtrot, a running walk, or an amble. All of these gaits are comfortable and cover ground rapidly. Unless you're a purist you'll probably be pleased with any of them.

There's no doubt that gaited mules are catching on, with some well-trained individuals selling for prices in five figures. In many respects they're a trail rider's dream.

This Tennessee Walker molly mule is used by her rancher owner to work cattle in Montana. Photo courtesy Dan Aadland.

Green Mountain Rosie

By Ron Silverthorn
Wickenburg, Arizona

While I was living in Missouri, I received a call from our daughter, Marie, who lived in Vermont. She wanted me to find her a fifteen-hand mule gentle enough for her two daughters to ride. While Missouri has a lot of mules, if you don't know the mule community, it can—and did—involve a good deal of driving and looking.

Eventually, I spoke with Sue Cole, publisher of *Mules and More* magazine. She recommended I call her son, Loren Basham. This turned out to be a good thing, as he had recently acquired Rosie from South Dakota. I rode her and recommended that Marie purchase the mule.

The following three paragraphs were written by Marie at the time she nominated Rosie—who was later accepted—into the Versatility Hall of Fame.

Green Mountain Rosie was purchased over the telephone, from a mule dealer in Missouri, in the spring of 2000. While I had never owned a mule, or even ridden one before, I thought the mule would be good company for my horse, and perhaps my kids would trail ride with me. As it turns out, the kids weren't interested in riding, but Rosie has turned out to be more fun for me than I ever imagined.

Besides being such a wonderful pleasure-riding mule,

Rosie has competed and placed at local horse shows. She has also competed and placed against horses in 15- and 25-mile competitive trail rides in the mountains of Vermont.

Most of Rosie's points have been earned fox hunting with Guilford Hounds, a drag hunt, in Guilford, Vermont. Rosie joined the hunt field in the fall of 2000. Her "hound savvy" and a willingness to plow through the most challenging terrain got her promoted to a "whipping in" mount in the fall of 2001. While Rosie doesn't have a Thoroughbred's speed, she is very determined to keep up with the hounds and is extremely level headed.

While Marie really enjoyed fox hunting on Rosie, her youngest daughter, Kori, decided to enter Rosie in the local horse shows and fairs.

Eventually, Kori decided that she wanted to show a horse. So Grandpap swapped a fine Quarter Horse for Rosie. Rosie came back to Missouri at Thanksgiving 2002. Since that time, she has been my push-button mule. She is so dependable. When I retired in 2004, we moved to Wickenburg,

Rose doesn't have a Thoroughbred's speed, but she is very determined to keep up with the hounds and is extremely level-headed. All photos courtesy Ron Silverthorn.

These two photos show that Rose can be a bit mulish about such things as a costume class, but eventually she played the part of a unicorn quite well.

Arizona. She has carried me and many others safely for many a mile.

Wickenburg has lots of trails, from easy to really difficult. We ride in the desert and the Bradshaw Mountains. In addition to riding the trails around Wickenburg, I have ridden Rosie on about 200 of the 800 miles of the Arizona trail. The trail begins at the Mexico border and stretches to the Utah state line. We have camped and ridden with the Arizona Mule and Donkey Club on the Mogollon Rim and camped and rode with Wickenburg Horsemen in Monument Valley, Utah. Our Navajo

When Kori came for a visit, she set up a jump for her and her friend to jump with Rosie. She wanted to make sure Rosie hadn't forgotten how to do it.

guide pointed out where many of the John Ford movies, starring John Wayne, were filmed. That was a great experience.

In 2007, I took what was our longest trip with my young friend from Missouri, Mike Farley. During our travels, we rode in New Mexico, Utah, Colorado, Idaho, and Oregon. In Oregon, we camped at our friends Herb Bauer and Diane Wilhelm's. Diane graciously took us on trail rides near her home in John Day. Later, we trailered to the Sisters, Oregon, area and rode in the Cascade Mountains. Great experiences!

In 2008, I was invited by John and Sena Hauer to ride the Grand Canyon with them. Bill Cavin and I joined them at the South Rim of the Canyon. Bill on Happy and me on Rosie, along with the Hauers, rode our animals down the Bright Angel Trail. The Bright Angel Trail was well-maintained and about six feet wide in most cases. We were used to much narrower and rougher trails around Wickenburg.

We rode to Indian Gardens and stopped to rest before going on to the Colorado River. To get to Phantom Ranch on the far side of the river, you ride through a tunnel and make a sharp left turn onto a suspension bridge. Rosie and Bill's Happy weren't too sure about that bridge. We dismounted and they willingly were led across the bridge. When we left Phantom Ranch and came back to the bridge, they carried us across as though they had been doing it all their lives.

This is an example of mules wanting to be sure they won't hurt themselves. Once they knew the bridge was safe, no problem.

The scenery in the canyon was spectacular. Yes, you can look off to the side of your mule and see three or four hundred feet down.

In 2009, we spent the summer in Missouri and rode in the Ozarks. There are so many great places to ride in the hill country west of the Mississippi River.

My riding has slowed down the last two years due to family concerns. With any luck, Rosie and I will be following new trails this year and hopefully for many more years to come. Rosie is now nineteen years old and has received her second Versatility Hall of Fame award. She is sound and has provided a mule for dozens of friends and family. She has been from coast to coast and has seen more of the United States than most people. Having Rosie has allowed me to see backcountry I could never otherwise have seen. Paying attention to her ears and where she was looking has allowed me to see a bear and a mountain lion I wouldn't have seen. She has been a joy and a wonderful friend.

You can be sure that good, solid mules like Rosie are going to keep themselves and you safe.

Rosie at home in Arizona.

Miracle Mule Baby Born in Colorado!

By John Hauer,
Moab, Utah

It has historically been an accepted "fact" that since mules are hybrids, they cannot reproduce. The scientific reason given for their sterility is that horses have 64 chromosomes, donkeys have 62 and their offspring (mules) have 63. Even numbers of chromosomes are required for reproduction . . . almost always. Chromosomes are "structures" that serve as storage units for an organism's DNA. DNA stands for the unpronounceable name of a chemical that tells organisms how to grow. For example it tells the mule's body how long to make its ears, how to build its brain and to put the skin and hair on the outside of the body. It is theoretically impossible for mules to be sires or dams.

Mule fertility is so rare that the Romans had a saying, "Cum mula peperit" meaning "when a mule foals," or in modern terms, "when hell freezes over."

When they were doing research for the recently released book on mules, *The Natural Superiority of Mules*, John and Sena Hauer tried to find documented cases of molly mules giving birth. There were numerous rumors of mules giving birth in China, Albania, Estonia and other exotic places where DNA testing is not available. For some reason, the Hauers did not uncover information about mollies in Texas and Nebraska that had foals--more about that later.

The Hauers were excited and very interested when Colorado residents Larry and Laura Amos called on May 3, 2007, to tell them that one of their molly mules, Kate, had given birth to a little male equine. The baby would not technically be a mule (half horse and half donkey) since it would have to be either one-third horse and two-thirds donkey, or two-thirds horse and one-third donkey.

The mule momma, behind the paint horse, is guarding her miracle baby.

John immediately made arrangements to visit the Amos Ranch in order to photograph the mother and baby and take hair from each of them for DNA analysis.

Larry and Laura Amos own Winterhawk Outfitters in Colbran, Colorado. They guide elk hunters, take pack trips, and fishing trips to remote lakes and streams in the Flat Tops Wilderness. They have taught American soldiers the fine art of mule packing for use in Afghanistan and Iraq.

In their outfitting business, Larry and Laura use about 50 mules and 50 horses for their pack trips. In June of 2006, they bought Kate, an eight-year-old, fifteen-hand black/brown molly from Randy Pulliam, in Pleasant Plains, Arkansas. Randy had acquired the mule in 2005 at St. Joseph, Missouri. He said she was a very gentle and willing mule. He kept her in a pasture with several other mules, horses and a jack that pasture-breeds his mares in order to produce mule babies. The jack is named Step-and-a-half. The name comes from an injury caused when his foot got hung in a gate when he was a baby. Randy says when Step-and-a-half walks, he picks the injured back foot up much higher than his other feet. He is about fifteen hands tall, and 1,000 pounds, is good-natured, and produces good-natured foals. Randy is certain that Step-and-a-half is the sire of Kate's foal.

Randy said Step-and-a-half will follow a horse mare around the pasture for days, waiting for her to come into heat. He did not see any sign that Step-and-a-half was interested in Kate and it was hard for him to believe it when he heard she had given birth. Neither Randy nor the Amoses had any idea that Kate was destined to make history.

The Winterhawk wranglers had packed Kate during the summer of 2006, and said she was a strong and easy-going pack mule with a nice disposition. Larry said he was looking for pack mules when he saw an ad in *Mules and More* magazine. He contacted Randy and bought Kate and seven other mules from him. They were delivered in August of 2006.

Larry said, "I worked Kate all fall, and turned her out

This is the proud papa of the mule foal.

in early December in to a pasture by the house, along with about 50 other mules, and 50 horses. At the time, we had two horse mares that were due to have horse babies in the spring. On April 27, at about midnight, I woke up hearing a commotion in the corral. I went out to check, and didn't see anything unusual, and the horses and mules settled down. At 3 a.m. the horses were whinnying and the mules braying and stirring around. I went out again and looked around and didn't see anything of concern and went back to bed."

Larry continued, "I got up at 5:30 a.m., looked out the window, and saw Kate in the pasture with a foal. She and the baby were both worn out from fighting off the other horses and mules. Mares and geldings will sometimes steal babies from their mothers, and john mules may try to kill them. I went out and picked the little fellow up and carried him to the arena. One of the wranglers led the mother. The foal was shaky, but obviously nursing and getting nourishment." When asked what he thought when he saw Kate with a baby, Larry said, "I thought 'holy s#%!'"

Laura Amos said, "When Larry and I looked out the

Kate the molly mule had a very big belly but no one suspected she was pregnant with a foal.

Days later, the miracle baby was born. This is Amos, taking shelter under his mom.

window and first saw Kate standing in the pasture with her baby, they were right in the center of of a group of about 100 horses and mules. I turned to Larry and said, 'Where did THAT come from?' There was a definite commotion and Kate was defending the baby. I woke our daughter, Lauren, and we went out to see the momma and her new baby. Lauren skipped school and we looked at our miracle mule all day."

Laura said that they had a good winter and all of their mules and horses were fat, so they had not noticed that Kate was more than just fat. Laura said, "This is all very exciting, and I hope we can breed Kate back, to a horse this time." It was left up to Laura and Lauren to name the colt. They couldn't think of a name they liked that is appropriate for a miracle baby, so they decided to have a "Name Kate's Baby Contest."

Larry and Laura didn't know what to do or who they should notify about the unexpected event. They had recently read John's book, *The Natural Superiority of Mules*, and decided that because of his obvious love for the long-eared critters, John should be the first to know, and that he could advise them about how rare mule motherhood really is, and what they should do about such an unexpected event taking place right there in their corral.

John and Sena were somewhat dubious. They had heard of several instances of molly mules stealing a mule baby from a horse mare. In some cases, the molly had actually produced nourishing milk for her newly adopted baby. Larry assured them that there were no horse mares in their area that might have given birth to the baby mule. When John got to the Amos ranch and saw the mother and foal and watched as the little one suckled the molly and had white, frothy milk all over his nose, he had no doubt that the almost impossible had happened there on the Amos ranch. He was convinced that Kate was indeed a momma and not just a foster parent.

Larry pointed to a large pasture containing about 100 mules and horses that were all gathered close to the fence watching the activity in the mule mother's corral. Larry said, "John, do you want to check all of them to see if there is any indication that one of them might be this baby mule's mother?" John politely declined the offer, being already convinced that Kate was indeed the mother of the long-legged, long-faced, and extra-long-eared baby.

John had to do some research to locate a laboratory that works with equine DNA. The most obvious choice was the University of Kentucky (UK) in Lexington. Breeders of race horses frequently have DNA testing done at UK to prove the identity of the sires of their foals. On May 4, the hair collected from Kate and the baby was sent by express mail to the equine science lab at the University of Kentucky. Two weeks later, after thorough testing, the director of the lab called with the good news that the DNA of Kate matched that of her baby. The tests are extremely accurate, leaving no doubt that the molly mule, Kate, had conceived and given birth.

As further proof of Kate being the mother of the foal, John suggested having a vet draw blood for DNA analysis at a different lab. He also wanted to get a chromosome count for both Kate and her foal. Larry took the pair to Dr. John Harris in Grand Junction, Colorado, where a blood sample was taken from each animal. The blood samples were sent by Dr. Harris to the lab at the University of California at Davis. Again, the DNA analysis showed that Kate is the mother. Additional blood samples will have to be sent to the lab in special vials in order to get chromosome counts for momma and baby. The result of the chromosome analysis will be reported in an upcoming issue of *Mules and More*.

John and Sena were sure that mule owners, veterinarians, animal scientists, geneticists, and researchers throughout the world would be interested in knowing about the rare event. They notified Bill Loftus, the science writer at the University of Idaho. Bill was involved in the

mule cloning project sponsored by the University of Idaho and Utah State University that resulted in the first equine clone. Bill is well connected with veterinarians and other equine scientists and their equine publications. The next contact was with Sue Cole, publisher/editor of *Mules and More*. Sue expressed her interest in a story and photographs of Kate and her baby for the magazine.

When working on the cloned mule project, Bill Loftus did some research into the history of mules giving birth. Below are two of the stories he found:

The most recent reports of births to mule mammas in this country took place in Texas and Nebraska. In 1923, a molly named Old Beck was reported to have foaled on a farm in Texas. No test was available at the time to prove or refute maternity.

In 1984, Krause, a molly owned by Bill and Oneta Sylvester of Champion, Nebraska, had a mule baby that was named Blue Moon (once in a blue moon) and was bred again and had a second foal that was named White Lightning. (Lightning doesn't strike the same place twice.) The sire of both babies was a jack named Chester. Krause's babies were the first case of mule fertility to be scientifically documented. It was determined that both babies had 63 chromosomes and that Krause was indeed the mother.

Since Krause gave birth to her foals, all of the reported

This baby, Amos, a cross between a donkey and a mule, shows more donkey characteristics than the average mule. The baby's mystery breeding would have made it two-thirds donkey and one-third mule.

cases of mollies giving birth that have been tested have been refuted (until Kate's delivery). Some of the reported dams were the actual mothers of the babies but were not mules. These mothers were determined to be mulish looking horses or donkeys. Other "dams" were indeed mules, but the foals were not their own babies. They had either kidnapped or adopted the foal of a horse or donkey.

Colorado Kate has indeed made history.

Food for thought: John poses this question, "Since virtually all male mules are neutered before they have a chance to reproduce and no concerted effort has ever been made to breed mollies to either jacks or horse studs, it is not surprising that no cases of mule paternity and very few of mule maternity have been reported. Could it be that in spite of their odd number of chromosomes mules are not as infertile as has been assumed?"

THE ALBANIAN MOLLY'S MISCARRIAGE

In 1994, in Vilan, Albania, where mules are very valuable possessions, it was reported that a mule belonging to Jakup Muzhaqi started braying with pain after working all day in the field. The closest thing to a vet in the village was Shaqyri Cekani who had studied animal medicine for one year. "I thought it had developed colic and gave it an aspirin injection," Shyqyri recalled. "Then something covered with what looked like white plastic fell to the ground." A head and legs could be clearly seen. Cekani was certain that it was a premature fetus. "It scared all of us, so we threw it to the dogs."

Ali Muzhaqui, Cekani's older brother, decided that the mule had the devil in her stomach and should be destroyed. The town elders worried that the mule's miscarriage could be a sign from the devil and cause a catastrophe. Most of the 530 villagers wanted to see the evil omen destroyed, but no one would kill the mule for fear of making things even worse. And Jacup, who was an elder, objected to the proposed killing of his only mule and his most valued possession. The mule was worth more than $400 which was ten times the national average

yearly earning in Albania—a fortune in that remote village. The mule was spared and Jakup would have liked to sell it, but no one would buy a cursed mule.

The "vet's" father, Nezir Cekani, said, "We asked the mufti in the mosque of the village over the mountain if the end of the world would come because of the devilish event. The mufti said the earth will end but only after 600 years."

MOROCCAN CURSE/BLESSING

On August 27, 2002, Lalla, a sixty-year-old Moroccan farmer made the 20 mile round trip on her fourteen-year-old molly to the souk, the weekly village market. At the souk, Lilla had sold her bag of prickly pear and bought some salt and rice. Although, in accordance with Moroccan culture, the mule had no name, she was Lalla's most valuable possession. The mule was fit and well-muscled from daily work on Lalla's small farm and from being ridden and carrying Lalla's produce to market.

At the souk the mule was always left in a large fenced area with hundreds of other mules, horses, donkeys, camels, sheep, goats, and cattle. This trip to market had been as uneventful for both the woman and her mule as all the other parts of their lives.

The following day their lives were changed forever when the little mule gave birth to a cute, long-eared colt. Lalla had no reason to suspect that her mule was pregnant. The thought had never entered her mind, and now she was frightened and ashamed. In her culture such an unheard of event was sure to be considered a religious sign and a harbinger of doom. In order to conceal the cause of her anxiety and shame Lalla hid the mule and baby in a small shed.

The news of the miracle birth leaked out and then spread rapidly. Lalla's shame quickly turned to celebrity as curiosity overcame superstition, and people from other villages came on foot, on mules, on donkeys and on horses to see the good looking foal with the black and white face and extra-long ears. Many of the visitors brought gifts for Lalla, her mule and its baby. The baby looked like a mule with donkey features or a donkey with mule features. Rather than being cursed by the unusual event, Lalla had been blessed when her hard-working mule had given her another work animal that she would be able to rely on in the future. She was also the recipient of the recognition and generosity of her neighbors.

Soon after Lalla's mule gave birth the news reached Dr. Gigi Kay, an equine veterinarian with the Society for the Protection of Animals Abroad (SPANA), a group based in London, England, and dedicated to the care and welfare of working animals in North Africa and Middle Eastern countries. Dr. Kay realized that, if confirmed, the birth would be news of great scientific importance. She quickly arranged to travel to Lalla's village to see the mule and baby. Dr Kay reported that the mother and baby were in very good shape. It was her opinion that Lalla's mule was the birth mother of the foal.

NAME THE BABY MULE CONTEST

The winning name in contest was Winterhawk's Kool Mule Amos.

It was obvious from the beginning and became even more apparent as the baby grew older that the father was indeed a donkey. The body shape, long ears, and light-colored rings around the eyes were very donkey-like.

Six-year-old Lauren and baby Amos became great friends. Lauren enjoyed "hanging out" with Amos And even did some Crayola art depicting her new friend.

Word of the miracle baby spread quickly and the event was heralded on the Paul Harvey show. Larry and Laura Amos received letters, emails, phone calls and visitors on a regular basis.

Unfortunately at about age three-and-a-half, little Kool Mule Amos became the victim of a winter ice storm and didn't live long enough to answer many of the questions raised by the miracle birth in the mountains of Colorado.

For more information about the good work done on behalf of work animals (mainly mules and donkeys) in third world countries, see SPANA's website at www.spana.org.

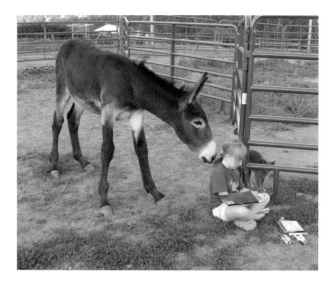

Mule baby Amos takes a liking to his new little friend, Lauren.

Lauren put her artistic skills to use featuring Amos.

On the Trail with Herb and Diane

By Sena Hauer

Herb Bauer and Diane Wilhelm enjoy their mules in as many facets as the colorful creatures exhibit.

Both longtime horse riders, their familiarity with the long-eared creatures grew throughout the 1990s when they had the opportunity to raise and train several mule foals. Herb and Diane were living in Oregon, where mules are prized for their ability to pack into the extreme terrain of the Wallowa Mountains and the Eagle Cap Wilderness. That country is so vast, deep, and rough that multi-day pack trips are the only way to see it.

Herb Bauer and his brother Jerry were raised on a ranch near Mancos, Colorado, where his family ran sheep in the nearby San Juan Mountains. Herb, pictured below as a child, has owned mules for most of his life, using them to pack and ride. This picture, taken circa 1934, shows the brothers on two donkeys named Pete and

Maude. Note the old pair of stilts leaning against a shed in this photograph. Those boys knew how to have old-fashioned fun!

Diane Wilhelm and her mules are the "Shady Ladies" of the Chief Joseph Days parade in Oregon.

The couple now splits their time between Oregon and Wickenburg, Arizona, where the mild winters and beautiful Sonoran desert offer riding galore and a community full of equestrian friends.

Herb's experience with donkeys and mules began when he was a small boy growing up in Mancos, Colorado. His family ran sheep in the nearby San Juan Mountains, and they used mules for ranching, hunting, and packing. Industry in those mountains didn't just involve ranching, though, as miners had long prospected for silver and coal, often using donkeys in their endeavors.

"Up behind the ranch there was a lot of coal mining activity. When the mines would play out or quit, the miners would turn the donkeys loose," recalled Herb. "My brother and I would catch them if we could, and then ride them. We had two donkeys named Pete and Maude."

Mancos is located at the base of two different land formations; the extreme alpine San Juan Mountains on one side and the Four Corners Colorado Plateau country on the other. Thousands of prehistoric Native Americans inhabited these lands between 550 AD and 1300 AD. Mesa Verde National Park is near Mancos, and Herb's grandfather was the first superintendent of that park in the early 1900s. The Bauer family purchased the Mancos ranch that had been owned by the Wetherill family. In 1888, Richard Wetherill and a fellow cowboy named Charlie Mason were the first known white men to discover the ruins of Mesa Verde. This country is rich in Native American history, and mules were important tools in the rough ranching activities there.

Decades later, Herb's foray into raising saddle mules came after ending up with a load of mares from Missouri that had been bred to have baby mules. He and Diane proceeded to raise seven foals, and they still keep and ride two descendants from that original load.

With that first herd of young mules, Diane said she had a lot of learning to do. "I had to take a Brad Cameron clinic just so I knew what a mule was," she laughed. She and Herb were working with a pair called Ella and Della who were trained to pack, drive, and ride. They still have Ella, who they ride and drive regularly. Dusty, a 1999 model that they also raised, is Diane's mainstay for trail rides, parades, and game events.

"I've always liked mules," says Herb. "My family had a ranch and we ran sheep, and I needed to use mules for packing all of the time.

"There's nothing like a mule," continued Herb. "They are stout and smart and just great. I love them. If you have a good mule, it's priceless. If it's a bad mule, it's because someone has mistreated it."

Diane has spent thousands of hours on the back of a mule since raising those first babies. She takes an annual pack trip with friends into the Wallowas when she is in Oregon each summer. She also participates in the Chief Joseph Days parade the third week of every July in Joseph, Oregon, and has competed in events at the nearby Hells Canyon Mule Days where she has won many buckles and ribbons with her mules.

Wanted: Dead or Alive , in the Gold Rush Parade in Wickenburg, Arizona.

Diane Wilhelm is a sheriff you don't want to mess with. She and her mules Dusty and Ella are the hit of the Gold Rush Day parade in Wickenburg, Arizona.

Diane Wilhelm packs her mules Dusty and Ella in the Oregon wilderness.

Hells Canyon Mules Days, held in Enterprise, Oregon, was started in the spring of 1981 when local ranchers and packers met with representatives of the Wallowa County Chamber of Commerce and USDA Forest Service to explore the idea of putting together a new county event.

"As a result, the mule—tough, intelligent, individualistic, often maligned, but the mainstay of the many packers and outfitters working in Wallowa County—was elevated to center stage for the first annual Hells Canyon Mule Days celebration on September 19 and 20, 1981," says the official history of the event. "Hells Canyon was an appropriate title because that area owes most of its early settlement and development to the mule, which predominantly

These mules came in handy on an elk hunting expedition near the Bauer Ranch in Colorado in 1950.

Herb Bauer with Dusty, one of several mule babies he and Diane Wilhelm raised in the 1990s. Dusty, now in her teens, continues to be Diane's choice saddle mule.

served as a major means of transportation to gain access to this rugged region of the county."

These celebrations are held at the base of the Wallowa Mountains and Eagle Cap Wilderness. "This is one of the most spectacular mountain ranges in the country, and it's certainly my favorite," says Diane. "They call it America's

Little Alps because there are a lot of steep granite mountain peaks. It's so vast that you have to pack in to see it."

Diane indulges the playful side of her mules by dressing up for parades and events. In a recent Chief Joseph Days Parade, she and her friend Jean Hauxwell dressed as saloon girls and rode their mules. They were the "Shady Ladies," and the mule Diane led was packing an old-fashioned wash tub holding a mannequin dressed as a lady of the evening.

Herb and Diane spend long winters in Arizona, where Diane is active in Gold Rush Days, the Wickenburg Horsemen's Club, and the Las Damas Women's Riding Organization. Diane is a regular participant in the Gold Rush Days Parade, where she has dressed as a sheriff, leading a mule that was packing a pretend dead outlaw. She has honored her late friend and mule lover Marj Hastie in an empty saddles ceremony using her mules, and she has dressed as a knight in armor.

Diane has fun with

Diane Wilhelm in front and the late Marj Hastie were trail leaders aboard mules on the annual Las Damas all-women five-day ride in 2012.

her mules. She organizes regular gymkhana events in her backyard arena and invites neighbors from all around to bring their critters to practice and compete for fun in an obstacle course.

"It's a challenge to work with mules but it's rewarding," says Diane. "If you watch them, they will tell you what's going on around you. They are loyal and they will take you places that most horses won't go."

Diane Wilhelm riding with friends in the Flat Tops Wilderness near Trapper's Lake, Colorado.

Diane Wilhelm riding in her bloomers on dress-up day at the Las Damas Annual Five-Day ride in Arizona.

Days later, Diane and Dusty were dressed in shining armor.

Herb Bauer and Diane Wilhelm

From Our Barn Door

The view from our barn door.

Why Moab?

John Ford: Looking down the Colorado River past Fisher Towers and Castlerock, with the LaSal Mountains as a backdrop, he exclaimed, "That's the greatest site I've ever seen!"

John Wayne: "Because Moab is where God put the West."

John Hauer: "Because Moab is the best place, perhaps in the world, for trail riding on mules and horses."

Ridley Scott, director of *Thelma and Louise*: "I have seen more wonderful scenery in a single day around Moab than any other day I have scouted."

Movie director George Sherman: "The wide variety and startling beauty of scenic features is without comparison . . . the best I have found anywhere in the world."

Stewart Udall, former Secretary of the Interior, describes this area as "acre for acre, the most beautiful country in the world."

During the first four years of the '90s, scenes from twenty-three movies were filmed in this area. The best-known included *Thelma and Louise*, *Geronimo*, *City Slickers II*, and *Forrest Gump*.

Nowhere else that I know of can you find a major river flowing through a beautiful red rock desert within sight and easy driving distance of mountains that reach almost 13,000 feet into the sky. In the desert, you find a variety of

Durango loves the scenery as viewed from her favorite rock.

Collard lizard.

lizards, waterfowl, songbirds, snakes, coyotes bobcats, and other desert, and riparian-dwelling creatures. The mountains are home to elk, bears, mountain lions, and small lakes full of trout.

The best way to describe this land, with its buttes, mesas, spires, cliffs, gigantic freestanding rocks, and the glorious red-rock color throughout, is one word: Western.

The region encompasses 11,576 square miles, more than 90 percent of which is public land. Most of the public land is off-limits to motorized vehicles, but is accessible to equestrians. Mules love it here!

Moab is known as the mountain bike capital of the world. It has also been discovered by four-wheelers, Jeeps, hikers, and runners. For some reason, it remains relatively unknown to those who are best equipped to experience the beauty of the area: trail riders on mules and horses.

Guests we take on trail rides invariably appreciate the scenery and often ask me if we ever get tired of it or take it for granted. The short answer is no. A longer answer is that every day we are awestruck, inspired, and almost overwhelmed by the incredible beauty of this magic place. We enjoy sharing it with others and seeing it through their eyes.

THE MOLLY MULE AND THE RATTLESNAKE

In 2012, Sena was leading a group of German tourists on a trail about a mile east of our corrals. I was in the middle of the group, relaxed and enjoying the scenery and conversation. I was riding my fourteen-year-old molly, Durango. When a rattlesnake crossed the trail in front of the horse ahead of us, Durango appeared to be outraged. She pointed her ears at the snake and backed about 10 times faster than I ever knew she could move in that direction.

Duchess in Miner's Basin.

The snake took refuge in a bunch of tumbleweeds at the base of a juniper tree. One of the tourists insisted that he had to have a photograph of the snake, which was very angry and loud. Much to Durango's chagrin, I got the lon-

Faded midget rattlesnake.

gest stick I could find and lifted the tumbleweeds for the photographer to get his photograph. The rattlesnake was showing his unhappiness at being disturbed by rattling as loud as he could. Behind me, Durango pulled back on the rein and snorted to let me know she thought I was crazy. The tourist was happy to get his photograph and the other eight tourists thought he was crazy.

The snake event took place about eleven months ago. Since that time, I have ridden Durango down that trail at

Durango, worrying about snakes.

least sixty times. Every time we get close to the juniper tree, she takes a detour of about twenty yards to stay a safe distance away from the snake tree. To me, this seems like ample proof that mules have great memories. It also demonstrates their superior intelligence and sense of self preservation. All of the other animals on that ride were horses and none of them paid any attention to the rattlesnake.

A MAJOR CONTRIBUTOR TO CIVILIZATION . . . THE DONKEY

The mule's sire, the donkey (also known as the ass in the bible and as burro in much of the world) has not been given the attention and credit he deserves. The quote below is from *Donkeys of the West* by William G. Long.

Long states that his purpose in writing the book is to develop "a little more understanding, sympathy, respect, and kindliness for one of the least appreciated and most misunderstood animals on this earth." (We believe the mule deserves that title in the United States, but the donkey undoubtedly has earned the title on a worldwide basis.)

"[This] kindly, gentle eyed, velvety nosed, radar eared, non-aggressive creature has been man's uncomplaining companion and burden bearer throughout all history.

"The usual reward for the donkey's loyal service has been ingratitude, neglect, abuse, and ridicule.

"The donkey's reaction, even to intolerable torment, seems to be expressed in stoical silence, punctuated by cataclysmic sound, drooping ears, bowed head, disconsolate eyes and a general appearance of dejected resignation as though he were saying to himself, 'Oh hell, what's the use?'

"No creature more readily makes a response to kindness than the burro. It is as faithful as a dog, and returns attention with equal eagerness. Every mother donkey is more than justified in admonishing every adolescent colt, 'My child, never forget the nobility of your donkey ancestry! And never, no never, make a human of yourself!'

"Our debt is great to this the diminutive kinsman of the horse. For, though we picture Atlas upholding the earth, has not the ass for unnumbered ages born Asia, Northern Africa and a goodly portion of the Western world upon its shoulders?

"A well-known prospector was want to ask what he would do if he suddenly found a million dollar claim. 'I would build a monument 8,000 feet high on top of Telescope Peak and dedicate it to burros. Such a monument would inadequately express the debt today's world owes that little beast.'

"Old-timers maintain that the burro is in reality one of the shrewdest animals on the Western plains. A horse can easily outrun a burro on the desert, but in rough mountain country the burro can run a horse sick."

The mule's predominantly admirable qualities stem from his donkey ancestry.

PHILOSOPHERS

We believe that mules are very philosophical.

Can you imagine what these three mules were thinking while they gazed into the Grand Canyon?

If you have an idea that you want to share with us, send it to hauer@mymules.com.

The Three Philosophers. Photo taken by Lori Greenstein. Courtesy of the Arizona Office of Tourism.

A NOTE FROM THE GRAND CANYON ASSOCIATION

The Grand Canyon Association published the following statement:

"For far longer than Grand Canyon has been a national park, mules have carried people and supplies into and out of the canyon. Early miners also used mules to haul ore to the rim. Since 1887, mules have carried terrified tourists down and up the trails, and beginning in 1902, the Kolb brothers made their living photographing mule-mounted 'dudes.' Today, in this age of space travel and the Internet, mules perform the same roles they have for more than a century at Grand Canyon. For saddle-sore tourists who have braved a

journey into the canyon astride a mule, the memories of their exhilaration from the ride and awe from the view will stay with them for a lifetime."

The Park Service has reduced the number of mule rides allowed in the canyon, and it is rumored that they may eliminate them completely. If you care, you can contact the Grand Canyon Association at www.grandcanyon.org.

SERVING OUR COUNTRY

This soldier and his mule served our country during World War II.

WHAT PEOPLE SAY ABOUT MULES

The Bible speaks of the stubbornness of people at least seven times. Not once does it state or imply that mules are stubborn.

History, written or painted or photographed, neglects to mention that right behind the heroic military leader, the intrepid explorer and legendary cowboy, was a mule doing a job, his shoulder to the collar, hauling a supply wagon or a cannon, being ridden by an intrepid mountain man, or packing the supplies that made these undertakings possible. Faithful and tough, he contributed greatly, but did not share in the glory.

In his diaries George Orwell reported that the high price of mules in Arabia was "due to their being ridden by rich men, the mule being in fact the badge of wealth."

In 1846, at Fort Bridger, Wyoming, mules sold for $40 per head, a horse could be had for $25.

If a mule gets his way once, he will remember it a long, long time. For a mule, one experience constitutes a fact.

A mule's temperature has to be a two-degree increase before they sweat. Their hair absorbs the water and puts it back into the skin.

Every evening, the mules in my string compare the notes they've taken during the day, create a game plan, with alternate plays, and execute that plan the moment they see me the next morning, depending on my body language!

Back in the olden days a picture of a farmer plowing with an old mule warmed many a heart. That was America at its best, and truly the family farmer and his mule were special.

Those who know them best are well aware that "mules need a job."

In the 1700s, Columbus introduced mules to the New World by shipping them to America on his second sea voyage.

The gestation of a horse foal is eleven months; the gestation of a donkey foal is twelve to thirteen months, and the gestation of a mule foal is eleven to twelve months.

There are a few naturally bred wild mules roaming around on BLM land in the West.

The mule can handle both heat and cold better than the horse. In the presence of immediate danger, the donkey has a tendency to fight first, run second; and the horse has a tendency to run first and fight second. The mule has both influences available to act upon. Mules often think it over for a while before reacting, and then they may decide that doing nothing is the best choice.

When a mule gets in a "tangled situation" which could be dangerous he will usually not let fear take over. He can switch into a logic mode and figure out a solution, rather than trying to fight his way out.

The term "mule skinner" did not come about because the teamsters dealt harshly with their mules. The term originated because it was said that the packers and teamsters were so proficient with their swearing that they could peel the hide off of a mule with their profanity.

A doctor said that if you chew gum while riding a mule you will be exercising every muscle in your body.

A Montana packer said, "I never ask too much of my

mules, and they never refuse." That's the kind of relationship to strive for with your mule.

Donley Hewitt, a farrier in South Dakota, said, "Mules will definitely treat you like you treat them. They are a cautious animal and far more independent than horses."

A mule has the special ability to be able to stand on two feet if one front foot and the back foot on the opposite side are picked up.

Riding your mule is a fun, relaxing way to commune with nature and share time with your friends. It is also much cheaper than a psychiatrist.

Ad in a Santa Fe newspaper: "We will carry the US mail and passengers from Independence to Santa Fe for four years commencing July 1, 1857, in stage coaches drawn by six mules."

The most important products of trade in the West were precious metals and mules.

More views enjoyed by Honey Bee, Durango, and other mules.

John and Sena Hauer at the top of the "Top of the World" trail, which overlooks the Colorado River Canyon and their ranch.

Old Blooth had a lot of fun playing with the girls, and he also knew how to work. In this photograph, taken in 1914, he and one of his friends are pulling a road grader to improve a road along the Columbia River just north of Rufus, Oregon.

For many years mules were the source of power for building and maintaining roads.

The Natural Superiority of Mules

MULE GALLERY

ATTACK ON THE MULE TRAIN

Charles M. Russell, 1894

Oil on Canvas

Courtesy Sid Richardson Collection of Western Art, Fort Worth, Texas

MEXICAN PACK MULE
Charles M. Russell
Wax Sculpture
Courtesy Buffalo Bill Historical Center, Cody, Wyoming; Gift of Dr. Armand Hammer and Charles Stone Jones 49.60

Inscription on base reads: Pack mule made of wood carved in 1910 to show pack rigging used in Mexico as seen in 1906
"Double Diamond" hitch used – leather blind is also used by packer as a quirt.

Don't know how it come to put this Chingow's bridle rein in the wrong hand. couldnt wave it when I did notice.

Choteau Montana
Dec 16 1914

C R Russell

Heres one of them nut letters I was talking about.

I want to make a picture of a Russian Cassack will you tell me what particular shades of blue and yellow you use to get the sky opposite a sunset – like in "Jumped". Also what colors for where the sun is hitting on the snow like that little picture on the west wall in your library.

Yours

Joe De Yong,
Choteau,
Montana,

ILLUSTRATED LETTER TO CHARLES RUSSELL

Joe De Yong, 1914

Watercolor on toned paper

Courtesy Buffalo Bill Historical Center, Cody, Wyoming; Gift of William E. Weiss 77.60

Jo De Yong was a protégé of Charles Russell

THE BELL MARE

Charles M. Russell, 1910

Oil on board

Courtesy Gilcrease Museum, Tulsa, Oklahoma

DAYDREAM
Bonnie Shields
Acrylic
Courtesy Bonnie Shields, The Tennessee Mule Artist

BURRO, KEAMS CANYON, ARIZONA
William R. Leigh
Oil on Canvas
Courtesy Gilcrease Museum, Tulsa, Oklahoma

MULES AT THE ROCK CORRAL
Terry Maddox
Hand-Tinted Lithograph
Courtesy Terry Maddox, pencil artist

BLUE RIBBON MULE
Terry Maddox
Hand-Tinted Lithograph
Courtesy Terry Maddox, pencil artist

SANTA FE TRADE
Frederic Remington, 1904
Courtesy of the Frederic Remington Art Museum, Ogdensburg, New York

ARMY MULE WITH HARNESS MARKS
Frederic Remington
Oil on canvas
Courtesy Buffalo Bill Historical Center, Cody, Wyoming; Gift of The Coe Foundation

UNTITLED
Frederic Remington
Oil on board
Courtesy Buffalo Bill Historical Center, Cody, Wyoming; Gift of The Coe Foundation 54.67

THE BELL MARE

Frederic Remington, 1903

Oil on canvas

Courtesy Gilcrease Museum, Tulsa, Oklahoma

EVERETT BOWMAN, ALL-AROUND CHAMPION COWBOY
OF THE WORLD, 1935 & 1937
Clyde "Ross" Morgan
Bronze
Wickenburg, Arizona

TIME TO RE-TIRE
Leslie Thrasher, 1926
Fisk Automotive Tire Advertisement

"TOUCH OF EAR" DRAFT MULE TEAM

Courtesy of J. Mack Bohn, Diamond JK Ranches

Syril, Oklahoma

SEEN ON THE HIGHWAYS AND BYWAYS OF AMERICA

INSPIRATION AFTER A MULE RIDE
Taylor Flanders, age 11
Watercolor and construction paper collage
Courtesy of the artist

THE TOY WAGON CHRISTMAS CARD
Jack Sorenson
Courtesy of Jack Sorenson Fine Art.

Santa sometimes has to rely on mules when his reindeer are tired.

The art work of Jack Sorenson has been featured on the covers of more than five dozen western magazines. In 1996, his work was picked up by the Leanin' Tree Greeting Card Company and he is today one of their bestselling artists. Find more at jacksorensonfineart.com.

ELK OMLETTE
Courtesy of Clark Kelley Price

This incident happened to Robin Obrian who now lives in Georgia. When he was a young man he was a packer for the park service in Yellowstone. He commissioned me to paint this personal experience for him.

It happened on the Thoroughfare trail between Turpin Meadows and Hawks Rest, about a 30-mile ride. He was packing in and encountered this bull elk on the bend of the trail. The bull was in the rut and on the fight. He lowered his head as if to charge. The whole outfit scattered. Two of the mules wound themselves around a lodgepole pine and broke the paniers, and food flew everywhere, and the bull disappeared. It took Robin quite a while to put everything back together. Fortunately, nobody was hurt and it left Robin with quite a memory.

When he received the painting, he said I nailed it, which was double pay for me. Just a side note: a few short years later, Robin was flying combat missions in the Korean War. He survived that, too.

—Clark Kelley Price

WALKER PARTY, 1863
George Phippen
Courtesy of Lynn Phippen.

The original painting is on display at the Prescott Public Library, Prescott, Arizona. It illustrates the historical arrival of a group of gold prospectors led by the famous mountain man, Joseph Walker, to camp by Granite Creek where the city of Prescott, Arizona, is now located. The Walker Party was a "mule outfit," using only mules for riding and packing, a very expensive but successful adventure.

George Phippen was a master of Western history and was the famous cofounder and first president of the Cowboy Artists of America.

ON TIME FOR SUPPER
George Phippen
Courtesy of Lynn Phippen.

Lynn was told by his artist father, George Phippen, that stagecoach companies commonly used horse teams only in town. At the next stop out of town they switched to mules because mules were better built for pulling, were smarter, more dependable, more surefooted, had harder, more durable hooves, could do twice as much work on the same amount of feed, and naturally live much longer than horses. The mules were more expensive but paid for themselves in the long run. The old mountain men preferred the use of mules for all of the above reasons, as well as the fact that the Indians had a harder time stealing them.

MULE RESOURCES

Below is a list of resources for the mule-minded. You may also contact the author, John Hauer, at P.O. Box 696, Moab, UT 84532, or 435-259-8015, john@mymules.com or visit his website at www.backcountrymules.com.

ASSOCIATIONS AND ORGANIZATIONS

Al Kaly Shrine Mule Train
Mr. Gale Fortney
5019 Half Moon Drive, Colorado Springs, CO 80915
719-596-5248

American Donkey and Mule Society
P.O. Box 1210, Lewisville, TX 75067
972-219-0781
www.lovelongears.com
lovelongears@hotmail.com

American Mule Association
P.O. Box 1349, Yerington, NV 89447
775-463-1922

Back Country Horsemen of America
P.O. Box 1367 Graham, WA 98338
1-888-893-5161
www.backcountryhorse.com
peg2@Mashell.com

Caballos Del Sol Benefit Trail Ride
Diane Lovett
928-634-2767
Lovett@sedona.net

Canadian Donkey and Mule Association
2417 Holly Lane, Ottawa, ON KIV0M7
613-731-7110
www.donkeyandmule.com
gkkraut@telus.net

TrailMeister is the largest directory in North America for horse and mule trails and camping areas. www.TrailMeister.com is the web address

Earth Walk
www.earthwalk.org
303-357-7120

North American Saddle Mule Association
P.O. Box 112, Chester, NH 03036
603-483-2669
www.nasma.net
lpackard@msn.com

Red Rock Ride: Call 435-679-8665 to obtain more information about riding in the national parks or saddling up for the Red Rock Ride.
www.redrockride.com
ridemule@color-country.com

Shriners Children's Hospitals
800-237-5055
www.shrinershq.org

PERIODICALS

Mules and More
P.O. Box 460, Bland, MO 65014
573-646-3934
www.mulesandmore.com
mules@socket.net

Western Mule Magazine
P.O. Box 46, Marshfield, MO 65706
417-859-6853
www.westernmulemagazine.com
ben@westernmulemagazine.com

BOOKS AND VIDEOTAPES

Jody Foss's books can be ordered directly from the author.
Mules Across the Great Wide Open, $19.95
In the Company of Mules, $24.95.
Send personal checks or money orders to Box 225, Tomales, CA 94971. Price includes priority shipping.

Meredith Hodges's video training series and books are designed to help you learn and apply her mule training methods so that the training process becomes resistance-free for you and your mule. The program can be used for other types of animals. Hodges has also written a mule book for children (of all ages) titled *Jasper, the Story of a Mule*. For more information, contact Hodges at www.luckythreeranch.com or toll-free at 800-816-7566.

Matthes, F.E. (1927). *Breaking Trail Through Bright Angel Canyon*. Mike Quinn/Grand Canyon Museum.

Dr. Robert Miller has written numerous books and produced four educational video tapes about horses and horsemanship. *The Revolution in Horsemanship* is a classic that all horse and mule lovers should own. 800-284-3362 www.robertmiller.com

Robinson, Betty, and Gorden, Pat. *Horse Trails in Arkansas and Oklahoma*. Saddle Bags Press, 2004. This 136-page guide may be purchased from Saddle Bags Press, P.O. Box 255, London, AR 72847 prepaid for $21.95, shipping included. The guide features detailed information on length of trails, fee requirements, facilities, trailhead parking, trail markings, difficulty rating, points of interest, headquarter contacts, GPS trailhead coordinates and agency websites.

Taylor, R. (1922). *Grand Canyon's Long-Eared Taxi*. Grand Canyon Natural History Association: Grand Canyon, AZ.

SADDLES AND EQUIPMENT

McClintock Saddle Works
25077 Viejas Blvd., Descanso, CA 91916
619-445-3946
www.mcclintocksaddles.com

McClintock Saddle Works, "Purveyors of Fine Mule Accoutrements": Saddles, chaps and chinks, canteens, Pressure Relief Pad (helps saddles fit better) and many other products to make your riding experience a celebrated joy.

Wyoming Outdoor Industries
For a catalog call 800-725-6853
www.wyomingoutdoor.com

Owned by Steve Richards, Wyoming Outdoor Industries is a leader in low-impact packing, camping, hunting and calling supplies.

MULES FOR SALE

Backcountry Mule Ranch
John and Sena Hauer
P.O. Box 696, Moab, UT 84532
435-259-8015
www.backcountrymules.com
john@mymules.com

Hawleywoods Mule Farm
Loyd Hawley
203 East Brush, Prairie Grove, AR 72753
Hm: 479-846-2819 Farm: 479-846-3084

Pair-A-Dice Mule Farm
Loren Basham
22801 Highway C, Belle, MO 65013
573-859-6793

MULE RIDES

Canyon Trail Rides
P.O. Box 128
Tropic, UT 84776
435-679-8665
www.canyonrides.com

Pete and Keela Mangum and family provide the only trail rides into the Grand Canyon from the north rim and in Bryce and Zion national parks. The Mangums feel that everyone should "experience the view of the Grand Canyon between the ears of a sure-footed mule."

Rainbow Bridge Outfitters
P.O. Box 310075
Mexican Hat, UT 84531

Eric and Charlene Atene offer trail rides in the Navajo Mountain area. The trip follows a trail used by the Navajo elders before roads were built in the area. They also sponsor overnight camping, scouting trips, drop camps and adventure tours with packstock anywhere in the Rainbow Plateau region.

Winterhawk Outfitters
Larry and Laura Amos
Silt, CO
970-876-2623
www.winterhawk.com

Larry and Laura are full-time outfitters in the Flat Tops Wilderness in Colorado. They offer high-country hunting on mules and horses, trout fishing and summer vacations for families. They also have a professional outfitters, guides and packers school which is approved by the Colorado Department of Higher Education.

Grand Canyon Mule Rides
888-297-2757
www.grandcanyon.com/gcnmule.html

These mule rides have been going into the canyon since 1891. The one-day and overnight rides leave from the south rim of the canyon. Reservations must be booked well in advance.

BOOKS AND VIDEOS

MULA
J&S Productions, 805-695-0164
"Tough. Intelligent. Always ready to do the job. Riders, drivers, packers, and mule traders know his secrets and sing his praises. He was the long-eared hero of the Old West."

Grand Canyon Mule Ride
Don Briggs Film and Video
Box 788, Sausalito, CA 94966
"A must for those who have taken the mule trip into the Grand Canyon, and for those who haven't, this is as close as you're going to get to the real thing."

Corazon Vaquero: The Heart of the Cowboy
Gary McClintock, 619-445-3946
This DVD is a 65-minute documentary featuring the Californianos of Baja. The The Vaqueros (Cowboys) of Baja were using mules 70 years before Southern California was settled. The vaqueros found that horses didn't work well in the rough desert and mountainous country of Baja. For more than three hundred years the vaqueros and their families have lived on ranches without roads. They utilized mules and hinnies in very spectacular ways in order to cope with their environment.

That Son of a Gun Had Sense
By Lonny Thiele
Lonny Thiele is an award-winning writer, journalist, and mule historian. Growing up in Missouri and serving as an agriculture reporter for a Missouri newspaper put him in

contact with a lot of old-timers who farmed with mules before the coming of the tractor. Thiele says, "There were 300,000 mules in Missouri in 1930. Where there was a mule, there was a story." In 2007 he started a three-year odyssey, interviewing seventy-eight elderly people who had worked with mules in their youth. The result is a 298-page book chock-full of great stories about mules. The book is a must read for mule lovers. To order a book, mail $24 to Lon Thiele, PO Box 884, Poplar Bluff, MO 63902.

MULE TRAINING CLINICS

Brad Cameron
982 Honey House Lane, Corvallis, MT 59828
406-961-1381
www.muletrainer.com

ARTISTS

Terry Maddox
2055 Ridgeway Drive
Eugene, OR 97401
541-344-0069
www.terrymaddox.com
tmaddoxart@aol.com

Terry is a pencil artist who enjoys working with mules as subject matter because of their "relaxed manner, subtle intelligence as well as artistic subject quality."

Bonnie Shields
230 Gold Creek Road
Sandpoint, ID 83864

Bonnie is a self-proclaimed "mule freak." She owns five mules and a donkey and says, "it takes every one of 'em to keep me on the trail." In addition to her art, Bonnie produces many mule and donkey related items. You can see her work at www.bonnieshields.com

Jack Sorenson
sorensonart@gmail

Though born in 1954, Jack Sorenson grew up living the Old West lifestyle that he now depicts in his work. He grew up living and working at Sixgun City, a dude ranch and frontier town situated on the rim of the Palo Duro Canyon and owned by his father. When many teenagers spent their adolescence working in retail or fast food, Sorenson worked as a stagecoach driver, a performance gunfighter, and a horse trainer. A naturally gifted artist since childhood, Sorenson began painting full-time in 1974.

Sorensons Gallery representation: Joe Wade Fine Art in Santa Fe New Mexico

PHOTOGRAPHERS

Avalon Photography
Jolene Bertrand
St. Louis Park, MN
952-922-6300
www.avalonphotoinfo.com
jolene@avalonphotoinfo.com

Avalon Photography is a Minnesota-based company that specializes in portraits of families, children, pets, and equine photography.

Mary S. Corning
Four Winds Resources
503-554-1624
www.fourwindsresources.com

Freelance writing and photography, natural horsemanship, life enhancement workshops

Curtis Martin Photography
PO Box JJ, Palisade, CO 81526
970-464-1427
www.cmartinphoto.com

images@cmartinphoto.com

Curtis shoots stock and assignment photographs of the real West: cowboys to executives, canyonlands deserts to the San Francisco streets.

Dan Norris
Canyon Color Graphics
44 North 100 West, Moab, UT 84532
800-891-6635
www.ancientimagescards.com
dan@ancientimagescards.com

Dan offers photographic services, cutting-edge graphic design, image scanning, and printing. Business cards to catalogs.

Guy Tillett
Western Wildlife Images
10108 Romel, Black Hawk, SD 57718
605-787-4530
gktilt@aol.com

Guy is a wildlife artist and photographer.

Ray Tysdal
813 Glendale Lane, Rapid City, SD 57702
605-772-7760

Ray is a fine art photographer who has developed a highly stylized black-and-white format of animal photography.

PHOTOGRAPHY CREDITS

Courtesy Al Kaly Shrine 65, 67, 68; courtesy Arizona Office of Tourism 158; courtesy Dan Aadland 139, 140, 141; courtesy Emily Aadland 140; courtesy Eric Atene 116; Avalon Photography 1 1 (inset), 77 (inset); courtesy J. Mack Bohn 178; courtesy Buffalo Bill Historical Center, Cody Wyoming 165, 166, 173, 174; Shari Cameron 114; courtesy Cattle Kate catalog 72; Central Missouri State University 73; Valerie Chase 115; courtesy Charles Gremp Photography 101; courtesy Sue Cole 2, 70 (right), 86, 87, 92, 94, 95; courtesy Colorado Mule Riders 82; Troy Cooke 128; Helen Eden 38; Taylor Flanders 180; courtesy Frederic Remington Art Museum, Ogdensburg New York 172; courtesy Jody Foss 97, 98; Four Winds Photography 112, 113; courtesy Gilcrease Museum, Tulsa Oklahoma 28, 167 169, 175; Pat Gordon 40, 41, 43, 44, 45, 47; Grand Canyon National Park Museum Collection 49, 50, 51, 52, 54 (left, top right), 55, 56, 58, 59; Lori Greenstein 158; Ira Grostin 29 (far right top, bottom); John Hauer 20, 68, 71, 87 (left), 105, 163; Sena Hauer iii, xii, xiii, xvi, 4, 71 (bottom), 88, 89 (right), 90, 95; courtesy Loyd Hawley 36, 37, 39; Carol Hillard 66; courtesy Meredith Hodges 31, 32, 34, 35; Bruce Hucko 5; Brett Johnson 126; Anthony Leonard 3 (left); Charlie Leonard 2; Library of Congress, Prints & Photographs Edition, FSA-OWI Collection v, 64; Janet Lowe 134, 135, 136; courtesy Sharon Lynn 104, 106, 162; Grant Macfarlane 122, 123, 124, 125; courtesy Terry Maddox 170, 171; Curtis Martin 9, 78, 96; courtesy Pat MacNamara 72; Garry McClintock 84; Dave McMahen 42; courtesy Robert Miller 15, 17, 18; Dan Norris132; Northern Arizona Cline library Special Collections NAU.PH.660.121; courtesy Sharon Northrup x; Christa Paterson 103; courtesy Lynn Phippen 183, 184; Quince Tree Photography 10; courtesy Clark Kelley Price 182; Richard Ranz 46; courtesy Steven Richards 79, 80; Steve Rush 138; courtesy Al Sammons 108, 109, 110; courtesy Bonnie Shields 168; courtesy Sid Richardson Collection of Western Art 164; courtesy Ron Silverthorn 142, 143, 144; courtesy Jack Sorenson 181; Guy Tillett 3 (right); Ray Tysdale vi, 1 (background top left); courtesy United States Military Academy at West Point 29; courtesy University of Idaho 21, 23, 26; courtesy U.S. Army Center of Military History 63; Western History/ Genealogy Department, Denver Public Library 68, 70; courtesy Mary von Koch 131; courtesy Carol Lucas Whiteside 117, 118, 119; Fred Whitney 60, 61

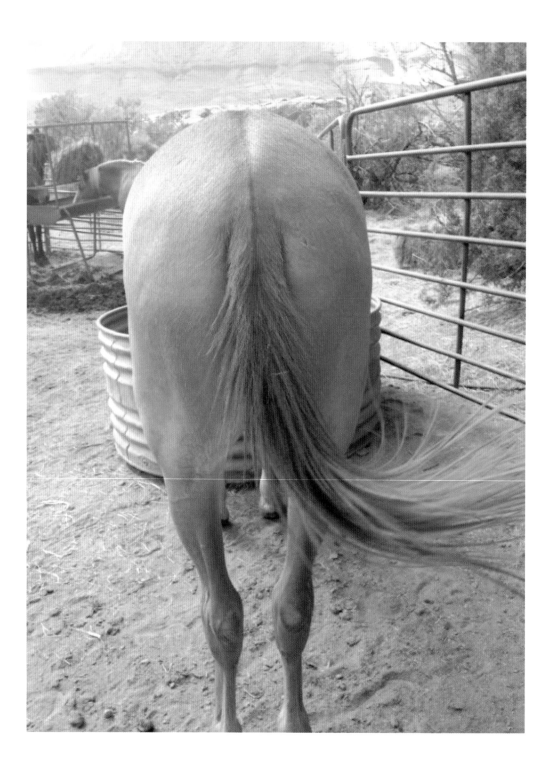